The Internet and New Social Formation in China

There are billions of Internet users in China, and this number is continually growing. This book acknowledges the various purposes of this Internet use, and provides a study about how the entertainment-consuming users form into publics through the mediation of technologies in the era of network society. It questions how individuals, mediated by new information and communication technologies, come together to form new social categories. The book goes on to investigate how public(s) is formed, with particular focus on how fans become publics in a society that follows the logic of network. Using textual analysis, network analysis, online surveys and in-depth interviews, this book provides a rich description of the process of constructing new social formation in contemporary China.

Weiyu Zhang is Associate Professor in the Department of Communications and New Media at the National University of Singapore.

Media, Culture and Social Change in Asia

Series Editor
Stephanie Hemelryk Donald, University of New South Wales

The aim of this series is to publish original, high-quality work by both new and established scholars in the West and the East, on all aspects of media, culture and social change in Asia.

1 Television Across Asia
Television industries, programme
formats and globalisation
*Edited by Albert Moran and
Michael Keane*

2 Journalism and Democracy in Asia
*Edited by Angela Romano and
Michael Bromley*

**3 Cultural Control and
Globalization in Asia**
Copyright, piracy and cinema
Laikwan Pang

**4 Conflict, Terrorism and the
Media in Asia**
Edited by Benjamin Cole

5 Media and the Chinese Diaspora
Community, communications
and commerce
Edited by Wanning Sun

**6 Hong Kong Film, Hollywood and
the New Global Cinema**
No film is an island
*Edited by Gina Marchetti and
Tan See Kam*

7 Media in Hong Kong
Press freedom and political
change 1967–2005
Carol P. Lai

8 Chinese Documentaries
From dogma to polyphony
Yingchi Chu

9 Japanese Popular Music
Culture, authenticity and power
Carolyn S. Stevens

**10 The Origins of the Modern
Chinese Press**
The influence of the Protestant
missionary press in late
Qing China
Xiantao Zhang

11 Created in China
The great new leap forward
Michael Keane

**12 Political Regimes and the
Media in Asia**
*Edited by Krishna Sen and
Terence Lee*

**13 Television in
Post-Reform China**
Serial dramas, Confucian
leadership and the global
television market
Ying Zhu

14 Tamil Cinema
The cultural politics of India's
other film industry
Edited by Selvaraj Velayutham

15 Popular Culture in Indonesia
Fluid identities in
post-authoritarian politics
Edited by Ariel Heryanto

16 Television in India
Satellites, politics and
cultural change
Edited by Nalin Mehta

**17 Media and Cultural
Transformation in China**
Haiqing Yu

18 Global Chinese Cinema
The culture and politics of hero
*Edited by Gary D. Rawnsley and
Ming-Yeh T. Rawnsley*

**19 Youth, Society and Mobile
Media in Asia**
*Edited by Stephanie Hemelryk
Donald, Theresa Dirndorfer
Anderson and Damien Spry*

**20 The Media, Cultural Control and
Government in Singapore**
Terence Lee

**21 Politics and the Media in
Twenty-First Century Indonesia**
*Edited by Krishna Sen and
David T. Hill*

**22 Media, Social Mobilization
and Mass Protests in Post-colonial
Hong Kong**
The power of a critical event
*Francis L. F. Lee and
Joseph M. Chan*

**23 HIV/AIDS, Health and the
Media in China**
Imagined immunity through
racialized disease
Johanna Hood

**24 Islam and Popular Culture in
Indonesia and Malaysia**
Edited by Andrew N. Weintraub

25 Online Society in China
Creating, celebrating, and
instrumentalising the
online carnival
*Edited by David Kurt Herold
and Peter Marolt*

**26 Rethinking Transnational
Chinese Cinemas**
The Amoy-dialect film industry in
Cold War Asia
Jeremy E. Taylor

**27 Film in Contemporary
Southeast Asia**
Cultural interpretation and
social intervention
*Edited by David C. L. Lim and
Hiroyuki Yamamoto*

28 China's New Creative Clusters
Governance, human capital,
and investment
Michael Keane

**29 Media and Democratic Transition
in South Korea**
Ki-Sung Kwak

30 The Asian Cinema Experience
Styles, spaces, theory
Stephen Teo

31 Asian Popular Culture
Edited by Anthony Y. H. Fung

**32 Rumor and Communication in
Asia in the Internet Age**
Edited by Greg Dalziel

**33 Genders and Sexualities in
Indonesian Cinema**
Constructing gay, lesbi and waria
identities on screen
Ben Murtagh

**34 Contemporary Chinese
Print Media**
Cultivating middle class taste
Yi Zheng

**35 Culture, Aesthetics and Affect
in Ubiquitous Media**
The prosaic image
Helen Grace

**36 Democracy, Media and Law in
Malaysia and Singapore**
A space for speech
*Edited by Andrew T. Kenyon, Tim
Marjoribanks and Amanda Whiting*

37 Indonesia-Malaysia Relations
Cultural heritage, politics and
labour migration
Marshall Clark and Juliet Pietsch

**38 Chinese and Japanese Films on
the Second World War**
*Edited by King-fai Tam,
Timothy Y. Tsu and Sandra Wilson*

**39 New Chinese-Langage
Documentaries**
Ethics, subject and place
Kuei-fen Chiu and Yingjin Zhang

**40 K-pop – The International Rise of
the Korean Music Industry**
*Edited by JungBong Choi and
Roald Maliangkay*

41 China Online
Locating society in online spaces
*Edited by Peter Marolt and
David Kurt Herold*

**42 Multimedia Stardom in
Hong Kong**
Image, performance and identity
Leung Wing-Fai

43 Television Histories in Asia
Issues and contexts
*Edited by Jinna Tay and
Graeme Turner*

**44 Media and Communication in the
Chinese Diaspora**
Rethinking transnationalism
*Edited by Wanning Sun and
John Sinclair*

45 Lifestyle Media in Asia
Consumption, aspiration
and identity
*Edited by Fran Martin and
Tania Lewis*

**46 The Internet and New Social
Formation in China**
Fandom publics in the making
Weiyu Zhang

The Internet and New Social Formation in China

Fandom publics in the making

Weiyu Zhang

Routledge
Taylor & Francis Group

LONDON AND NEW YORK

First published 2016 by Routledge

2 Park Square, Milton Park, Abingdon, Oxfordshire OX14 4RN
711 Third Avenue, New York, NY 10017

Routledge is an imprint of the Taylor & Francis Group, an informa business

First issued in paperback 2017

British Library Cataloguing in Publication Data
A catalogue record for this book is available from the British Library

Library of Congress Cataloging in Publication Data
Names: Zhang, Weiyu, author.
Title: The internet and new social formation in China : fandom publics
   in the making / Weiyu Zhang.
Description: 1 Edition. | New York : Routledge, 2016. | Series: China policy
   series ; 45 | Includes bibliographical references and index.
Identifiers: LCCN 2015032551| ISBN 9781138799264 (hardback) |
   ISBN 9781315756141 (ebook)
Subjects: LCSH: Social media--China. | Internet--Social aspects--China. |
   Social stratification--China. | China--History--21st century.
Classification: LCC HM1206 .Z484 2016 | DDC 302.23/10951--dc23
LC record available at http://lccn.loc.gov/2015032551

ISBN: 978-1-138-79926-4 (hbk)
ISBN: 978-1-138-47721-6 (pbk)

Typeset in Times New Roman
by Taylor & Francis Books

Contents

List of illustrations   x
Preface   xi
Acknowledgement   xiii

1   Publics, fans, and social media   1

2   Popular culture and digital technologies   15

3   Rear window to movies: from fans to subaltern publics   31

4   Ten years after: from subaltern to regular publics   49

5   Online translation communities: from consumers to prod-users   60

6   *House of cards*: from entertainment to politics   75

7   Douban versus Renren: fan objects as network nodes   88

8   Weibo publics: celebrities as network nodes   107

9   Fandom publics: social formation in the network society   124

Index   142

List of illustrations

Figures

2.1 Number of Internet users (in ten thousands) in China, 2007–2013   16
2.2 Money (in Yuan) spent on cultural consumption in China,
    2005–2012   17
2.3 Levels of satisfaction with leisure-relevant issues among Chinese
    (percentages of people who are satisfied), 2006–2012   18
2.4 Number of titles of books, magazines, newspapers, and
    audio/video products produced in China, 2005–2012   19
2.5 Hours of radio and TV program produced and aired in China,
    2005–2012   20
2.6 Number of movies produced in China, 2005–2012   20
2.7 Market revenues (in 100 million Yuan) of movies, online games,
    and online videos in China, 2005–2012   21
7.1 Historical traffic trends: reach percent   92
7.2 The network structure of Douban   98
8.1 Yao Chen's Repost Network based the Top 100 Reposters (Before
    and After De-centralization)   116
8.2 Xu Xiaonian's Repost Network based on the Top 100 Reposters
    (Before and After De-centralization)   117
8.3 Li Kaifu's Repost Network based on the Top 100 Reposters
    (Before and After De-centralization)   118

Tables

3.1 Private movie watching organized by Rear Window, 2000–2003   42
7.1 Bridging and bonding social capitals perceived by Renren versus
    Douban users   100
8.1 Descriptive statistics of PM 2.5 updates by selected celebrities   114
8.2 Results of content analysis of selected celebrities' PM 2.5 updates   114
8.3 Significant simple bivariate correlations between user comments
    and celebrity updates   115

Preface

It has been almost 20 years since China introduced the Internet to the everyday life of its citizens. Yet China is still not a democracy. This has deeply puzzled those who believed that the Internet is a democratization force. Some attributed the cause to the tight control of the Chinese government. Others blamed the ordinary Chinese people for being drowned in material pleasures. Still others suggested that China is such an exceptional case that it cannot be understood using existing frames. So what has actually happened on the Chinese Internet, if the majority of its users did not spend much time on advocating for democratic revolutions? More intriguingly, how has Chinese society changed since the presence of the Internet, in the midst of other economic, political, and cultural developments? Is China indeed an exception, without any reference value for our understanding of other parts of the world?

Much of my focus in this book is on the entertainment-seeking Internet users in China. Although sharing with popular culture scholarship in recognizing the importance of trivial practices such as watching online videos, I emphasize how new social formations emerge out of such practices, and under which circumstances evolve into politically functioning publics. The fans I have talked to and researched range from movie fans, fans of foreign reality TV shows and TV dramas, fans who went a step further to translate and disseminate such foreign-language content, and fans whose fan objects are celebrities instead of cultural products. These ordinary fans have done much creative works and modified the Chinese reality little by little, bit by bit, along the years. Whether these changes introduced by fandom publics are good or bad really depends on the value system one uses to make the judgment.

Another purpose of this book is to defy the myth of Chinese exceptionalism through empirically supported theorization. Oftentimes, China is a complicated mosaic that one can see the traces of pre-modernism, modernism, and post-modernism simultaneously. As the industrial factory of the world in the twenty-first century, China is going through what the developed world has already gone through, but in a vastly different social condition, namely the Network Society. Understanding China's side of the story will help understand how the non-Western players in this new social structure could have experienced different social transformations, albeit the shared space of the global network society. In addition, the transformations China's network society has been through would nevertheless influence other parts of the world. Through an in-depth discussion of the network logic, Chinese empirical evidence is used to construct a theoretical concept (i.e. fandom publics) that might be informative for other network societies.

The book was inspired by my personal experience of getting online in the 1990s, especially the group of movies fans I met through online forums. The resources I have relied on in this book are mainly first-hand and longitudinal (15 years) data from the fans themselves, including both their discourses and their online/offline activities. Through following the actors themselves, I endeavor to provide a description not of a moving target, but of how the target moves. Other than the academic readers I hope to reach and have a conversation with, I imagine that online fans in China can read this manuscript as accounts of their own communities, memories, and histories. Practitioners who want to find out how to foster and reach such fans may also find this work relevant.

The book can be read either in the set sequence or by individual chapters that interest you. Chapter 1 and 9 are two theoretical chapters, in which you can find the concept, fandom publics, being introduced against existing definitions of the public(s), explained in view of the three network theories, and criticized through various critical frames. If you wish to understand how to draw theoretical inspiration from this book to study other contexts, these two chapters would be most useful. If you are a casual reader of this book who is interested in Chinese online fandom, Chapter 2 gives you a review of the big picture whereas Chapter 3–8 describe five fascinating cases that will never bore you. For those who are techie and curious about the technological implications, Chapters 7 and 8 explicate the network logic to understand the Internet of people, the Internet of things, and the Internet of both.

Weiyu Zhang
Glasgow, UK
July 2015

Acknowledgement

When I started my field trips to Guangzhou and Nanjing back in 2002, I hadn't decided whether I would pursue my PhD degree, not to mention an academic life. I was naively drawn to the group of movie fans I met on the Internet, who shared with me this youthful passion for movies. I remember it was a sunny afternoon and I finished my last interview in Guangzhou. My interviewee, whom I contacted through leaving a message on Rear Window to Movies, decided to send me back to the train station. It just so happened that there was a bookstore beside the train station. One second before I stepped into the station entrance, my interviewee shouted, hold on! He rushed into the bookstore and rushed out with a book in his hands, a book written by the then rising Chinese movie director Jia Zhangke. I sometimes find it fascinating to observe how, in the late 1990s and the early 2000s, Internet users in China seemed to be a group of idealists who did not mind being brought to places and people by serendipity. I wish the Chinese Internet had stayed just so, but the reality quickly became so complicated that one book cannot sufficiently account for it. During the decade following the completion of my master thesis, I travelled to the United States for my PhD study, a five-year-long journey full of moments beyond my imagination. I migrated back to Asia and settled down in Singapore, struggling to prove that I deserve a corner in the academic world. From the moment I began to put up this book, my memory flashed back to that sunny afternoon in Guangzhou that made me believe that I absolutely loved what I was doing. This book, to me, is not only a work about the 20-year development of the Chinese Internet but also a memoire of my personal growth or lack of such.

There are many people who have accompanied me, at different moments, for different lengths, along the journey leading to this book. I will have to first thank all the individuals who have been my research subjects, no matter whether they would like to be named fans. The key figures of Rear Window to Movies, including Weixidi, Vain, Bonney, Huang Xiaoxie, Tengjin Shu, Gu Xiaobai, Bei Taixi, and many others, kindly shared with me their life experience in both 2002 and 2011. I am particularly grateful for all interviewees from the online translation community, which has been a major source of inspiration for quite a while. I felt guilty that in late 2014, some major downloading websites such as shooter.cn were forced to close down and I kept wondering whether it was because of my academic paper that drew the unwanted attention. Many online fans, whose contribution may not be directly recognized in this book, have also made this book rich through their day-to-day active and creative participation in the consumption and reproduction of fan objects. Thanks to their works, it is no exaggeration to say that it has been my great pleasure to write this book.

Students and colleagues have direct contribution to some parts of this book. I want to acknowledge that Chapter 5 is based on collaboration between me and a PhD student Chengting Mao. Chengting has an unusual sense of sympathy for her research subjects, reminding me of my Hong Kong years. Chapter 6 is a side-project when my master advisee, Lize Zhang, and I were working on a book chapter on Chinese fans of American reality shows. Lize is talented and despite being only a Master student, has shown tremendous potential to be an academic. Chapter 7, again, is based on collaboration between me and a Master graduate, Rong Wang. Rong is now studying at the University of South California, doing fabulous research on Social Networking Analysis and Development Communication. Chapter 8 is based on collaboration with Prof. Jia Dai and my Master student, Yang Tian, both of whom worked at Tsinghua University when we first initiated the project. Their diligent work ethic has driven me to complete this book project.

Along the years, there were a few academic institutions that have been the best venues for generating and sharing the ideas stated in the book. First of all, the Chinese Internet Research Conferences in 2015 (Edmonton, Canada), 2014 (Hong Kong), 2013 (Oxford, UK), 2011 (Washington, DC, USA), 2009 (Philadelphia, USA), 2007 (Texas A&M, USA) have given me the opportunities to hear the most expert comments from the best scholars in the field. I cannot thank this academic community enough for providing me a spiritual home. The China Communication Association regularly sponsors sessions on the topic of China and the Internet, which have enriched my thoughts on the same topic. The conference on "Networked China: Global Dynamics of Digital Media and Civic Engagement" organized by Steven Reeves and Wenhong Chen marked the height of such sharing moments. It was during this trip to Austin, Texas, that I started to form my key arguments. I cannot forget the summer of 2010 I spent in Beijing either, when I was invited to join the Joint Summer School held at Chinese University of Communication and the Young Scholar Forum at Renming University. I extend my gratitude to Lei Zhang and Weizhen Lei for showing me the vivid discussions happening in the Chinese academic circle. Last but not least, I am in debt to the East Asia Institute and Institute of South Asian Studies at National University of Singapore. Yongnian Zheng kindly allowed me to stay at EAI for a semester, during which I not only focused my energy on writing but also benefited from the non-stop conversations among economists, political scientists, sociologists, and policy experts housed in EAI. Robin Jeffery enlightened me about research in the Asian region through talking about his life-long research experience in India.

My academic friends are the treasure I discovered along this journey. I want to take a deep bow to a group of friends who have been my never-failing critics and want to tell you that I kept your voices in mind when writing this book. They are Bingchun Meng from the London School of Economics, Ming Jiang from the University of South Carolina, Elaine Yuan from the University of Illinois, Chicago, Jing Wu from Beijing University, Jie Xu from the University of Villanova, Ingrid Hoofd from Utrecht University, Jack Qiu, Francis Lee, and Lokman Tsui from the Chinese University of Hong Kong, Fei Shen from the City University of Hong Kong, and Guobing Yang from the University of Pennsylvania and Zhongdang Pan from the University of Wisconsin, Madison. My colleagues at NUS have helped me keep my sanity. They are Leanne Chang, Iccha Basnyat, Denisa Kera, Anne-Marie Schleiner, Tracy Loh, Francesca Nathan, Jing Ying Chiang, Peichi Chung, Carol Soon, Tan Tarn How, and Gayathri Dorairaju. Here are my heroes, who have set the bar so high that I know that I will always have space for growth: Mohan Dutta, Millie Rivera, Paul Lee, Joseph Chan, Vincent Price, and Martin Fishbein. A special thank goes to Dr. Chan, who generously offered his excellent photography work as the cover of this book.

I want to dedicate the last line to my family, my father Zengliang Zhang, my mother Sumei Li, and my sister Yan Zhang, for your unconditional support.

1   Publics, fans, and social media

Fundamental to the debate around social media should be the idea of social formation or the new forms of social collectivities. How do socially mediated individuals come together to form new social categories? The inquiry has been carried out in the vibrant discussions on virtual communities (Baym, 2000; Jones, 1995; Rheingold, 1993). Communities, taken away from their nostalgia of intimate interaction and dense connection (Bell and Newby, 1976; Bernard, 1973), are transformed by the modern conditions of society, salient among which is the rapid evolution of technologies. Whereas the exploration of virtual communities focuses on the style in which they are formed, maintained, and imagined, an important purpose of community seems to be neglected. A community is a social unit that connects individuals and society (Friedland, 2001). Watson (1997, p. 102) stated the purpose of community in one question: "How does a group struggle for greater representation in the larger society?" While the network approach of community measures the individual relational network and limits the function of community to social support (Wellman, 1999), the political connotation of community, implied in Watson's question, remains unexamined. The notion of public, as a noun, refers to a specific social category that appears as a political actor (Splichal, 1999, p. 2). Community members become a public only if they engage in open contestations on issues that have consequences on their lives but are not under the members' full and direct control. A further question needs to be asked: How do socially mediated individuals come together to act as political collectivities?

A tradition of examining new media as public sphere took roots in a Habermasian model of a universal discursive space for rational–critical debate (Habermas, 1989). As a revision of the Habermasian bias towards a bourgeois public sphere, subaltern or counter-public spheres (Fraser, 1993) were proposed as an empirically more accurate and normatively more inclusive lens to look at the political potential of new media. The shared academic interest here is to understand how new media provide infrastructural support to such spheres and whether the support is sufficient to reach the democratic ideal, be it the universal and rational ideal of Habermas, or the inclusive and engaging ideal of Fraser. Public in public sphere(s) is an adjective that describes a nature or an attribute of the sphere(s) (Splichal, 1999, p.17). This tradition does not pay much attention to public as a noun. Habermas merely used "a body of private persons assembled" (cited in Fraser, 1993, p. 10) to indicate a public. To Fraser (1993, p. 14), counter-publics mainly refer to "members of subordinated social groups." The former casts too wide a net to capture an ephemeral social category that has been infamously claimed as phantom (Lippmann, 1925). The latter assumes the procedure of formation a done deal, jumping too fast from social groups to political publics. In other words, the public sphere(s) approach to examining the political aspects of new media suffers from the lack of focus on public(s), the actors who act in the discursive arena of open contestations. The public sphere(s) without public(s) has distracted our inquiry from describing the process through which virtual community members become online publics, and more pertinent to this book's focus, how social media redefine this process.

The thought on public(s) as a social category can be traced back to the Chicago school of sociology that has been intrigued by the impact of Industrial Revolution in the twentieth century (e.g., Blumer, 1946; Park, 1904/1972). Other American and European intellectuals, including Dewey (1927), LeBon (1895/1960), Mills (1956), and Tarde (1890/1903), also contributed significantly to the theorization of public(s). In these efforts, public(s), as a developing social entity, is often contrasted with two collective concepts which are believed to be modern entities, namely mass and crowd. Community is left out of the comparisons as the concept was constructed as a pre-modern sociological category that inspires the reflection on the changes brought by Industrial Revolution (Calhoun, 1980). Consistent across the comparisons is an interest in finding out the role that the modern communication media play in shaping these social entities. The relations to modern media, at least partially, differentiate public, crowd, and mass. A communicative model of public (Price, 1992) argues that a public has to form itself via discussion and debate, which highlights the role of media in enabling such discursive exchanges. In other words, a public has to be mediated in a massified modern society.

The necessity of mediation in social formulation directs our attention to another common social category seen in modern societies, namely audiences. Fans, as the most actively engaged audiences, have a close association with media products but the concept was rarely seriously considered as comparable to public(s), largely due to its everyday connotation of obsession and irrationality (Hills, 2002, p. ix). Recent studies point out that the opposition between fan culture and formal politics is a normative construction rather than an empirical separation (Van Zoonen, 2005, pp. 1–4). Contrary to the popular representation of fans as atomized and dangerous individuals (Jensen, 1992), fans have been found to be socially connected and creatively engaged (Fiske, 1992). Van Zoonen (2004) argued for three connections between fan culture and politics: fan communities are structurally equivalent to political constituencies; the two entities make use of and value similar repertoires of activity; and the emotional investments fans often make are crucial to civic engagement. If political purpose is not alien to fans and their activities, it is without much difficulty to admit that fans can act as publics in certain circumstances.

The transformation from fans to publics is now largely built upon the mediation of information and communication technologies (ICTs) such as the Internet and mobile phones, which are considered the foundation of a network society (Castells, 1996; Rainie and Wellman, 2012). Cyberspace does not merely provide an online replication of the offline fandom and, rather, intersects with fans' relationships in such a way as to alter fan practices and identities. As Hills (2002, p. 172) said, "(t)he mediation of 'new media' must be addressed rather than treated as an invisible term within the romanticized 'new'." Parallel to this argument is to argue that the mediation of social media significantly influences the manner in which fans become publics. Baym (2007) found that social media, as a recent phase of new media development, not only overcome the constraints of geographic locale but also transcend the boundary of disparate online platforms. The fashion of "networked collectivism" provides fans a complex ecosystem of sites to connect. Jenkins (2006) argued that ICTs support the networked practices of fans and their collective intelligence, which have the potential to foster political activism.

This chapter introduces a theoretical discussion of how the network logic of new ICTs leads to new ways of forming publics. It opens with a review of different conceptualizations of public, with an emphasis on the contrast between European, American, and Chinese definitions. Whereas "public" is defined in the West by its distinction from "mass" and "crowd" against the background of the Industrial Revolution, Chinese history has witnessed a conceptual evolution that stresses the oppositional relationship between "public" and "private" along the moral dimension. Both Western and Chinese definitions, however, seem to encounter the term's contemporary discontinuation when fandom becomes the raw material from which publics are forged. Fandom seems to contradict the Western notion of public due to the popular understanding of fans as isolated, obsessive, and irrational. It also contradicts the Chinese notion of public, as fans are categorized as private individuals and their fandom as pursuing self-interests. These contradictions invite us to reconsider the boundary between public and private and the social conditions in which the boundary is drawn. It is argued that network society, in contrast to mass society, is becoming the dominating logic of social formation in China. The social conditions associated with the network society urge us to redefine public as a relational concept, which illustrates the network logic (in contrast to the hierarchy logic) of connecting individuals and building visibility. The chapter concludes with an outline of the book.

Crowds/masses/ publics vs. audiences/fans

Starting from the days of the Chicago school, the conceptualization of public has always been driven by inquiring about the formation of social collectivities under different societal conditions. During the period when society became massified, the concern was that destructive and violent crowds seemed to mark the era. Many scholars (Tarde, 1890/1903; Park, 1904/1972) tried to define public through its contrast to crowd. Crowds, as LeBon (1895/1960, p. 10) believed, are mentally inferior and essentially "barbarian." Individuals in crowds are anonymous, emotional, and unconscious of their critical agency, which results in the rapid spread of spontaneous imitation of even the most violent behaviors. This fearful description of crowds was no longer prominent in recent scholarship when terms like "the wisdom of crowds" (Surowiecki, 2004) present a fresh look at loosely structured and collectively unreflective associations. Surowiecki (2004) argued that if the individuals in crowds can be diverse, independent, and decentralized, an aggregation of the private judgments leads to intelligent collective decisions. He suggested that if informed individuals can be spared from the contagious influence that suppresses their agency, crowds are able to generate better outcomes than the situation in which individuals can fully communicate with each other through either emotional imitation or rational discussions. However, this elimination of what Park (1904/1972, p. 79) calls "primary reciprocity" from crowds only makes them more like masses.

Mass, as another concept constantly in comparison to public, was considered more worrisome than crowd to displace public (Blumer, 1946). Similar to what has been listed in Surowiecki's book, individuals in masses are largely anonymous, highly heterogeneous, and have very little interaction or communication. An aggregation mechanism, such as an opinion poll, might be used to pool their intelligence. What binds together the masses is not shared emotion as in crowds but a common focus of attention. Different from crowds in LeBon's sense, masses are so geographically dispersed and physically separated that they are not able to act effectively together. Mills (1956, p. 304) estimated that modern conditions appeared to be more favorable to mass rather than public because "fewer people express opinions than receive them" from mass media and the authorities that control the channels of political action penetrate the mass. The mediation through mass communication channels contributes to the formation of masses due to the systematic control over these channels by authorities, which successfully eliminates an autonomous sphere of communication between individuals.

The concept, public, differs from crowd in its critical ability to "think and reason" whereas crowd only has "the ability to feel and empathize" (Park, 1904/1972, p. 80). In addition, it differs from mass in the prominence of communication taking the form of disagreement and discussion surrounding a particular issue. Public also differs from Surowiecki's intelligent crowd for the same reason: communication, in particular discussion, has to be a central mechanism that connects individuals in a public. In short, a communication mode of critical discussion separates public from crowd and mass. What is shared among the three concepts, however, should not be underestimated. All of them are "initial routes to the creation of wholly new social entities" (Price, 1992, p. 26). They are bonded by a collective force: emotional attachment in crowd, critical discussion in public, and mere attention in mass. None of them has evolved into formally organized collectivities, in which roles, norms, and traditions become fixed, and therefore, serve as "empirical preliminary stages" (Park, 1904/1972, p. 80) leading to social changes.

The conceptual distinction discussed above indicates a fundamental interest in the "associational relationships" (Emirbayer and Sheller, 1999) during the transformation of social morphology (Castells, 1996). One pillar of such transformation is the mechanism of mediation. When crowds are made possible through the "primary reciprocity" that is contagious and emotional, the emergence of masses is often attributed to the one-way communication mode of mass media (e.g., newspapers and TV). The mass circulation of popular texts (in the form of media products, sports events, celebrities, and more) also leads to the formation of another social category, audiences (Livingstone, 2005). A widely held view seeking to oppose audiences and publics puts the concept of audience closest to the concept of mass, in terms of passivity and isolation (Hartley, 2002). An alternative view, however, argues that as mediation becomes an irreversible reality, no publics can be formed without being audiences or, media users because media bring visibility or popularity that the concept of public entails. Yet audiences "sustain a modest and often ambivalent level of critical interpretation, drawing upon—and thereby reproducing—a somewhat ill-specified, at times inchoate or even contradictory sense of identity of belong which motivates them towards but does not wholly enable the kinds of collective and direct action expected of a public" (Livingstone, 2005, p. 31).

Among those most actively engaged audiences are fans. A negative image is often associated with fans in popular wisdom and mass media representations (Hills, 2002, p. ix). Fans are often depicted as atomized, manipulated, obsessed, and irrational, who in many aspects resemble crowds (in term of enthusiasm and emotionality) and masses (in terms of shared attention and lack of communication). However, academics found that fans are communicative by interacting with each other through various media (Baym, 2000); creative by engaging in interpretive and expressive practices that both enjoy and challenge the texts provided (Hellekson and Busse, 2006), and committed by investing their enduring emotion into the fan objects (Grossberg, 1992).

With the rebuttal against the anti-social and agency-deprived definition of fans, the contrast between fans and publics seems to dwell on one dimension: ration versus emotion. The normative notion of public prescribes rationality as the key feature of the communicative action seen in publics (Habermas, 1984). Specifically, a public, defined as private individuals coming to a public sphere to debate, thus has to conform to the principles of the discursive space, such as providing "validity claims" (Habermas, 1979). This rationality bias has been challenged from historical, theoretical, and empirical angles (Fraser, 1993). Historically, the reason-focused bourgeois public sphere has excluded subordinated and disempowered social groups based on such claims as that they are not capable of reasoning. Theoretically, the insistence on rationality limits the legitimate forms of expression to reasoned arguments and downplays the importance of other discursive means such as story-telling and emotional appeals. Empirically, non-rational expressions have been and are widely used in public contestations, making the exclusive focus on rationality a futile theorization. It is proposed that our definition of public shall loose its normative constraint, i.e., the rationality bias. Publics are connected through disagreements and discussions, which can take any forms of discursive expressions. Back to the fundamental question Watson (1992) asked, a public emerges when the individuals, who share the attention on certain issues, makes efforts to represent themselves to the larger society through engaging in debates among themselves as well as with other societal members. Fans, therefore, can become publics when they try to represent their interests and put up their appeals in front of the larger society.

Public as just vs. private as unjust

When Splichal (1999) reviewed the concepts of public, publicness, and publicity in American and European traditions, he noticed that in contrast to public as a specific social category (e.g., the Chicago School) or publicness as a specific nature of particular activities or spaces (e.g., Habermas), publicity has been used as a moral principle by political philosophers such as Kant and Dewey. The principle of publicity, according to Kant, means that the maxim of all actions that affect the rights of other human beings is that these actions have to be made public (cited in Splichal, 1999, pp. 63–64). Implied in this principle of publicity is that without such publicity, there would not be justice because human beings whose rights are affected by the actions would not be able to raise their objections and stop the actions, especially when the actions refer to the actions of the state or other political authorities. As Splichal's (1999) review extended, it becomes clear that publicity as a moral principle is not the most popular usage of the concept in the Western context. In contrast, the moral dimension of the concept public is almost the most important understanding of the word in China.

Mizoguchi (2011) traced the historical evolution of the Chinese words *Gong* (public) and *Si* (private) among major Chinese thinkers and contrasted the conceptualizations with their Japanese counterparts. He found that the origins of the two words indicate a relationship of opposition. The word *Gong* has been explicitly defined as the opposite of *Si*, which can be seen in the layout of the Chinese character *Gong* as the upper part *Ba* looks like a person's back and the lower part a character element of *Si*. The first century AD *Shuo Wen Jie Zi* thus etymologically analyzed that *Gong* means "turning one's back to the private" (*Beisi wei gong*). In addition, a moral preference is shown in this oppositional relationship. Whereas public is good and just, private is wicked and unjust. This moral dimension is distinct from either the economic or the political dimension of the concept, whereas *Gong* in its economic sense means proprietorship owned by collectivities (in contrast to individuals) and *Gong* in its political sense refers to the state/central government (in contrast to citizens/local communities). Although public is sometimes equivalent to official/governmental in political and economic contexts (Rowe, 1990), its moral dimension clearly differentiates itself from *Guan* (official). A governmental official or even a government is bad or corrupt if self-interest instead of public interest is pursued. Meanwhile, citizens (*Min*) are not morally superior when they engage *Guan* from the perspective of their self-interests. That is why in Chinese, conflicts can be seen between *Guan* and *Min* but never between *Guan* and *Gong*. Other than the reason that *Guan* and *Gong* are sometimes interchangeable in political and economic contexts, *Gong* is a transcendental moral that governs our judgment about both *Guan*'s and *Min*'s behaviors.

The modern word *Gong Min* (publics) is thus a value-laden concept, rather than a descriptive term. The Chinese definition shares with the Chicago School in its emphasis on the normative meaning of the word but the two traditions emphasize different norms. The Chicago School, when contrasting public to crowd and mass, focuses on the rational critical discussions that enable a discursive relationship among the individual citizens. The Chinese *Gong Min*, by giving private individuals (*Min*) a prefix (*Gong*), stresses the moral rightness the individual citizens have to embrace when they act as a social entity. In other words, it is not the mediation of rational debate that channels the formation of a public but the ultimate justice being pursued gives the individuals the qualification of being a public. Therefore, *Gong Min* does not bear the burden of the norm of rationality as the Western public does, but imposes a different type of burden that is the moral rightness of justice. When social groups merely represent their self-interests in front of the larger society, they would not be qualified as *Gong Min*. Only if these groups are able to articulate their self-interests with the backup of moral rightness or frame their appeals in a sense of justice for all, they could be seen as defending public interest and thus serving *Gong*.

Fans, apparently, do not always live up to this high moral expectation. Instead, popular wisdom often looks down at fans as morally subordinate because their self-interests have little common ground with public interests. As we know that fans are often the minority among audiences, their enthusiasm towards the fan objects constantly faces scrutiny from the majority of a society. There are instances in which their fandom offends the majority and elicits moral condemnation. However, such high moral grounds are hard to reach for any social entities that are trying to advocate for certain issues. By dismissing these efforts as private individuals pursing for self-interests, the complicated dynamics in a network society remains hidden and the tensions are narrowly understood as conflicts between *Guan* and *Min*. It is again proposed that our definition of public shall loose its normative constraint, and this time, the moral rightness bias. One public can be motivated by the self-interests of that particular collectivity and does not have to appeal to justice for all. Different publics can be in conflict with each other when pursing their own interests. Such self-serving efforts are not necessarily unjust or wicked.

I propose that we go back to the origin of the Chinese characters of *Gong* and *Si* so we can be less biased by the moral interpretations that evolved along with the changes of historical conditions. What *Si* indicates in its character layout is basically enclosing, a graphical metaphor of setting up fences to make the land or resources someone's own. If *Gong* is the opposite of *Si*, public means to disclose, to be open, to make visible. Visibility thus becomes the main take from this etymological analysis of *Gong*. Dayan (2005) made a similar argument by stressing that publics differ from spectators or audiences because publics also perform to be seen. In other words, publics engage in collective performance to make themselves visible to the larger society. Such visibility of publics reaches its new height when social media allow any users to broadcast themselves to the entire world on a daily basis (Baym and Boyd, 2012). The critiques on both the Western and Chinese conceptualization of public make it clear that our examination of this social category has to focus on how individuals are connected and visibility in front of the larger society is built through the mediation of new ICTs.

A relational concept of publics

If we take the normative emphasis away from the conceptualization of public and focuses on the term as a social category, the social conditions in which collective entities are formed become critical. The transformation of social morphology from the industrial to network society (Castells, 1996) indicates that social formation has to follow a different logic now, namely, the network logic. The network logic is used in contrast to the vertical-hierarchical logic, which is the dominant organizational structure in the industrial society (Castells, 2005, p. 5). Both American Fordism and Soviet Statism are good examples of such top-down, one-way, rigid hierarchies. The power of network in the industrial society is suppressed because the communication technology at that time is not able to afford large, complex networks. Although networks are not specific to twenty-first century societies, the network logic becomes the most efficient organizational form now thanks to new ICTs, which organize human coordination through electronic information flow with great flexibility, scalability, and survivability (Castells, 2005, p. 6).

Social formation, including the formation of publics, has to happen under the mandate of this network logic. The augmentation of human capacity of information processing enables social actors to (re)organize their efforts in networks of unprecedented size and manage the high degrees of organizational complexity that come with them. In other words, publics "are communicating more and more through complex networks that are bottom-up, top-down, as well as side-to-side" (Ito, 2008, p. 3) and networked publics are in contrast to the passive audiences or consumers, in terms of their networking capability powered by ICTs. My definition of publics is thus oriented towards "associational relationships" (Emirbayer and Sheller, 1999) that are formed in the distinct social conditions of the network society. A relational concept of publics emphasizes first, the enhanced self-selection and self-organization of communication networks, indicated in terms such as "networked individualism" (Wellman, 2002) or "networked collectivism" (Baym, 2007); second, the mediation of ICTs, which organize "sparsely-knit individuals with little regard to space" (Wellman, 2002, p. 10) and restructure the publics through their distinct affordances (Boyd, 2010); third, visibility achieved through the associational relationships among individuals and their constant performances (Dayan, 2005; Papacharissi, 2014).

Outline of the book

This book is guided by a theoretical interest that goes beyond the approaches typically used in new media studies, i.e., virtual communities and online public spheres. It attempts instead to rejuvenate the classic notion of public and provide a fundamental discussion of how publics are formed in the era of network society—in contrast to the mass society era, when the concept, public, was first developed. This focus on publics as political actors who struggle for representation in front of the larger society also distinguishes the book from many works on Internet politics, which usually restrict their examination to political actors who primarily engage with governments or other political institutions such as parliaments or elections. Instead, this book takes a step back to examine a rudimentary social category—fans—and how this social entity becomes a political collectivity that could be considered publics. Engaging with political institutions is only one of the many interactions they undertake to make themselves visible. Their engagement with other publics, local and global commercial forces, and different levels of political power comprises the wide spectrum of their activities.

The empirical interest in fans and fan groups leads to an account of the blurring boundary between cultural and political spheres found in the social realities of China. As much as fan culture is currently studied, this book attempts a sociopolitical reading of Chinese fans, based on fans' own narratives and activities. As an epistemological nuance, this book addresses the application of Actor–Network Theory. This methodological approach was inspired by Bruno Latour (2005), who argues that we should "follow the actors themselves" and not limit our examination to the existing collectivities—which must be acted out by actors in order to exist. In other words, I try to provide a description not of a moving target, but of how the target moves. Latour's dynamic epistemology is particularly suitable for a book that models change rather than stability, and things-in-making instead of things-done. The book builds on an ethnographic work that spans the years between 2000 and 2014. The data used in this book take various forms, including participant observation in a variety of online spaces (e.g., discussion forums, blogs, microblogs, social networking sites); textual analysis of online contents; in-depth interviews and re-interviews with key participants; online surveys of average Internet users; and network analysis of both human and nonhuman components.

Chapter 1, the current chapter, introduces the central argument of the book with a theoretical discussion of how the network logic of new ICTs leads to new ways of forming publics. After reviewing the European, American, and Chinese definitions of public, the contradictions between the traditional conceptualization and the modern social category, fans, are elaborated on. These contradictions invite us to reconsider the boundary between public and private and the social conditions in which the boundary is drawn. Instead of inserting too much normative expectation to the concept, public, I propose to use a relational concept of publics in order to trace the developing procedure of forming social entities that function as political collectivities in an ever-changing China.

Chapter 2 opens with an empirical review of the development of popular culture in China, including its most recent phase of digitalization. The importance of entertainment-seeking among Internet users is confirmed through user data (e.g., CNNIC) and industry reports, as well as media coverage. Despite its empirical prominence, academic endeavors to understand the phenomenon of popular culture on the Chinese Internet have been scarce. The second part of the chapter attempts to explain why these entertainment-seeking netizens have not become a focus of research on China and Internet. The ideological and structural biases implied in the relative lack of discussion of online fandom are explored, and the book's intellectual orientation is further explained with an emphasis on the technologies.

Chapter 3 focuses on one of the most influential online communities of movie fans, Rear Window to Movies. Using data from 14 in-depth interviews, an online survey with 185 respondents, and participant observation over two years, the discourse that emerges from fans' engaged discussions is identified and contrasted to the state and commercial discourses. The activities fans engage in to disseminate their discourse to the larger society are documented in detail. When these fans develop their own discourse and make it visible to the majority of social members, they become a public. The subaltern nature of this public has to be acknowledged, however, due to the relatively limited reach and influence of their discourse.

In Chapter 4, Rear Window to Movies fans were revisited 10 years after the original study to trace the dynamics of the Chinese Internet and the fandom it mediates. Another set of 15 in-depth interviews, as well as a decade-long continuous participant observation, yielded evidence of how the social network, initiated and stabilized in cyberspace, transforms the subaltern public into the regular public. Some of the movie fans who share their thoughts and feelings about movies became "freelance movie reviewers" through their connections with mass media executives. Later on, popular online reviewers were able to enter the moviemaking process through their connections with both independent filmmakers and directors in the commercial movie industry. These reviewers can promote their standards of quality not only through their online criticism, but also through creative work (e.g., screenwriting) that is directly connected to the production of movies.

The connectivity of contemporary fans allows for creativity in their interpretation and reinvention of fan objects. Fans are no longer merely consumers, passively receiving what they are offered. They become users and producers in one (i.e., prod-users). Chapter 5 expands the boundary of fan objects from movies to any foreign-language content, including both entertainment and information. Fans' creativity is demonstrated by the phenomenon of the online translation community. Volunteer translation arose in the context of pirated VCD/DVDs, when the translation of foreign movies was often of poor quality due to the limitations of those doing the pirating. When the Internet became the main source of free foreign content, translating such content into Chinese required volunteers. This chapter traces the history of the online translation community, analyzes the ICT-based mechanism that makes the collaboration possible, and investigates volunteers' motives for contribution. The potential of such fan creativity to foster a civic culture is discussed in this chapter.

As a special case of online foreign content, American political sit-coms represent a genre of fan objects that issues a political invitation to its consumers. Chapter 6 focuses on the content itself, which has been deliberately ignored in previous chapters. Whereas publics can form around any issue, those that form around foreign content such as American political sit-coms have unique features, such as being prompted to embrace democratic values. Through a textual analysis of posts on a Baidu discussion board for *House of Cards* fans, this chapter shows how Chinese fans interpret American reality shows according to two themes of contradiction: authentic/unauthentic and foreign/indigenous. More importantly, this chapter demonstrates how the interactions among fans enabled by such fan communities reshape the meaning-making process of viewing and enjoying foreign content.

A turn is taken in Chapter 7 with a more profound effort to discover the network logic. Social networking sites (SNSs) in China are even more diverse than in American and European contexts. This chapter examines Douban, a SNS that connects users not only through social ties but also via fan objects such as books, movies, and music albums, in contrast to a Facebook-type SNS, Renren. Network analysis and an online survey of users clarify the different structures and effects of relationship-oriented SNSs and interest-oriented SNSs. This network logic, which resonates with Castells' argument, can be viewed as the social-formation principle of the network society.

In Chapter 8, the network logic discussed in the previous chapter is used to analyze Weibo, and in particular, the celebrities on Weibo. The fan objects here are the celebrities themselves, and they serve as network nodes that connect not only their fans but also topics that emerge from different domains. These celebrities' capacity for meta-connection allows their followers the access to discussions of various topics and to be in touch with each other. However, the concentration of celebrities as critical nodes in the network also brings vulnerability to the networked publics.

The concluding chapter, Chapter 9, locates the book's findings in a broader theoretical context, building conversations with a diverse range of conceptual traditions. After a review of concepts such as "mediated publics" and "networked publics," I attempt to clarify the network logic through contrasting three network theories, namely, Social Network Theory, The Network Society, and Actor–Network Theory. The network logic that mandates the formation and maintenance of fandom publics is illustrated by synthesizing various empirical findings scattered among different chapters. Then, I delve deep into the visibility fandom publics have to achieve and the performative dimension of the concept. Through a comparison to the concepts of "issue publics" and "affective publics," the style and aesthetics of the co-performance of fandom publics are explicated. Finally, I provide critiques of the concept, fandom publics, via four critical frames, namely, democratization, post-Marxism, post-colonialism, and post-modernism. Through an active and reflective engagement with such critical traditions, I end this book with a proposal of looking at power as seduction, rather than power as coercion, or exploitation, or hegemony, or knowledge.

Bibliography

Baym, N. (2000). *Tune in, log on: Soaps, fandom, and online community*, Sage, Thousand Oaks, CA.

Baym, N. (2007). The new shape of online community: The examples of Swedish independent music fandom. *First Monday*, 12(8). Retrieved from http://firstmonday.org/htbin/cgiwrap/bin/ojs/index.php/fm/rt/printerFriendly/1978/1853.

Baym, N. and Boyd, D. (2012). Socially mediated publicness: An introduction. *Journal of Broadcasting & Electronic Media*, 56(3), 320–329.

Bell, C. and Newby, H. (1976). Community, communion, class and community action: The social sources of the new urban politics, in *Social areas in cities: Vol. II. Spatial perspectives on problems and policies*, eds D. T. Herbert and R. J. Johnston, Wiley, Hoboken, NJ, pp. 189–207.

Bernard, J. (1973). *The sociology of community*, Scott & Foresman, Glenview, IL.

Bourdieu, P. (1993). The field of cultural production or: The economic world reversed, in *The field of cultural production: Essays on art and literature*, ed. R. Johnson, Columbia University Press, New York, pp. 29–73.

Boyd, D. (2010). Social network sites as networked publics: Affordances, dynamics, and implications, in *Networked self: Identity, community, and culture on social network sites*, ed. Z. Papacharissi, Routledge, New York, pp. 39–58.

Boyd, D. M. and Ellison, N. B. (2007). Social network sites: Definition, history, and scholarship. *Journal of Computer-Mediated Communication*, 13(1), article 11. http://jcmc.indiana.edu/vol13/issue1/boyd.ellison.html.

Blumer, H. (1946). Collective behavior, in *New outlines of the principles of sociology*, ed. A. M. Lee, Barnes and Noble, New York, pp. 167–222.

Calhoun, C. J. (1980). Community: Toward a variable conceptualization for comparative research, *Social History*, 5(1), 105–129.

Castells, M. (1996). *The rise of the network society*, Blackwell, Oxford and Cambridge, MA.

Castells, M. (2005). Informationalism, networks, and the network society: A theoretical blueprint, in *The network society: A cross-cultural perspective*, ed. M. Castells, Edward Elgar, Cheltenham, pp. 3–48.

Chu, Y. C. (2002). The consumption of cinema in contemporary China, in *Media in China: Consumption, content and crisis*, eds S. H. Donald, M. Keane, and Y. Hong, Routledge, London, pp. 43–54.

Dayan, D. (2005). Mothers, midwives and abortionists: Genealogy, obstetrics, audiences and publics, in *Audiences and publics: When cultural engagement matters for the public sphere*, ed. S. Livingstone, Intellect Ltd, Bristol, pp. 43–74.

Dewey, J. (1927). *The public and its problems*, Holt, Rinehart & Winston, New York.

Emirbayer, M. and Sheller, M. (1999). Publics in history, *Theory and Society*, 28, 145–197.

Fiske, J. (1992). The cultural economy of fandom, in *The adoring audience: Fan culture and popular media*, ed. L. A. Lewis, Routledge, London and New York, pp. 30–49.

Fraser, N. (1993). Rethinking the public sphere: A contribution to the critique of actually existing democracy, in *The phantom public sphere*, ed. B. Robbins, University of Minnesota Press, Minneapolis, MN, pp. 1–32.

Friedland, L. A. (2001). Communication, community, and democracy: Toward a theory of the communicatively integrated community, *Communication Research*, 28(4), 358–391.

Grossberg, L. (1992). Is there a fan in the house? The affective sensibility of fandom, in *Fan culture and popular media*, ed. L.A. Lewis, Routledge, London and New York, pp. 50–68.

Habermas, J. (1979). *Communication and the evolution of society*, Beacon Press, Boston, MA.

Habermas, J. (1984). *The theory of communicative action, Vol. 1: Reason and the rationalization of society*, trans. T. McCarthy, Beacon Press, Boston, MA.

Habermas, J. (1989). *The structural transformation of the public sphere: An inquiry into a category of bourgeois society*, MIT Press, Cambridge, MA.

Hartley, J. (2002). *Communication, cultural and media studies: The key concepts*, Routledge, London.

Hellekson, K. and Busse, K. (2006). *Fan fiction and fan communities in the age of the Internet*, McFarland, Jefferson, NC.

Hills, M. (2002). *Fan cultures*, Routledge, London and New York.

Jenkins, H. (2006). *Convergence culture: Where old and new media collide*, New York University Press, New York.

Jensen, J. (1992). Fandom as pathology: The consequences of characterization, in *The Adoring Audience: Fan culture and popular media*, ed. L. A. Lewis, Routledge, London and New York, pp. 9–29.

Jones, S. G. (1995). *CyberSociety: Computer-mediated communication and community*, Sage, Thousand Oaks, CA.

Ito, M. (2008). Introduction, in *Networked publics*, ed. K. Varnelis, MIT press, Cambridge, MA, pp. 1–14.

Latour, B. (2005). *Reassembling the social: An introduction to Actor-Network-Theory*, Oxford University Press, Oxford.

LeBon, G. (1895/1960). *The crowd*, Viking, New York.

Li, Y. (2010). *Cinephilia: The history of a culture*, Fudan University Press, Shanghai.

Lippmann, W. (1925). *The phantom public*, Harcourt Brace Jovanovich, New York.

Livingstone, S. (2005). On the relation between audiences and publics, in *Audiences and publics: When cultural engagement matters for the public sphere*, ed. S. Livingstone, Intellect Ltd, Bristol, pp. 17–42.

Mills, C. W. (1956). *The power elite*, Oxford University Press, Oxford.

Mizoguchi, Y. (2011). *The evolution of the concepts "public" and "private" in China* [in Chinese], Beijing, China: SDX Joint Publishing.

Papacharissi, Z. (2014). *Affective publics: Sentiment, technology, and politics*, Oxford University Press.

Park, R. E. (1904/1972). *The crowd and the public and other essays*, University of Chicago Press, Chicago, IL.

Price, V. (1992). *Public opinion*, Sage, Newbury Park, CA.

Rainie, H., and Wellman, B. (2012). *Networked: The new social operating system*, MIT Press, Cambridge, MA.

Rheingold, H. (1993). *The Online community: Homesteading on the Electronic Frontie*, MIT Press, Cambridge, MA.

Rowe, W. T. (1990). The public sphere in modern China. *Modern China*, 16(3), 309–329.

Shefrin, E. (2004). Lord of the Rings, Star Wars and participatory fandom: Mapping new congruencies between the Internet and media entertainment culture. *Critical Studies in Media Communication*, 21(3), 261–281.

Sontag, S. (1996). The decay of cinema, *The New York Times*, February 25. Retrieved from www.nytimes.com.

Splichal, S. (1999). *Public opinion: Developments and controversies in the twentieth century*, Rowman & Littlefield, Lanham, MD.

Stalder, F. (2006). *Manuel Castells*. Polity, Cambridge.

Surowiecki, J. (2004). *The wisdom of crowds*, Anchor Books, New York.

Tarde, G. (1890/1903). *The laws of imitation*, Holt, New York.

Theberge, P. (2004). Everyday fandom: Fan clubs, blogging, and the quotidian rhythms of the Internet. *Canadian Journal of Communication*, 30, pp. 485–502.

Van Zoonen, L. (2005). *Entertaining the citizen: When politics and popular culture converge*, Rowman & Littlefield, Lanham, MD.

Watson, N. (1997). Why we argue about virtual community: A case study of the phish. net fan community, in *Virtual culture: Identity and communication in cybersociety*, ed. S. G. Jones, Sage, Thousand Oaks, CA, pp. 102–132.

Wellman, B. (1999). The network community: An introduction, in *Networks in the global village: Life in contemporary communities*, ed. B. Wellman, Westview Press, Boulder, CO, pp. 1–48.

Wellman, B. (2005). Little boxes, glocalization, and networked individualism, in *Digital cities*, eds M. Tanabe, P. van den Besselaar, T. Ishida, Springer, Heidelberg, Germany, pp. 10–25.

Zhang, W. and Mao, C. (2013). Fan activism sustained and challenged: Participatory culture in Chinese social media. *Chinese Journal of Communication*, 6(1), 45–61.

Zhang, W. and Wang, R. (2010). Interest-oriented versus relationship-oriented social network sites in China. *First Monday*, 15(8). Retrieved from http://firstmonday.org/htbin/cgiwrap/bin/ojs/index.php/fm/article/view/2836/2582|.

Zhu, Y. (2002). Chinese Cinemas economic reform from the mid-1980s to the mid-1990s. *Journal of Communication*, 52(4), 905–921.

2 Popular culture and digital technologies

Li Yuchun is a Chinese female singer and actress who appeared on the cover of one issue of *Time Magazine* as the popular idol of China. She made her fame through wining a nationwide singing contest, *Super Girl*, in 2005. Before Li Yuchun became the household name via her performances on TV, another Chinese female Furong Jiejie (literally meaning Sister Lotus), far less good looking and talented than Li, had already made waves on the Internet and received extensive coverage by the mass media a year earlier. Furong Jiejie started to be noted when she posted many of her own portrays on Tsinghua University's Bulletin Board System, arguably one of the most active online communities among Chinese college students. Along with these pictures, Furong Jiejie spoke highly of her own appearance and talent in a very genuine tone, which amused the Internet users who apparently disagreed. It seems that Li Yuchun is the TV idol and Furong Jiejie is the Chinese Internet's own superstar. However, the fact is both figures have earned their position in Chinese contemporary popular culture through both new and traditional media. Li Yuchun's fan groups were largely based on the Internet, with the Baidu Postbar as a prominent leader. These fan groups were able to mobilize thousands of votes and make their idol the final winner of the contest. Meanwhile, Furong Jiejie started to appear on TV or newspapers for commercial purposes after she became so well known by the Chinese Internet users. Both females are not the type of diva one often sees in the Chinese mainstream: Li Yuchun is a tomboyish girl who does not wear fancy dresses and Forong Jiejie is not even pretty. The cultural transformation such female celebrities symbolize is so fast that scholars can barely keep up with the changes.

This chapter opens with an empirical review of the development of popular culture in China, including its most recent phase of digitalization. The importance of entertainment seeking among ordinary Chinese in general and Internet users in particular is confirmed through user data (e.g., CNNIC), industry reports (e.g., iResearch), media surveys (e.g, Xiaokang Magazine), and national statistics on the cultural industry (e.g., Statistics Bureau). Despite its empirical prominence, academic endeavors to understand the phenomenon of popular culture have not picked up the momentum until the 1990s. The second part of the chapter attempts to review existing English language literatures on studying popular culture in contemporary China, with an emphasis on how historical contexts shape our inquiry. The last part of this chapter explains why the entertainment-seeking netizens have not become a focus of research on China and Internet and how existing theoretical frameworks are incapable of describing and explaining online popular culture. The book's intellectual orientation is further explained through proposing a perspective of technological centralism when studying online popular culture.

The supply and demand of cultural products

China has 5.64 billion Internet users (Chinese Internet Network Information Center [CNNIC], 2013), and this number is still growing. Between 3 and 4 billion users connect to the Internet for entertainment, such as reading literatures, listening to music, watching videos, and playing games. Roughly 70–80% of Chinese Internet users also seek information from the Internet (online news, search engines, etc.), including a large amount of entertainment information. Entertainment has consistently been the second most popular type of Internet activity (lower than information seeking) since the CNNIC adopted its current breakdown of usage behaviors. From January 2007 to January 2013, the number of online gamers and video watchers almost tripled (see Figure 2.1). Reading online literatures, much of which is user generated content, is also a popular pastime, with the number of users doubled during the five years between

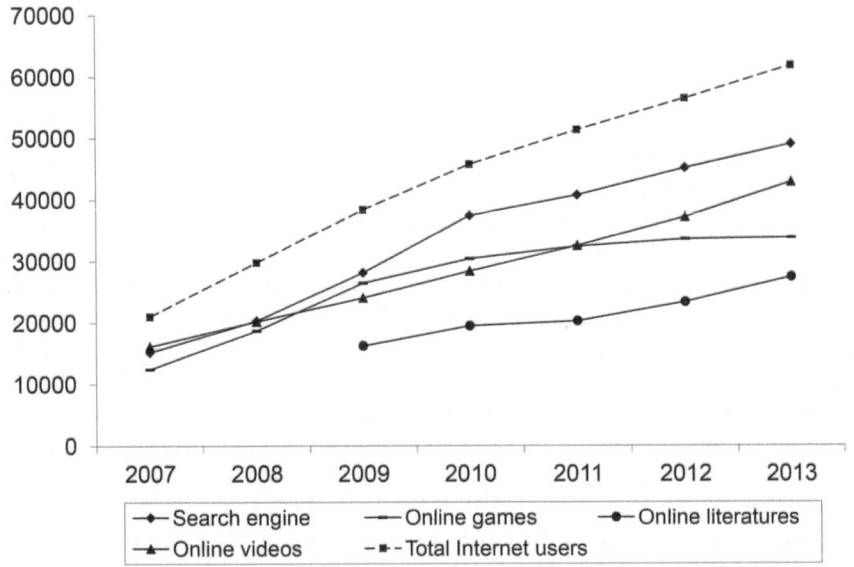

Figure 2.1 Number of Internet users (in ten thousands) in China, 2007–2013
Source: CNNIC.

2009 and 2013. Listening to music on the Internet was one of the users' favorite online activities, too. Although the statistics only lasted till 2009, the trend was obviously fast shooting up. Is entertainment-seeking a unique behavior pattern that belongs to Chinese netizens? Are the Internet users particularly playful compared to the hard-working majority of the Chinese population? The answer is no.

If development means the enhancement of living conditions (Zhang and Chib, 2014), both material goods and cultural consumption are part of modern life. The consumption of cultural goods is a phenomenon that is only possible after a market of such goods comes into being. Actually, one definition of popular culture (Gold, 1993, p. 908) puts its emphasis on a mass market, for which cultural products are produced. If we look at the big picture of popular culture in China, both the supply and the demand side of the mass market of cultural products have gone through tremendous changes over the years. At the demand side, we witnessed a steady increase in money spent on consuming cultural goods among both urban and rural families (see Figure 2.2). From year 2005 to 2012, cultural consumption per person in an urban family has increased from 526 yuan to 1214 yuan and the increase was largely attributed to the consumption of services, in contrast to the consumption of devices such as television sets and computers. The increase, however, was much slower among the rural families, with cultural consumption per person

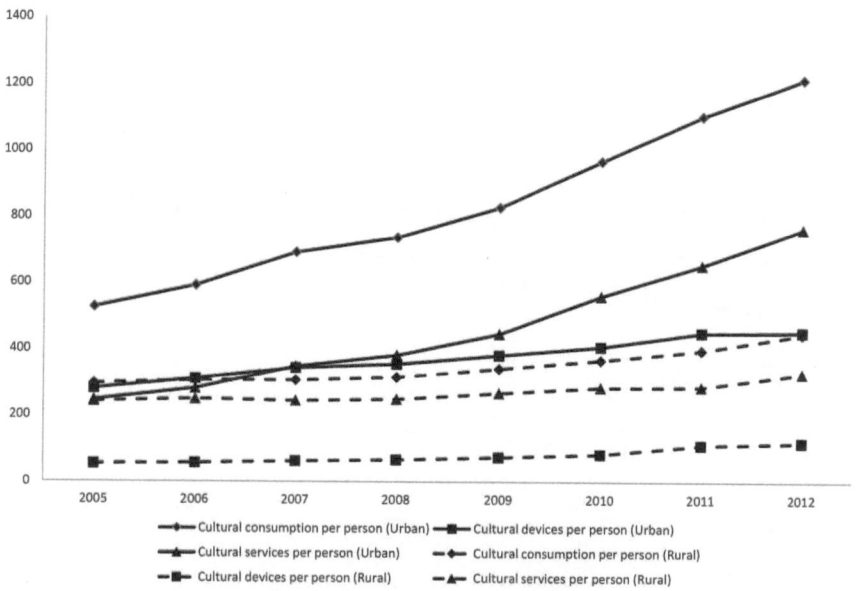

Figure 2.2 Money (in Yuan) spent on cultural consumption in China, 2005–2012
Source: *The Statistics Yearbook of Cultural Industry* (2013).

changing from 295 yuan to 445 yuan. From these numbers, we can see that popular culture and its consumption are more of an urban phenomenon.

In addition to money, the amount of free time is also critical for Chinese to enjoy leisure and entertainment. A recent report (China Tourism Academy, 2013) of leisure activities shows that on average, Chinese urbanites had 3.6 hours leisure time on a weekday, 5.3 hours on a weekend day, and 6.1 hours on a holiday in 2012. The amount of leisure time Chinese rural residents have is highly seasonal. During the high season of farming work, there were on average 3.8 hours spent on leisure. And when the farming work was not heavy, the hours increased to 5.1. These numbers, compared to developed countries such as the US, are relatively low. For instance, the American Time Use Survey (Bureau of Labor Statistics, 2013) shows that the annual average of leisure time among Americans was 5.1 hours in 2012, a number that is close to Chinese urbanites' weekend average and rural residents' low season average. A longitudinal survey conducted by *Xiaokang Magazine*, a magazine published by Qiushi Journal, an "organ of the Central Committee of the Communist Party of China" (http://english.qstheory.cn/), shows that the level of satisfaction with leisure spending and leisure activities have both increased over time whereas the satisfaction level with leisure time kept the same since 2005 (see Figure 2.3). When both money and motivation are available but time is limited, the Internet has taken a leading position in leisure activities because of its convenience and flexibility. The 2012 Xiaokang survey, along with many other studies (e.g., Yin, 2005), confirms that the favorite Chinese leisure

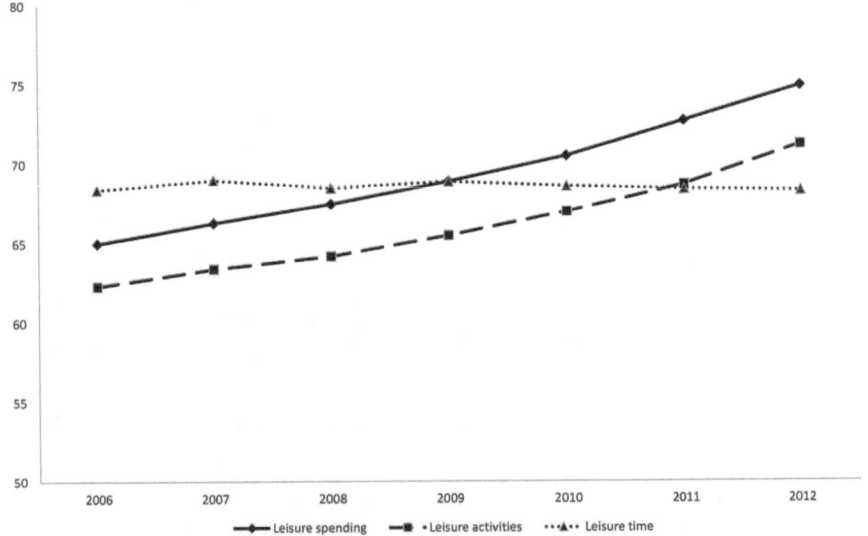

Figure 2.3 Levels of satisfaction with leisure-relevant issues among Chinese (percentages of people who are satisfied), 2006–2012
Source: *Xiaokang Magazine* (2013a).

activity is to go online (Xiaokang Magazine, 2013b), followed by traveling, watching movies, shopping, watching TV, and so on.

With abundant money but limited time at the dispersal of Chinese urbanites, the needs for cultural consumption seemed to be met by an enthusiasm of the media producers. At the supply side, we witnessed a rapid growth in the pro- duction of cultural goods, especially the electronic and digital ones. Except for books, traditional media products such as newspapers and magazines have been staggering in their growth (see Figure 2.4). One may argue that it is, at least partially, because that newspapers and magazines are under strict license quota enforced by the government. A further examination of the sales number (i.e., number of copies sold) shows that still, there is virtually no growth in magazine sales and the increase of newspaper sales is about 10% from 2005 to 2012 (National Bureau of Statistics of China, 2013). Books, despite the big jump in number of titles printed, actually were not better sold over the years. Audio/video products in the format of CDs, VCDs, DVDs, and blu-rays even had a decrease in titles produced whereas there was no change in copies sold. What have been growing fast are radio programs, TV programs, and movies. The hours of both radio and TV programs produced have increased over 20% from 2005 to 2012 (see Figure 2.5). The number of regular movies has had a 65% growth during the same time period (see Figure 2.6). Different from the print media, such growths in production were paralleled with the growths in sales. For

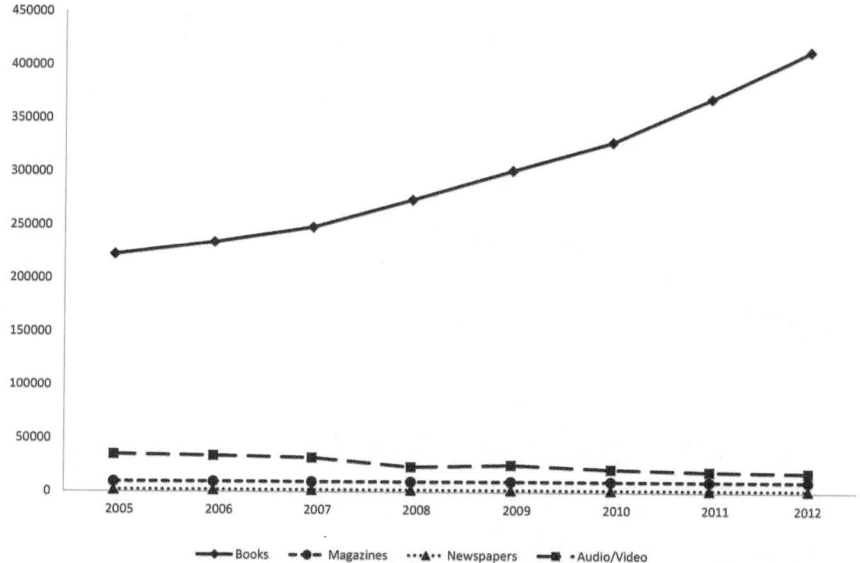

Figure 2.4 Number of titles of books, magazines, newspapers, and audio/video products produced in China, 2005–2012
Source: *The Statistics Yearbook of Cultural Industry* (2013).

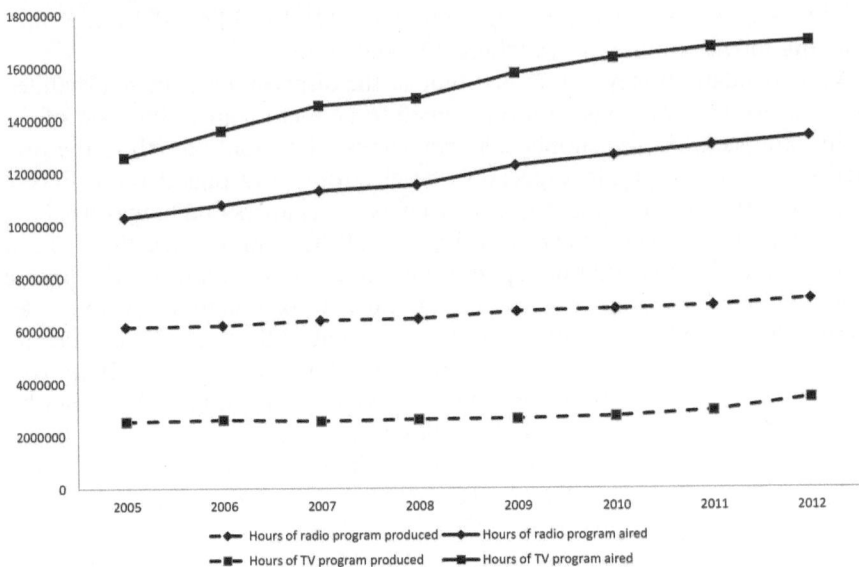

Figure 2.5 Hours of radio and TV program produced and aired in China, 2005–2012
Source: *The Statistics Yearbook of Cultural Industry* (2013).

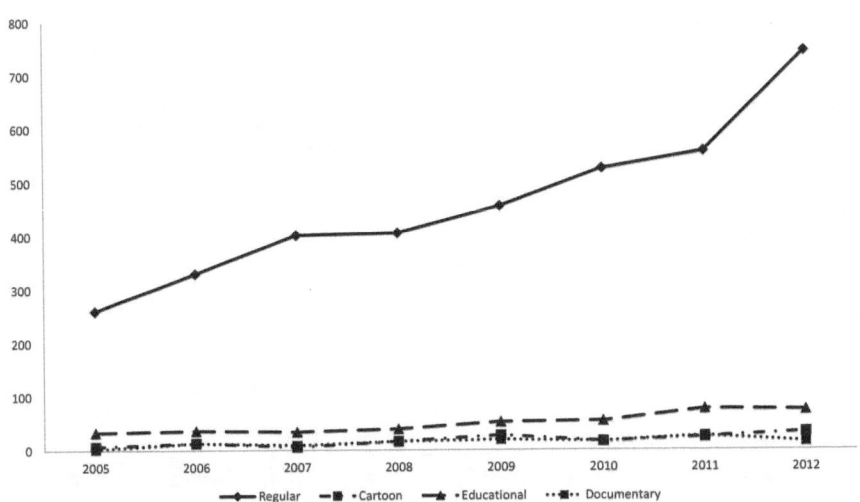

Figure 2.6 Number of movies produced in China, 2005–2012
Source: *The Statistics Yearbook of Cultural Industry* (2013).

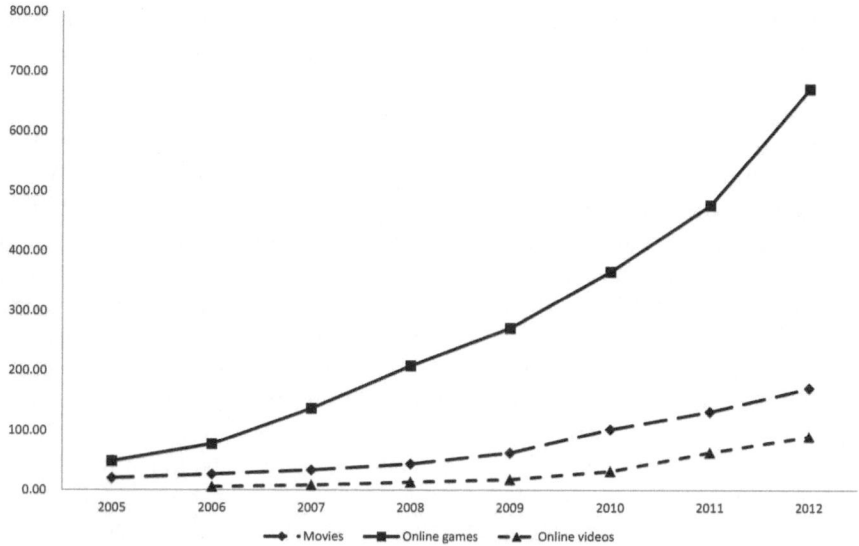

Figure 2.7 Market revenues (in 100 million Yuan) of movies, online games, and online videos in China, 2005–2012

Source: Multiple reports from CNNIC and iResearch (www.iresearch.com.cn).

instance, the box office income of movies has had an 88% leap from 2005 to 2012 (see Figure 2.7).

Whereas the growth of electronic cultural products is impressive, the speed at which digital cultural goods flourish can only be described as explosive. Online games had the market revenue of 4.8 billion in 2006 and the number became 67 billion, 14 times larger in 2012. The market revenue of online videos in 2012 was about 20 times larger than the number in 2006. In contrast, the box office income of movies was eight times larger in 2012 than in 2006. It is without doubt that digital cultural products have become one of the dominant material formats of popular culture in China. Both usage data and market statistics suggest that cultural consumption, which is often considered entertainment-seeking behavior; is nevertheless central to ordinary Chinese's everyday life. Without fully understanding cultural consumption and its recent phase of digitalization, our knowledge about both China and the network society would be incomplete.

The unpopular scholarship of popular culture

Despite the empirical prominence of popular culture in China, scholarly investigation on the topic is still scarce. First of all, we have to acknowledge that this is not just a problem of Chinese scholarship. Popular culture studies in general have been ignored in the academic community till the late 1960s and early 1970s (Lent, 2013) and in the case of China, the 1990s. The reasons for ignoring popular culture studies in the Chinese context are both similar to and different from those in an American or European context. Similarly, popular culture in China is often considered as low, in contrast to high culture or fine art (Zhong, 2010, pp. 3–4). Academics, as part of the intellectual elite, are thus not supposed to work on such issues of little taste. The dismissal of popular culture in China is further reinforced in a historical era that follows the closure of Cultural Revolution. Wang (1996) named the 1980s a period of "high culture fever," during which China's post-revolutionary utopian vision reached its new height among the intellectual elite till 1989 brought an abrupt ending to the heated debate. Meanwhile, the marketization introduced by Deng Xiaoping ironically brought some members of the intellectual elite unprecedented popularity, leading to both fame and money (Zha, 1995). The intellectual elite who were given or witnessed this sudden celebrity were perplexed by this radical transformation. Zha (1995) very well documented the internal and external struggles experienced by the once-to-be fine artists, illustrated in the example of Chen Kaige, one of the most well-known fifth generation film directors. Another iconic example that marks the transition from the 1980s to 1990s is Wang Shuo, whose hooligan literature written in the 1980s specifically targeted the sense of superiority of intellectuals and became bestsellers in the 1990s (Wang, 1996). The ignorance of popular culture studies in the 1980s can thus be understood as an antagonistic stand against the low, tasteless, and quickly commercializing mass culture, devoid of ideological utopians.

When commercialization and consumption took roots in Chinese society during the 1990s, the local intellectuals seemed to retreat to the ivory tower by alienating themselves from the debate on cultural politics (Wang, 1996). Meanwhile, a burgeoning scholarly attention from English-speaking academics became evident (e.g., Lull, 1991; Chinoy, 1999). Considering that popular culture could be imagined as just another type of mass-consumed products that contribute to the economic growth of the country, cultural consumption as an economic activity has emerged as one significant characteristic of the 1990s' cultural scene. Chinese consumers were increasingly allowed to buy (not necessarily from the original producers) many cultural products that were not available before the open-up, starting from those from the Greater China (Hong Kong and Taiwan) to East Asia (Japan and Korea) to the Far West (US and UK). The influence of consumption was so profound that some scholars proclaimed that there was a "consumer revolution" (Wu, 1999; Davis, 2000), empowering Chinese to become citizens through their purchase power. It was believed that consumption brings Chinese citizens the consciousness of individual choices and eventually, the desire of defending their own rights to make such choices (Davis, 2006).

Apparently, the Chinese government has never naively treated cultural consumption as purely an economic activity. Policies and regulations regarding the production and distribution of cultural products have been in constant revisions in order to address the emerging challenges. The biggest threat to the ideological control during the 1990s was the beloved and hated globalization (Hockx and Strauss, 2006). On one hand, integration with the global market is inevitable and the government was under huge pressure from the global capitals to further open the cultural market, including increasing the quota for foreign imports and taking actions against the local piracy (Fung, 2008). On the other hand, a worry about surrendering to foreign cultures was prominent in the official discourse. Although nationalism was used politically to give the Chinese government additional legitimacy in the post-reform era, the fear of losing Chinese culture was at least partially sincere. In addition to controlling the influx of foreign cultural products, the government was provocative in pushing the local industry to both compete with the global capitals and perform ideological functions (Yu, 2009). As Link, Madsen, and Pickowicz (2002, p. 3) pointed out, this post-1989 era had a new central tension, which is between different aspects of globalization, in contrast to the tension between state and society that dominated the years after 1978 and before 1989.

The complexity regarding globalization has driven popular culture studies to go beyond the economic aspect and to investigate the production, distribution, and consumption of cultural products as social and cultural practices embedded with meanings. One thread of such research focused on the media reform, with or without discussing the implications of such structural transformation for popular culture. Among those which did (e.g., Lu, 2002; Yu, 2009), the implications were largely centered on the problem of modernity, or a cultural identity that is neither Communist nor Capitalist. Popular culture in this sense is not only seeable/hearable media content, but embodiment and expression of the confused identity of being Chinese in a modern society. Cinema studies have long been discussing this issue in their documentations and interpretations of Chinese movies (e.g., Lu, 1998; Zhu, 2003). However, what marked the complications of modern identity and popular culture in the 1990s were definitely TV programs, especially TV dramas. If popular music was more about youth culture (De Kloet, 2006), TV dominated the attention of the majority of population regardless of age. Quite a few volumes have been dedicated to studying Chinese TV (Lull, 1991; Chinoy, 1999; Curtin, 2007; Zhu, 2008; Zhu and Berry, 2009; Zhu, Keane, and Bai, 2008; Zhong, 2010; Zhu, 2014). They together provided a comprehensive examination of Chinese TV as an institution, the political economy of TV reform, the transnational and trans-border flow of TV content, the subgenres and styles of TV programs, and audiences' receptions and interpretations of the content. All of these aspects are linked to the idea of identity politics, in contrast to party or ideological politics.

Another group of studies have conceptualized popular culture as opposed to official culture, manifested in the time and space of living in contemporary China. Unofficial culture, as Link, Madsen, and Pickowicz (1989, p. 5) introduced, refers to "any kind of culture that has its origin in the social side of the tension between state and society." This definition has two layers of meanings: Firstly, folk or local culture that emerged before the institutionalization of a centralized Socialist state could be seen as lying at the other side.

This layer of meaning leads us to fix our eyes on traditions and rituals as well as their contemporary (dis)continuations, which were exactly what Wu and Murphy (1994) tried to record in their edited book. Secondly, the daily life lived by ordinary Chinese answers, resists and transgresses the official culture. This understanding is in line with Williams' (1958) well-known definition of culture, which means a whole way of life that is ordinary. Williams (1958) also emphasized that culture is both traditional and creative. This second layer of meaning coincides with this point in the focus on the creative ways ordinary Chinese use to bypass or to null the omniscient official power. Works that have followed this definition often had a strong flavor of ethnography, putting much attention to the thick description of the in-situ insights (e.g., Link, Madsen, and Pickowicz, 1989; Barme, 1999; Dutton, 2000; Link, Madsen, and Pickowicz, 2002; Wang, 2005). Equipped with this ethnographic methodology, the examination of unofficial culture often went far to include aspects of life that are rarely considered by popular culture scholars their subjects, such as marriages and divorces (Arkush, 1989; Zhang, 1989), rural migrant workers (Chan, 2002; Zhang, 2002; Sun, 2005), commercial nightlife (Feng, 2005), and consuming T-shirts (Barme, 1999). Although these rich ethnographic accounts provided us a broad view of the social mosaic, the emphasis on the opposition to the official is no longer appropriate when marketization, globalization, urbanization, social stratifications, power conflicts (e.g., those between the provincial and the central government), and identity struggles (e.g., those of gender, sexuality and ethnicity) all intersect with cultural practices and are shaping/shaped by culture.

Technological centralism in studying online popular culture

The development of Chinese popular culture during the last two decades in the twentieth century has shown us the extreme complexity of the subject. A simple binary framework that contradicts state and society has been replaced by a tripod structure that differentiates state, market, and society (e.g., Gries and Rosen, 2010). But I argue that this new framework still cannot capture the volatile boundaries among the three entities because these so-called entities are not really entire and undergoing breakdowns and re-inventions almost all the time. This lack of descriptive and explanatory power of existing frameworks is best illustrated in discussing the role of technology, in particular, information and communication technologies (ICTs). Neither the structure approach (e.g., the political economy of mass media) nor the audience approach (e.g., audiences' receptions and interpretations of TV dramas) nor the content approach (e.g., discourse analysis of films) was ready to incorporate technology in its meta-narrative. In most cases, technology takes a secondary position in such studies, as seen in terms such as "channels," "tools," and "status markers," which mean merely a material existence that is given meanings to. For instance, one storyline about ICTs tells us that both Chinese state and society are trying to use technology as an efficient tool to further their interests. On one hand, scholars investigate how the authoritarian state successfully maintains its power through ICTs (e.g., the sophisticated system of censorship; Qiu, 2007). On the other hand, scholars document how citizens, non-government organizations (NGOs), and other non-state players take advantage of the Internet to resist the totalitarian force of the state (e.g., online activism; Yang, 2010).

When viewing ICTs as an efficient tool to strengthen the state power, researchers first establish the oppressive nature of the state. Next, they analyze the persistence of authoritarian power despite of the transformational characteristics of ICTs. Consequently, the flagship area of censorship studies has received the most public attention, with an emphasis on surveillance, control, and the Great Firewall (Wang and Hong, 2010; Y. Zhao, 2008). These studies start from the assumption that ICTs are double-edged swords that both enhance individual freedom and facilitate state control, but the latter argument seems to be more pervasive. From technological means, infrastructure building, administrative arrangements, regulatory regimes to hegemonic control, Internet censorship in China indicates an unprecedented level of state control. A related thread of research establishes how the state takes advantage of public sentiment by manipulating nationalist jingoism to reinforce control (Pan, Lee, Chan, and So, 2001; Qiu, 2006; X. Wu, 2007).

Activism studies serve as a counter-theme to censorship research, focusing on participation, engagement, democracy, civil society, and the public sphere. The assumption is that the control of the state still leaves a large space of struggle for citizens and NGOs, empowered by the usage of ICTs as highly promising and fundamentally liberating (Yang, 2010). Although censorship research reveals a densely knit web of state control, Chinese citizens seem to be able to probe blind spots to promote social advancement in various situations. Public spheres flourished on the Internet to allow the public expression of opinions and debates (Cheong and Gong, 2010; Dai, 2007; S. Li, 2010; M. Wu, 2008; Zhang, 2012), which were rarely seen in the state-controlled commercial mass media (Reese, 2009). The challenges posed by the Internet for traditional media are discussed extensively in Y. Zhao's (2008) comprehensive book on the media regime in China. However, the democratization potential of the Internet in China is still contested and is far from settled, even after a decade of study (Huang, 1999; Taubman, 1998; Stanley, 2010; Yuan, 2010).

The censorship vs. activism dualism is a great example to show how simplistic our view of technology is. The ultimate question seems to rest upon who will win the battle with the tools of ICTs. If ICTs help activists win, a democratic government will emerge, and if ICTs stand at the side of censorship, the state will continue as an oppressive apparatus. Unfortunately, many studies on popular culture and ICTs in China fall into this dualist trap, too. They are obsessed with the question, whether online fandom of popular culture is empowering the state or the society. With the state/market/society framework getting well-known, the simplistic view takes one step further and asks whether popular culture facilitated by ICTs is empowering the global capitals, the state that is in conspiracy with capitals, or the society that is against both above. Zheng's (2007) book rightly pointed out that the Internet empowers all, with victory dependent upon particular circumstances. There won't be a simple answer to the "who wins" question, since the dispute is not a zero-sum game. For instance, ICTs may help capitalists in the global cultural industry to exploit fans but the fact would not automatically deny the potential of online popular culture to resist and revise other powers, including both the state power and social powers (e.g., gender discrimination).

Here I argue for a perspective of technological centralism to study the role of ICTs in any social changes, including the changes of popular culture. First of all, I have to make clear the distinctions between technological centralism and two other infamous terms, namely, technological essentialism and technological determinism. Both infamous terms are problematic not because of technology but due to the way they define technology. Technological essentialism tends to see technology as possessing a set of attributes that are necessary for technology to be technology. The most erroneous version of technological essentialism is to make a moral judgment of the attributes by saying that ICTs are essentially good or bad. Technological essentialism in disguise would say ICTs are essentially both good and bad, depending on how people use them (i.e., technological instrumentalism). This view is still essentialist because instead of carefully looking into the large variety of technologies that we call ICTs, it assumes that all ICTs are the same in the most bracketing and thus uninformative way, i.e., both good and bad. In addition, this view also implies that technology is neutral in nature and becomes discriminatory in the effects of its usage. For example, a computer is a computer and it only becomes a tool of crime when a criminal uses it to hurt people. Still this view ignores the historical and interactionist attributes of technology, which means that ICTs are not an autonomous force separated from state, market, society, and many other forces. Not all computers are of the same nature. Those computers that have been fully turned into criminal tools by terrorists are not neutral. Technological determinism is also wrong due to its logic of determinism. Similar to the binary view on the role of ICTs in China mentioned above, technological determinism is drawn to a fake binary about what is the cause and what is the consequence, as if there has to be an end of history. The majority of scholars now agree that technology does not fully determine the development of social relations and cultural practices (Baym, 2010). But we have to be aware that the other way around (i.e., social determinism or cultural determinism) is also wrong: social relations and cultural practices do not fully determine the development of technology either. Or in a milder tone, social structures and cultural values are so multi-dimensional that they do not foretell one direction of technological development. Therefore, what really matters in technological centralism is centralism, which refers to foregrounding technology along with other traditionally understood actors, without reducing technology to mere tools or representations of other important things.

It is equally important, if not more, to emphasize that what occupies the center of my inquiry of online popular culture is not just technology. Instead, what I try to foreground is a network of heterogeneous actors (Law, 1992, p. 379) that include an unlimited array of nodes including individuals, groups, organizations, institutions, technologies, physical objects, biological species, and many more. In other words, I am trying to take a network or relational approach (Bourdieu, 1989, p. 15; Latour, 2005, p. 12) to study my subject but this network is not just social in the sense that it does not limit itself to the relations among human actors. It is also not limited to the relations among a few over-generalized categories such as state, market, and society. Rather, this network of heterogeneous actors is always evolving, rendering any victory or failure temporary effects of the network (re)configuration. Although the subject of study is online popular culture, it cannot even be described without referring to its relations with other actors. My purpose of studying online popular culture is not to fix the phenomenon, or to make it another entry in the list of sociological terminologies, but to trace the trajectory of initiating, stabilizing, and dissolving a network, which is part and parcel of social formations in the network society.

Bibliography

Arkush, R. D. (1989). Love and marriage in north Chinese peasant operas, in *Unofficial China: Popular culture and thought in the Peoples Republic*, eds E. P. Link and R. P. Madsen, Westview Press, Berkeley, CA, pp. 72–85.

Barmé, G. R. (2013). *In the red: On contemporary Chinese culture*, Columbia University Press, New York.

Baym, N. (2010). *Personal connections in the digital age*, Polity, New York.

Bourdieu, P. (1989). Social space and symbolic power. *Sociological Theory*, 7(1), 14–25.

Bureau of Labor Statistics (2013). *Charts by topic: Leisure and sports activities.* Retrieved from www.bls.gov/tus/charts/leisure.htm.

Chan, A. (2002). The culture of survival: Lives of migrant workers through the prism of private letters, in *Popular China: unofficial culture in a globalizing society*, eds P. Link, R. P. Madsen, and P. G. Pickowicz, Rowman & Littlefield Publishers, Lanham, MD, pp. 163–188.

Cheong, P.H. and Gong, J. (2010). Cyber vigilantism, transmedia collective intelligence, and civic participation. *Chinese Journal of Communication*, 3(4), 471–487.

China Tourism Academy (2013). *Annual report of China leisure development, 2012–2013*, Tourism education Press, Beijing, China.

Chinese Internet Network Information Center (CNNIC) (2013). *The annual report of Internet development in China.* Retrieved from www.cnnic.cn/hlwfzyj/hlwxzbg/hlwtjbg/201307/P020130717505343100851.pdf.

Chinoy, M. (1997). *China live: Two decades in the heart of the dragon*, Turner Publishing, Nashville, TN.

Curtin, M. (2007). *Playing to the worlds biggest audience: The globalization of Chinese film and TV*, University of California Press, Berkley, CA.

Dai, X. D. (2007). The Internet in China: Unlocking and containing the public sphere. *China Quarterly*, 189, 196–198.

Davis, D. (ed.) (2000). *The consumer revolution in urban China* (Vol. 22), University of California Press, Berkeley, CA.

Davis, D. (2005). Urban consumer culture, in *Culture in the contemporary PRC* (No. 6), eds M. Hockx and J. Strauss, Cambridge University Press, Cambridge, pp. 170–187.

De Kloet, J. (2005). Popular music and youth in urban China: The dakou generation, in *Culture in the Contemporary PRC* (No. 6), eds M. Hockx and J. Strauss, Cambridge University Press, Cambridge, pp. 105–121.

Dutton, M. R. (ed.) (1998). *Streetlife China*, Cambridge University Press, Cambridge.

Feng, C. (2005). From ballrooms to teahouses commercial nightlife in Hainan since 1988, in *Locating China*, ed. J. Wang, Routledge, New York, pp. 133–149.

Fung, A. Y. (2008). *Global capital, local culture: Transnational media corporations in China* (Vol. 16), Peter Lang, Bern, Switzerland.

Gries, P. and Rosen, S. (eds) (2010). *Chinese politics: State, society and the market*, Routledge, New York.

Hardt, M. and Negri, A. (2000). *Empire*, Harvard University Press, Cambridge, MA.

Hockx, M. and Strauss, J. (eds) (2005). *Culture in the Contemporary PRC* (No. 6), Cambridge University Press, Cambridge.

Huang, E. (1999). Flying freely but in the cage: An empirical study of using Internet for the democratic development in China, *Information Technology for Development*, 8(3), 145–162.

Latour, B. (2005). *Reassembling the Social: An Introduction to Actor-Network-Theory*, Oxford University Press, Oxford.

Law, J. (1992). Notes on the theory of the actor-network: Ordering, strategy and heterogeneity. *Systems Practice*, 5(4), 379–393.

Lent, J. A. and Fitzsimmons, L. (eds) (2013). *Asian Popular Culture in Transition*, Routledge, New York.

Li, S. (2010). The online public space and popular ethos in China. *Media, Culture & Society*, 32(1), 63–83.

Link, P. Madsen, R. P., and Pickowicz, P. G. (2002). *Popular China: Unofficial culture in a globalizing society*, Rowman & Littlefield Publishers, Lanham, MD.

Link, E. P. and Madsen, R. P. (1989). *Unofficial China: Popular culture & thought in the Peoples Republic*, Westview Press, Boulder, CO.

Lull, J. (2013). *China turned on: Television, reform and resistance*, Routledge, New York.

Lu, X. (2002). Introduction, in *Chinese communication studies: Contexts and comparisons*, eds, X. Lu, W. Jia, and D. R. Heisey, Greenwood Publishing Group, Santa Barbara, CA.

Pan, Z., Lee, C., Chan, J. M., and So, C. K. Y. (2001). Orchestrating the family-nation chorus: Chinese media and nationalism in the Hong Kong handover. *Mass Communication & Society*, 4(3), 331–347.

Qiu, J. L. (2006). The changing web of Chinese nationalism. *Global Media & Communication*, 2(1), 125–128.

Qiu, J. L. (2007). The wireless leash: Mobile messaging service as a means of control. *International Journal of Communication*, 1, 74–91.

Reese, S. D. (2009). The future of journalism in emerging deliberative space. *Journalism*, 10(3), 362–364.

Stanley, R. (2010). Is the Internet a positive force in the development of civil society, a public sphere, and democratization in China? *International Journal of Communication*, 4, 509–516.

Sun, W. (2005). Anhui baomu in Shanghai: Gender, class, and a sense of place, in *Locating China*, ed. J. Wang, Routledge, New York, pp. 171–189.

Taubman, G. (1998). A not-so World Wide Web: The Internet, China and the challenges to nondemocratic rule. *Political Communication*, 15(2), 255–273.

Wang, J. (1996). *High culture fever: Politics, aesthetics, and ideology in Dengs China*, University of California Press, Berkeley, CA.

Wang, S. S. and Hong, J. (2010). Discourse behind the forbidden realm: Internet surveillance and its implications on Chinas blogosphere. *Telematics & Informatics*, 27(1), 67–78.

Williams, R. (1958). Moving from high culture to ordinary culture, in *Convictions*, ed. N. McKenzie, MacKibbon and Kee, London.

Wu, M. (2008). Measuring political debate on the Chinese Internet forum. *Javnost-The Public*, 15(2), 93–110.

Wu, X. (2007). *Chinese cyber nationalism: Evolution, characteristics and implications*, Lexington Books, Lanham, MD.

Wu, Y. (1999). *China's consumer revolution: The emerging patterns of wealth and expenditure*, Edward Elgar Publishing, Cheltenham.

Wu, D. and Murphy, P. D. (eds) (1994). *Handbook of Chinese popular culture*, Greenwood Publishing Group, Santa Barbara, CA.

Xiaokang Magazine. (2013a). *Chinese are still busy: Overtime work has influenced the quality of leisure.* Retrieved from http://xkzz.chinaxiaokang.com/xkzz3/newsview.asp?id=6275.

Xiaokang Magazine. (2013b). *Satisfaction with leisure is highest among the post-50s generation: Time, work, and income are barriers to leisure.* Retrieved from http://xkzz.chinaxiaokang.com/xkzz3/newsview.asp?id=6722.

Yang, G. (2010). *The power of the Internet in China: Citizen activism online*, Columbia University Press, New York.

Yin, X. (2005). New trends of leisure consumption in China. *Journal of Family and Economic Issues*, 26(1), 175–182.

Yu, H. (2009). *Media and cultural transformation in China*, Routledge, New York.

Yuan, W. (2010). E-democracy@China: Does it work? *Chinese Journal of Communication*, 3(4), 488–503.

Zhang, L. (2002). Urban experiences and social belonging among Chinese rural migrants, in *Popular China: Unofficial Culture in a Globalizing Society*, eds P. Link, R. P. Madsen, and P. G. Pickowicz, Rowman & Littlefield, Lanham, MD, pp. 275–299.

Zhang, W. (2012). Virtual communities as subaltern public spheres: A theoretical development and an application to the Chinese Internet, in *Virtual community participation and motivation: Cross-disciplinary theories*, ed. H. Li, IGI Global, Hershey, PA, pp. 143–161.

Zhang, W. and Chib, A. (2014). Internet studies and development discourses: The cases of China and India.*Information Technology for Development*, 20(4), 324–338.

Zhang, W. and Mao, C. (2013). Fan activism sustained and challenged: Participatory culture in Chinese online translation communities. *Chinese Journal of Communication*, 6(1), 45–61.

Zhang, X. (1989). How come you aren't divorced yet? in *Unofficial China*, eds. R. Madsen, P. Link, and P. G. Pickowicz, Westview Press, Boulder, CO, pp. 57–72.

Zhao, Y. (2008). *Communication in China: Political economy, power and conflict*, Rowman & Littlefield, Lanham, MD.

Zheng, Y. (2007). *Technological empowerment: The Internet, the state and society in China*, Stanford University Press, Stanford, CA.

Zhong, X. (2010). *Mainstream culture refocused: television drama, society, and the production of meaning in reform-era China*, University of Hawaii Press, Honolulu, HI.

Zha, J. (1995). *China pop: How soap operas, tabloids, and bestsellers are transforming a culture*, The New Press, New York.

Zhu, Y. (2008). *Television in post-reform China*, Routledge, New York.

Zhu, Y. and Berry, C. (eds) (2009). *TV China*, Indiana University Press, Bloomington, IN.

Zhu, Y., Keane, M., and Bai, R. (eds) (2008). *TV drama in China* (Vol. 1). Hong Kong University Press, Hong Kong.

Zhu, Y. (2014). *Two billion eyes: The story of China Central Television*, The New Press, New York.

3 Rear window to movies
From fans to subaltern publics

Cinema, according to Sontag (1996), is "an art unlike any other: quintessentially modern; distinctively accessible; poetic and mysterious and erotic and moral – all at the same time." As an artistic form, movies are popularly consumed even with the advent of the television era, on a smaller screen and within a more domestic space. New ICTs such as VCD, DVD, and online video streaming have further diversified the way movies are watched. Movies in China originated from the same artistic attempt to create an art that appeals to the large number of members in modern societies. As a cultural product, movies always invite the audiences to pay attention, to feel, to communicate, and to criticize. However, as Bourdieu (1993, p. 38) argued, cultural production is not just a matter of artistic creation as "(t)he artistic field is positioned within the larger field of power" (Shefrin, 2004, p. 263). Movies in China are subject to the same power hierarchy that is prevalent in the social structure. As an artistic object, movies have been differentiated from overt politics (although movies could be political) and given an ambiguous role of both mass entertainment and mass education (or propaganda) by the Chinese state. A Bourdieuian approach suggests that the complexity of the practice lies in the larger field of power struggle among political, economic, and social forces.

Cinephilia, the fandom of movies, became visible in China when VCDs and DVDs began to circulate (Li, 2010). Movie collecting became feasible, as piracy made access to banned (mostly Chinese) and unavailable (mostly foreign) movies easy; online websites facilitated their exchange and discussions. The early form of public sphere described by Habermas (1989, p. 29) started from the topics of art criticism, including literatures, theaters, music, and many other artistic works. A bourgeois public emerged out of the groups that discuss such matters in a rational–critical manner and the same group of publics turned to discussions on political issues when the social conditions became permissive. History seemed to repeat itself in China, although the coffee houses and salons that housed the European bourgeois public were replaced by the mediation of the Internet, especially discussion forums, blogs, microblogs, and social networking sites (SNSs).

This chapter answers Bourdieu's theoretical call by first introducing the power dynamics in the historical development of Chinese movie industry, in order to understand how online fandom of movies in China took its shape. After describing the political economy, this chapter continues to examine the discourse that arose from fans' heated discussions on movies, in contrast to the state, commercial, and, surprisingly, academic discourses on the same fan object. The Habermasian concept of public sphere is slightly entertained when the deliberativeness of such fan discourse is examined. However, what distinguishes my orientation from either Bourdieu's or Habermas' is clearly shown in the third section of this chapter, in which I document in details how these online movie fans go out of the confine of their online communities to perform in front of the larger society. They became a subaltern public through actively networking among themselves, with mass media, and with sympathetic commercial forces, around a shared object called movies. This networking logic dictates the formation of this Chinese subaltern public, the public of online movie fans. The discourse they create, therefore, becomes linkages that internally bond the individual fans of the subaltern public, and externally engage other nodes in the network. The political and economic powers become important nodes that co-define the network in which this subaltern public can perform itself into being. This case of a networked public is made even more explicit in the next chapter, when the subaltern public becomes a regular public that is often visible to the society.

The historical development of Chinese online cinephilia

The movie industry in China has been a state-monopolized enterprise for almost 40 years, following the policy that artistic practices have to serve as the propaganda tools for state control (Chu, 2002). The marketization of movie industry started in the late 1980s (Zhu, 2002), when the centralized studio system was reformed to force the state-owned movie production studios and distributors to gain financial independence. However, the production reform is accompanied with the close control of the movie content, ranging from censorship of the screenplays to banning of the finished movies, from edits of imported movies to subsidies to main-melody movies. The dilemma between the demand of marketizaiton and the lack of creativity did not help the state-owned studios and distributors to transit smoothly to a productive movie industry. The central government reacquainted the import of Hollywood movies in order to deal with the crisis faced by Chinese movie industry in 1995. Hollywood's high-cost production not only restored Chinese audiences' theatre-going habit but also became the new standard for quality films in contrast to the state-dictated ones. Another significant policy change in 1995 was that the state relaxed its production licensing policy, extending the right to produce feature films from 16 state-run studios to additional 13 provincial level studios. The production reform directly led to a temporary proliferation of Chinese domestic film production during the 1990s, most of which were cheap knockoffs of Hollywood entertainment films.

Further commercialization of the movie industry was seen in the early twenty-first century, indicated in a new policy that leads to an almost full opening-up of the Chinese movie industry. In 2003, the State Administration of Press, Publication, Film, and Television issued an order in which production, distribution, and theater management start to be fully open to local private capital. A year later, another order allowed foreign capital to join the Chinese movie industry through collaborating with local companies. Meanwhile, entry into the World Trade Organization in 2001 made the Chinese government increase the yearly quota for imported movies from 10 to 20. The number was recently raised to 34 in 2012. The first decade of the twenty-first century has witnessed an astonishing proliferation of commercial movies thanks to the loosened restriction of capital invested in the movie industry. Feature films produced in 2001, the birth year of "the first commercial movie" *Big Shot's Funeral*, numbered 88. In 2013, there were 638 feature films produced in mainland China (National Bureau of Statistics of China, 2014). However, due to the state control of content, most of these commercial movies do not directly address sensitive social issues.

Independent movies, which are produced, circulated, and shown outside the official institution (at first state-owned and later fully commercialized) were born out of the desire to provide an honest description of contemporary China. When the phenomenon of Chinese independent movies first surfaced, it was a response to the historical condition in the 1980s, when the centralized studio system was at the verge of bankruptcy and strict censorship left little space for artistic innovations. Among the most successful independent movie makers are the professionals trained inside the official institution (e.g., Beijing Film Academy) and they were forced to go underground as the studio system was in crisis and could not support their movie making. The so-called sixth generation of Chinese directors initially made their names through independent movies during the late 1990s and early 2000s. For example, Wang Xiaoshuai made his maiden work *The Days* with only 100,000 RMB. Then the production team started attending international movie festivals and competing for prizes, which exposed them to more alternative financial sources. Wang Xiaoshuai raised 3,000,000 RMB when he produced his third movie *Beijing Bicycle*. Some investors in these independent movies made profits through distribution in countries other than China. Other investors such as film festivals did not expect to get the money back at all.

Other than the production cost, these independent movies were also troubled by the fact that their movies did not go through the official institution and, therefore, cannot be legally shown to the Chinese public. An alternative distribution channel was obtained mainly through two means, the Internet and unofficial movie shows, both of which have been highly relevant to the pirate movie industry. The pirate movie industry provides Chinese audiences the access to such independent movies in a way summarized in Wang and Zhu's (2003) article: the demand for independent movies above ground is first transferred to the underground suppliers; then the domestic underground producers look for sources within China and if that fails, they turn overseas (e.g., a popular pirate version of Jia Zhangke's movie *The Platform* is its Japanese version); and, finally, from overseas the goods are smuggled back into the domestic underground. The introduction of broadband Internet, especially the video sites such as Youku and Tudou, made these pirate movies even more accessible to Chinese audiences. When movie fans organized unofficial movie shows outside the official theaters, the sources of these movies were often pirate VCDs and DVDs too.

A prominent change seen in the last decade with regards to Chinese independent movies was the return to the official institution of many independent movie directors. The leading figures of the sixth generation such as Zhang Yuan and Jia Zhangke now all make movies within the official confines, although without giving up their artistic preferences. Meanwhile, newcomers to the independent movie scene no longer face the challenges that their seniors encountered, thanks to the reduced entry barrier brought by both the further commercialization and new ICTs such as digital video cameras (DVs). The new challenges now are no longer just about how to circumvent the censorship system to get the release license (sometimes called the dragon label). Independent movie directors nowadays have to deal with competition from commercial films, struggling to find financial support for production and theaters for public release. While the earlier independent movies makers were mainly concerned by an over-controlling state, those who strive to make art movies in China now are primarily troubled by over-commercialization. Owing to the artistic and thus unpopular nature of such movies, independent movie festivals, such as the China Independent Film Festival, Beijing Independent Film Festival, and Yunnan Multi Culture Visual Festival, emerged as the platforms to publicize and promote such movies. These festivals, however, are made possible only if there is a certain degree of governmental tolerance, which is often offered in exchange of image building.

Movie fans existed in China long before the Internet was invented. Immediately before the Internet became a popular medium, the fandom around movies was shared and sustained through film magazines such as *Popular Movies*. After the Internet became widespread, mass media including film magazines, newspapers, and TV programs continued to function as virtual worships for movie fans. However, it was the Internet that first provided a space for Chinese movie fans to build their own communities. On one hand, these spaces, in contrast to the mass-mediated spaces, were more user-oriented in the sense that they did not have to serve the functions assigned to Chinese mass media, including both ideological and commercial functions. On the other hand, the discussions seen in the online spaces were as in-depth as, or even more profound than, discussions one can find in other channels. The academic and professional publications on movies, which were supposed to feature the most significant discussions, were void of such significance due to again, the ideological control. The online communities for movie fans laid the base for the emergence of an alternative discourse and, furthermore, the performance of such discourse in front of the larger society.

Chinese online cinephilia took shape during the transitional years in which the centralized studio system was painfully going through its rebirth and the constraints imposed on imported movies were still tight. When the Internet entered ordinary Chinese life around 1996, the online space quickly became a discursive sphere in which movie fans could exchange their views and feelings of the movies they watched, many of which through pirate VCDs and DVDs or unofficial movie shows that rely on such pirate sources. Rear Window to Movies, a discussion board exclusively focusing on movies, was one of the pioneers in providing ordinary Chinese movie fans an online space to discuss movies. When Rear Window was established at the end of 1998, it was hosted by a pioneering online community website, Xicihutong (xici.net). The website was organized as a system that hosts thousands of discussion boards on various topics, with over 100,000 such boards in 2003. Rear Window, during its heyday, was one of the largest discussion boards on xici, with more than 5,000 registered users who put this board on their favorites list and numerous daily visitors. Although the discussion board itself became less active over the years due to the emerging new technologies such as portal sites, blogs, micro-blogs, and SNSs, Rear Window as a name was still frequently mentioned in Chinese movie fans' conversations. A good example is that in 2013, the founder of Rear Window started an art movie line called "Rearwindow Film" for the sake of promoting independent movies. During its inaugural year, Rearwindow Film showed 15 art movies with the dragon label in more than 300 theaters, distributed among 70 cities. The empirical findings reported in this chapter capture a snapshot of Rear Window around 2001–2003, about three years after its foundation and the golden age of the discussion board.

Constructing the counter-discourse

An online survey of 187 Rear Window users was conducted in April, 2003. The survey showed that over 99% of users were aged between 18 and 35 years old and over 97% of them had a college degree. A significant amount of users (38%) were college students and, for that reason, about 27% of users had a monthly income lower than 500 RMB. However, compared to the general population, the majority of Rear Window users (63%) enjoyed a relatively high monthly income (higher than 1,000 RMB). A content analysis shows that film reviews were the most popular content on Rear Window, occupying about 67% of all the posts. Informational posts occupied a significant portion at 22%. Other posts were all less than 5%, which includes social interaction, tasks, and advice, as well as management announcements. Seventy-four percent of film reviews got replies with comments. Seventy-seven percent of the respondents of my survey participated or observed the discussions on the board. From these numbers, we can see that although there were diverse contents on Rear Window, discussions about movies played a leading role and provided the base on which the counter-discourse could emerge. In order to discover individual discursive statements about Chinese movies and industry, I used key words including Chinese films, Chinese directors, Chinese actors, Chinese movie prizes, pirate movies, and specific movie titles like *Hero* to search through all the posts. In addition, corresponding open-ended questions were asked in the online survey to see whether the statements were widely accepted by the users.

The state discourse claimed that audiences should be guided. In other words, the government should decide which kinds of movies are permitted to be released to the public. Thus the government controlled production and distribution and became the dominant producer of discourses regarding Chinese movies. The first official claim was "developing the mainstream melody, promoting the diversity" (Zhu, 2002), which means that ideological movies should be prioritized and, at the same time, commercial movies are allowed. The second claim was "arts for socialism and arts for the people," which obviously promotes that movies should facilitate cultivation of the socialism ideology. The third claim was often considered a balance to the above two ideological ones: "let a hundred flowers blossom and a hundred schools of thoughts contend." This double-hundreds claim implies that movies other than the ideological ones should be allowed. In order to define which kind of films are quality films, the state established three film prizes, which are the Golden Rooster Prize, the Baihua Prize, and the Huabiao Prize. Through these three state-controlled prizes, the state reinforced its definition of quality movies. In addition, reports and reviews of the prize-winners in the state-controlled mass media helped to disseminate this discourse. The discourse formed on Rear Window usually referred to the state discourse and voiced alternative views about quality Chinese movies. The counter-discourse is made up of a set of statements.

Statement 1: Chinese movies are in trouble because of the state-controlled institution

Although the state discourse admitted the difficulties that the Chinese movie industry was encountering, it attributed these difficulties to pirate VCDs and DVDs. In comparison, the Rear Window discourse claimed that it is the state-controlled institution that impedes the development of the Chinese movie industry. One user posted the following:

> User #1: It is a long way for the institution to reform. However after entry into the WTO, no reform means collective suicide. The results of a perfect reform have some characteristics:
>
> Persons with competence become active.
> *Life Time*[1] is shown publicly.
> Censorship is cancelled.
> Foreign movies are not dubbed.

Statement 2: Censorship is bad and useless

Censorship as the control tool for the state was described as necessary by the state discourse. The state discourse emphasized that censorship could be beneficial for both the movie industry and the audience. The discourse on Rear Window countered such a statement. Censorship is considered both evil and weak because the movie fans can still access the banned movies through unofficial means. Another user made the following statement:

> User #2: I have once been to the Film Bureau. ... To tell the truth, my impression of the Film Bureau is that this is a concentration camp for Chinese movies. I had to return to the street so that I did not feel as choky as when I was there.

Statement 3: State film prizes are bad and not worth caring about

State film prizes were the main method that the government used to promote its definition of quality movies. Rear Window users questioned the credibility of these film prizes and despised the prizes. In the online survey, most of the respondents said that the mainstream films were not worth watching. Two extreme words were cited, which were "shit" and "rubbish." The second popular attitude was that "it has nothing to do with me": I do not care about it and I have not seen such movies for a long time.

> User #2: Its (Huabiao Prize) taste decides that it cannot reflect what people think. It cannot guide the market and reflect box office sales either. This kind of prize is a waste, which has no meaning at all. There are actors who buy votes for the Baihua Prize. It lost its poor self-respect and said nothing for the audiences. The Golden Rooster has become an ill rooster. Its influence gets weaker. Not only are the sponsors hesitant to fund it, but the actors are also hesitant to join it. The most salient truth is prizes cannot promote box office sales and cannot reveal the quality of films. Prizes have become a lampoon and a senseless game within a small faction.

Statement 4: Independent movies are good in general but being banned has become a word of sales promotion

I expected that Rear Window users would classify independent movies as quality movies in their minds. In fact, users were very strict in judging what a quality movie is. Answering the open-ended question about independent movies, they said that most of the independent movies were good but they were aware of the fact that "being banned" has been used for sales promotion. From this statement, we can see that the subaltern public discourse is not subordinate to any grand discourses including that of independent movies.

Respondent #12: Most of the banned movies are quality movies, which were treated unfairly.

Respondent #29: Quality movies are easily banned. Some people make use of such a view and sell their movies under the name of "banned movies."

Respondent #61: We must treat the banned movies individually. We must know whether it is a real piece of art or just a camouflage to catch attention.

From the analyses above, we can see that the Rear Window discourse was formed mainly against the state discourse, with warnings about the commercial discourse. The discourse not only proposed another set of value judgments but, more importantly, provided a new identity for movie fans. The addressee of the state discourse was a receiver while that of the market discourse was a consumer, neither of which grants movie fans any discursive autonomy in judging the quality of movies. However, the Rear Window discourse defined audiences as reviewers who can distinguish between what is good and what is bad and, moreover, who can articulate these standards. In the state discourse, audiences were ignorant and should be told what is good and what is bad. In the market discourse, audiences were voiceless and they only needed to buy or not buy. However, in the Rear Window discourse, audiences had the ultimate say in making judgments and actions. Although the counter-discourse was clearly against the dominant state discourse and the emerging commercial discourse at that time, we need to understand how the counter-discourse was constructed in order to assess its deliberative nature (or lack of such). The following section selects one case, arguably the most critical debate on Rear Window, to illustrate to what extent, Rear Window both fulfilled and failed the ideal of the Habermasian public sphere.

To examine the deliberativeness of the Rear Window discourse, a debate on "whether Chinese movies are a kind of politics" was chosen for analysis. This debate began on July 9, 2002, and lasted for about two weeks. After one of the then board managers posted a summary on July 16, the debate began to decline. The debate completely ceased on July 21. The debate was ignited by an interview with Jia Zhangke, one of the prominent directors often named as the sixth generation. In this interview, the interviewer (User #3) harshly criticized another sixth-generation director Wang Chao and his movie *An'yang Baby*. He also criticized a book titled *My Camera Doesn't Lie*, which introduces eight young directors including Jia Zhangke and Wang Chao. Only two hours after this interview was posted, another post called *I Only Believe in Baby's Eyes* made strong arguments against the critiques. The author used an ID that was the same as the post title and, finally, it was found out that the ID owner was one of the authors of the book *My Camera Doesn't Lie*. The debate reached its first turning point when a reputable movie scholar posted an article on July 10. The author was a professor working in the Beijing Film Academy who was very active in promoting Chinese independent movies. He pointed out that the critique on *An'yang Baby* showed apathy towards Chinese independent movies, which struggle to exist in the tough political environment. At this stage, the focus of the debate shifted to which criterion should be applied when evaluating a movie, its art value or its political significance. The second turning point appeared after an ordinary user (User #4) wrote that even if we focused on political significance, Wang Chao only took advantage of politics to achieve personal fame and the real life of the lowest class was not honestly depicted in his movie. In response to User #4, the professor asked a final question for this debate, i.e., whether movies are a kind of politics.

There were in total 56 relevant posts when the analysis was made, among which 39 were posted by different IDs. More than half (56%) of the posts were written as a reply to statements made by other users, including both agreements and rebuttals. Seventy-four percent of the posts contained replies that explicitly expressed disagreements. We can see that a reciprocal conversation was the mainstream during the debate. A great majority (81%) of the posts demonstrated the reasons why they supported or opposed one opinion. Among the posts with reasons, 76% of them provided valid claims that are criticizable.[2] Meanwhile, the debate was not void of emotional expressions and, even worse, personal attacks. Two types of personal attacks were observed: the first type was quite obvious and users attacked each other with dirty words. The second type, without curses, often attributed the weakness of one argument to the weakness of the person who was behind the argument. For example, another professor working at the Beijing Film Academy criticized User #3 and one of his supporters (User #5) that "I consider User #3 as a youth loving literature and I am impressed by User #5's immaturity. I want to say that tricks cannot be played on all things in the world. And not all tricks could be forgiven because of juvenility." The content analysis shows that 51% of the posts contained this kind of soft personal attack.

If we look at the content of the debate, we can see that it was mainly a fierce competition between two contrasting, if not contradictory, views on what is considered a quality movie. What makes this debate particularly interesting is that the debate was not really between the two often imagined antagonistic entities (i.e., state vs. society). The first view is that Chinese movies should have political significance, or any Chinese movies that challenge state domination could be called quality movies. This view was often supported by a group of academics, including professors in universities and professionals within the independent movie institution. On the other hand, a group of folk[3] movie reviewers claimed that Chinese movies should reduce their political sensitivity, or a quality Chinese movie must in the first place have value as art. Academics had the advantage with their knowledge about Chinese independent movies, which was used as hard evidence supporting their arguments, and theoretical training, which strengthened their ability of arguing and counter-arguing. In contrast, other users only had their personal experience and did not have any inside stories. However, folk movie reviewers knew how to use the Internet effectively to express their opinions. For example, User #5 resigned as one of the board managers during the debate, in order to keep equal status with his opponents, which earned him compliments and support from many users. In contrast, the first professor revealed his real identity when he made his rebuttals. Although he intended to ask the participants to be responsible for their words even in a virtual space, the self-revelation of his offline identity received many critiques. A participant described this action as a "hijack" of the debate.

> User #6: This action is heroic but violent. It destroyed the happiness of anonymity that the Internet brings to us. Here is a free public space first of all. We do not have much discursive rights and have been very satisfied that we can speak here. Anonymity is very important here, with which we can speak out in spite of the burden of personal relationships, without which we will hesitate to speak out due to self-doubts of the immaturity of our opinions.

The content analysis demonstrates that the construction of Rear Window discourse was a process that involved both rational and emotional expressions, which cannot be completely cut off from the offline social hierarchy. The significance of such discursive construction lies not in its potential of realizing a Habermasian public sphere, but in giving a group of online movie fans, who had no voice before, a space to articulate their thoughts and to engage in debates with other discourses. Whereas the state and the commercial discourses are predominant in the mainstream media, the Rear Window discourse is clearly against these two interpretations of the Chinese movie industry and its challenges. More interestingly, the autonomy of the Rear Window discourse is further shown by its distance from the academic discourse, or the high culture fever discussed in Chapter 2, an elitist discourse that overlooks the desires and feelings of the ordinary Chinese. Although the historical condition of the Chinese movie industry in the early 2000s set up a stage for online movie fans to perform their discourses, my take on analyzing such a subaltern public is to focus on how they strive to perform in their own style on the stage, or even to find a larger stage for their performances. In other words, I do not see the existing structures as fixed and pre-determining and, instead, I am interested in making explicit the structuration and re-structuration done by various entities, best described using a language of network, nodes, linkages, and disconnections.

A networked subaltern public

A subaltern public is completely enclaved if its discourse never travels out of the safe space of its community (Squires, 2002). We can even argue that an online community of movie fans cannot be seen as a public unless their members and their discourses have a certain degree of visibility. Although the openness of the Internet already granted Rear Window some visibility, the reach of this virtual space, as shown in our demographic analysis of the users, was restricted to the better educated, better paid, but underdeveloped middle class who were interested in movies. The networking practices of Rear Window users thus became necessary conditions in which these movie fans, first gathered on an online discussion board, were able to become a public that performs its political appeals, although these appeals were still at the margin compared to the mainstream discourses at that time. This section reviews two prominent networking practices that not only connect the individual members of Rear Window into social contacts but also connect the Rear Window public to other forces including those of society, the market, and the mass media. The first practice is termed Private Movie Watching (PMW), an activity that shows movies (both legal and illegal; both Chinese and foreign) in a physical locale that is often not part of the official movie theater system. The other practice is the constant interaction (sometimes conflicts) with the mass media, a practice that is both a blessing and a curse for the subaltern public to make their discourse visible. The problem, as shown in detail later, laid precisely in the mediation process of mainstream Chinese media when visibility was striving to be enhanced.

PMW showed movies that were inaccessible through official channels such as movie theatres or legally sold VCDs or DVDs. The organizers collected these movies from the pirate movie industry and through their personal contacts with independent directors and producers. PMW became a nationwide phenomenon around 2000, mushrooming in many cities such as Beijing, Shanghai, Guangzhou, Nanjing, Wuhan, Chengdu, Kunming, Shenyang, and Taiyuan. Quite a number of audiences watched Chinese independent movies in this way. Thirty-five percent of my survey respondents said that they had attended such activities at least once. As one of the four most important PMW in the country[4], PMW organized by Rear Window was first proposed and run by the founder of Rear Window and his friends, lasting from June 2000 to December 2002. But the activity was temporarily closed at the end of 2002, right before the 16th People's Congress because the state had tightened its control during the sensitive period. However, when state control loosened, Rear Window managers re-organized their PMW in a bar starting from late 2003. The evolution of Rear Window's PMW (see Table 3.1) shows the flexibility of this subaltern public. When oppression decreased, the subaltern public made use of various resources to increase its visibility by networking among themselves and with other forces. However, when their activities provoked sanction, they turned back to focus on their internal activities, which could keep their online discursive space safe.

In contrast to the relatively easy access to movies thanks to both the pirate movie industry and the directors and producers themselves, the resources for showing movies were hard to get, which at least required a large, empty space and some equipment. That is why organizers of PMW must cooperate with other social and commercial forces, because government regulations would not allow official theaters to be formally involved in this. PMW organized by Rear Window mainly cooperated with two kinds of forces: universities and commercial entities. Some active Rear Window users who were undergraduate students initiated the collaboration with universities. They often asked the student unions in their universities for support so that they could rent or borrow space in universities. The movie shows were open to the public although the main audiences were students, who appreciate art movies more than the general public does. Nearly all European art movies were shown at universities (see Table 3.1). More importantly, the state often gave more freedom to academic activities since the influence of these activities was limited.

Table 3.1 Private movie watching organized by Rear Window, 2000–2003

Locale	Time	Ticket fare	Movies shown	Reasons for termination
Multimedia center in a university	June 2000 to August 2000	5 RMB per person	European art movies	Renovation of the center
Multimedia classroom in a university	September 2000 to February 2001	Free	European art movies	Closure of the classrooms during winter vacation
Multimedia Center in a university	March 2001 to August 2001	2 RMB per person	European art movies, banned movies and Taiwan movies	Closure of the center during summer vacation
A shopping mall selling electronic goods	August 2000 to March 2001	Free	Japanese movies, Korean movies, and others	Bankruptcy of the shopping mall
An official movie theater	November 2001 to August 2002	10 RMB per person, 50 free tickets each time, 20% discount for students	Korean movies, Taiwan movies, Oscar winners	Change of theater manager
Amphitheater in a university	November to December 2002	1 RMB per person	Taiwan movies	Termination by the cooperator, the student union of the university
A bar	November 2003	Free	Chinese independent movies and European art movies	Termination by the bar owner

Watching movies at universities could wear the mask of academic activities. However, the collaboration was not stable due to fast changing university policies. For example, the renovation of the spaces, the beginning of winter or summer vacation, the 16th People's Congress, and even the approach of final exams could be the reasons for termination.

Compared to universities, commercial corporations were more predictable during their collaboration with Rear Window. Their aim was to attract consumers and make money. Commercial outlets included a shopping mall that sells electronic products, such as VCD/DVD players, speaker systems, and TV/displays. To them, the movie fans were potential consumers because the fans watch movies a lot at home and need the products. The shopping mall and Rear Window agreed that the mall would provide equipment and space, a small theatre which was meant for previewing electronic products, while Rear Window was responsible for looking for movies, organizing shows, and advertising on the Internet. After the bankruptcy of the shopping mall, Rear Window worked with a movie theatre, which was of course state-owned. This collaboration was particularly telling because PMW emerged precisely because the movies shown were not accessible in official theaters. The tricky reality was that the entire movie industry was under huge pressure to gain financial independence, an order issued by the central government. Chinese movie theatres had to survive on their own after the state stopped funding them. Thus the manager of this particular movie theater wanted to risk working with Rear Window in the hope that Rear Window could bring young movie fans to his theatre. After half a year's collaboration, the theater found that they could not make money from the collaboration because Rear Window users were just a small social group and not the general young audiences they expected. They became very passive in helping with arranging the movie shows and the manager who had decided to work with Rear Window was transferred to another movie theatre in the suburbs. The collaboration had to end. When the study was conducted in 2003, the ongoing PMW was held in a bar. Rear Window showed many Chinese independent movies and European movies there. The bar profited from audiences purchasing drinks and foods; the entry fee was totally free.

PMW is a networking practice that connects individual members of the Rear Window community by giving them the chance to sit inside the same physical space to enjoy the movies they all love. Many interviewees told me how they became good friends with each other through first attending then helping with such activities. The friendship built over the years of struggling to find sponsors and locations for showing the films they felt passionate about was the foundation upon which the network of a subaltern public could grow into a network of a regular public that was often visible in the society. PMW also functions as a recruitment tool for Rear Window to attract young users, especially college students, to join the fandom of movies. Many active members, some of whom later became the board managers, were made aware of Rear Window through participating in PMW. In addition to being a social (i.e., among individuals) networking practice, PMW also functions as a networking practice that connects social forces (e.g., the universities), commercial forces (e.g., the shopping mall and the bar) to these movie fans. Although these other forces definitely had their own goals to achieve during the collaboration, their support nevertheless strengthened the presence of this subaltern public in a larger network of powers. The fact that their support made this node of online movie fan community stronger allowed this subaltern public to sustain itself and provide impressive performances in front of the larger society. One format of such performances was interaction with mass media. I call it interaction because the mediation process went both ways: the mass media tried to represent Rear Window and its discourses in ways that serve their needs; the Rear Window public strived to influence the representation through actively managing their relationship with the mass media staffs.

When Internet penetration was not as high as now, the mass media were the main channels through which subaltern discourses could reach wider audiences (Felski 1989). Fourteen percent of the respondents knew about Rear Window from the mass media. The close relationship between Rear Window and mass media could be further seen in the demographics of users: 12% of the users were news editors or reporters, who ranked third in the occupation category. That is why interaction between Rear Window and mass media often occurred as personal contact between users, some were folk movie reviewers and others were mass media personnel. For instance, the board managers introduced the discussion board on newspapers or editors recruited writers from the board to supply content for their publications. It was Rear Window that provided the opportunity for them to meet each other, which was almost impossible before virtual space became available.

Rear Window was primarily used by mass media as news sources. Mass media reported the activities of Rear Window such as PMW and asked managers or active participants for interviews. Meanwhile, the interviewees from Rear Window used these opportunities to propagate their own discourse. A lot of the national media have reported Rear Window, such as *Southern Weekend* and *Hunan TV.* Although most news reports framed Rear Window as a new phenomenon that could bring users many benefits, some of them talked about Rear Window from an official point of view with caution. For instance, one newspaper commented: "The government department must pay attention to the administration of these civil organizations and their activities."

The other form of collaboration between Rear Window and mass media was that mass media recruited writers from Rear Window. At the same time, the users who became media writers created their own fame from this collaboration and, more importantly, disseminated the subaltern discourse to the wider public. More than half of the Rear Window users (51%) had contacts with mass media, and 18% of them wrote for the mass media, regularly or irregularly. The Rear Window users were recruited by all kinds of mass media, from national media to local press, and from general media to professional publications. Mass media personnel preferred looking for writers from Rear Window because Internet users were part of their target market. Online writers who were favored by Internet users would attract the same people in the offline world, they believed.

> Editor #1: Why did I pay attention to the Internet? The first reason is that I recognized its importance. The Internet users are vogue youths who are overlapping with my target readers. ... I must make my readers overlap with the Internet users and then the Internet users will buy my newspaper.
>
> (January 30, 2003)

However, there were risks for being under the spotlight on mass media. It could attract the attention of the government and elicit strict sanctions. Furthermore, media outlets were often out of the control of Rear Window users. Sixty-four percent of Rear Window users who were also media writers agreed that there are clear differences between posting online and writing for the mass media. They found that they must obey some rules of the mass media and cannot write as personally or freely as on Rear Window. Their opinions were selectively disseminated to the wider public. Owing to the double-edged effect of collaboration with the mass media, 68% of the respondents thought that Rear Window should maintain a distance from the mass media and should not contact mass media by its own initiative. Sixteen percent of the respondents thought that Rear Window should actively cooperate with the mass media and obtain media exposure as often as possible. Only 3% of the respondents thought that Rear Window should totally isolate itself from the mass media. Interviews with both Rear Window writers and mass media editors confirmed this observation.

> User #6: I was disgusted with the editors who often asked me to provide some sexy photos of the stars when I wrote about the Korean movies for them. ... It is totally impossible that the media do not have any limitations. There are definitely guides that forbid some discourses. We were once to be the guests in a radio program; I saw that the guidelines were posted on the wall, indicating what kind of things could never be mentioned. All were there. It was serious.
>
> (February 5, 2003)

> Editor #2: The authors from the Internet like writing things with an unconstrained style. ... Some authors could write very good articles online, but I felt that these articles are not appropriate to publish in the magazines. In addition to the inappropriate style, the content of the articles is often inappropriate to publish in magazines. For example, movie reviews that talked about the sensitive topics like religion or politics. You can speak about it freely on the Internet but cannot on mass media. Mass

media pay attention to the leadership effect and they must have the "correct propaganda guide."

(January 28, 2003)

Interaction with mass media is made possible through the networking practices between managers and active members on Rear Window on the one hand, and reporters and editors working for mass media on the other hand. Those Rear Window users who became media writers were able to introduce to the wider public the discourse they co-constructed within the safe space of Rear Window, centering around the theme of what are considered quality movies if our standards are no longer those defined by the state or the market economy. They made visible the alternative criteria to ordinary Chinese people and encouraged them to make judgments by themselves. However, their discourse had to be processed by the gatekeepers in the mass media. The radical aspects of the discourse were compromised and the wider public may not be able to fully understand the original discourse from the subaltern public. Although at the action level, networking was occurring among individuals, their connections actually revealed a deeper and less visible network among the powers as well as the effort to re-structure such power dynamics. Using writers from Rear Window to supply content for mass media was not purely a personal favor mass media personnel performed for the subaltern public, it was a decision made to address the dilemma between commercialization of mainstream media and political control from the government. Although it was also unfair to say the motivation of mass media personnel was completely interest-driven, considering that many of these reporters and editors were themselves active users of Rear Window and shared a passion for movies with fellow users, their representation of the Rear Window discourse to the wider public had to be a modified version in order to satisfy both censors and readers.

Rear Window to Movies, an online discussion board that had attracted ordinary Chinese movie fans, was first of all an online community for these fans. However, the active discussions fostered in this virtual space enabled the construction of an alternative discourse about Chinese movies that was against the state and the commercial discourses. The discursive construction was made possible through heated debates that were full of both reason and emotion. It is thus inappropriate to say that Rear Window constituted an online public sphere due to both its limited scope (i.e., not universal) and its lack of rationality. Meanwhile, Rear Window was actually more than just a subaltern public sphere. The users of Rear Window took a step further to represent their discourse in the mass media and to reach the larger society through working with other social and commercial forces to show movies in an unofficial way. I argue that such networking practices that bring visibility to their discourse turned the movie fans into a subaltern public. This subaltern public, although constrained by the historical and structural conditions, nevertheless had the potential to change the game precisely because it plugged itself into the network of powers and managed to sustain its presence over time. Internet technology definitely played a critical role in making such a lasting presence possible through functioning as a safe space for community building and networking among the members themselves. While we cannot deny that the general market-ization reforms are game changers, the Rear Window public were not merely responding to such changes but actively taking part in the changes, although not without risks of being appropriated, misunderstood, or even sanctioned. The constant interaction (sometimes conflicts) with mass media serves as a great example to show how the subaltern public earned its visibility through collaborating while struggling with other powerful nodes in the network. This networking logic of forming publics is more clearly seen 10 years after Rear Window users became a regular public speaking for Chinese movies, which is going to be the focus of next chapter.

Notes

1 A banned movie by *Zhang Yimou*.
2 "Criticizable" (Dahlberg 2001a) is judged in two steps: the first step is to see whether the poster talked about his/her reasons as the only truth that everyone should agree with. If not, I examined whether there were replies criticizing these reasons. Both "with the reasons as only truth" and "without critiques" are sorted as "not criticizable."
3 Here I used the word "folk" to refer to the majority of social members who primarily locate in the real life world. The reason why I did not choose "citizen" is that civil society in China is still being formed. The term folk provides a less defined but more inclusive view of the people who are establishing an order that is other than the state or the market logic.
4 Huang Xiaoxie. The Watchers of Chinese Movies. *Nanfang Weekend.* March 19, 2001.

Bibliography

Bourdieu, P. (1993). The field of cultural production or: The economic world reversed, in *The field of cultural production: Essays on art and literature*, ed. R. Johnson, Columbia University Press, New York, pp. 29–73.

Chu, Y. C. (2002). The consumption of cinema in contemporary China, in *Media in China: Consumption, content and crisis*, eds S. H. Donald, M. Keane, and Y. Hong, Routledge, London, pp. 43–54.

Dahlberg, L. (2001). Extending the public sphere through cyberspace: The case of Minnesota E-Democracy, *First Monday*, 6(3).

Felski, R. (1989). *Beyond feminist aesthetics: Feminist literature and social change.* Harvard University Press, Cambridge, MA.

Habermas, J. (1989). *The structural transformation of the public sphere: An inquiry into a category of bourgeois society*, MIT Press, Cambridge, MA.

Li, Y. (2010). *Cinephilia: The history of a culture*, Fudan University Press, Shanghai.

National Bureau of Statistics of China. (2014). *China Statistical Yearbook 2014*. Retrieved from www.stats.gov.cn/tjsj/ndsj/2014/indexeh.htm.

Shefrin, E. (2004). Lord of the Rings, Star Wars and participatory fandom: Mapping new congruencies between the Internet and media entertainment culture. *Critical Studies in Media Communication*, 21(3): 261–281.

Sontag, S. (1996). The decay of cinema, *The New York Times*, February 25. Retrieved from www.nytimes.com.

Wang, S. and Zhu, J. J. H. (2003). Mapping film piracy in China. *Theory, Culture, and Society*, 20(4), 97–125.

Zhu, Y. (2002). Chinese Cinema's economic reform from the mid-1980s to the mid-1990s. *Journal of Communication*, 52(4): 905–921.

4   Ten years after

From subaltern to regular publics

During the last week of 2011, I travelled on an international flight, an inter-city fast train, a domestic flight, and took numerous taxi journeys to map out three cities, Nanjing, Shanghai, and Beijing. I was not able to cover other major cities where Rear Window alumni live, such as Guangzhou and Shenzhen. I had to turn to the Internet for help: two interviews were conducted through online chats, including one interviewee living in another time zone. Most of my interviewees were located in Nanjing when the study was first conducted in 2003. Many of these Nanjing-bound users migrated to other major cities for a job and the kind of job they took was often related to movies. Many Rear Window users who were invited to write for the mass media eventually became mass media employees, specializing in movie-relevant writing. For instance, a well-known Rear Window user moved to Shanghai to work for a professional film magazine for six years and, recently, made a career change to work for a movie company. Some Rear Window users who were not satisfied with writing about movies made by others became movie makers themselves, creating movies for Chinese audiences in the capacity of playwrights and directors. Still other users, no matter how active they had been, became silent and distant from their passion for movies.

Although not all Rear Window users evolved into members of a regular public, some prominent figures in this networked public have made impressive performances that the larger society cannot ignore. The girl who became a playwright had 276,081 followers on Weibo as of July 10, 2014. The girl who had moved to Shanghai to work as a media professional hosted a personal blog that attracted over 1,600,000 clicks during 2004–2006. The boy who wrote the most popular post on Rear Window, co-authored a screen play that earned more than 10 million RMB box office sales. Moreover, their performance on mass media no longer had to be compromised because they were now the gate-keepers themselves. The contrasts between now and then are not small. What has happened during all these years, I argue, is the formation of a regular public following the network logic: firstly, the enhanced self-selection of communication networks leads to the networked individualism that marks the performance style of many Rear Window alumni; secondly, the mediation of ICTs, especially blogs, SNSs, and microblogs, organize these geographically sparse individuals into a cohesive public; and, finally, the visibility of this regular public and its political appeal is further achieved through connections among individuals supported by technologies, which imply a deeper social structure that connects different powers.

This chapter focuses on revisiting Rear Window to Movies and its associated fandom 10 years after the original study to trace the development of the Chinese Internet and the user activities it mediated between 2003 and now. Another set of 15 in-depth interviews, as well as a decade-long continuous participant observation, yielded evidence of how the network, initiated in cyberspace and stabilized through both online and offline connections, transforms a subaltern public into a regular public.

The performance style of networked individualism

In the last chapter, I have talked about the Rear Window discourse that is different from the state, the market, and the academic discourse on what is a quality movie. The last decade could be seen as a period of further development in promoting the folk standards of quality movies. Folk standards are in contrast to the other discourses that exclusively focus on the objects of movies themselves. As one of the interviewees, Carpenter, said, the folk movie reviewers consider movies as something in between the physical forms of sights and sounds and the psychological mechanisms of the audiences. The fan objects here are not merely movies per se, but the intersection between movies and individual experiences. The folk movie reviewers do not care much about the techniques used in the movies, nor do they really favor one certain genre of movies. What matters to them is the simple although illusory feeling that the movie talks to their individual experiences. The standards they utilize to evaluate movies are thus simply whether the sights and sounds can evoke their emotional and rational reflections on their personal histories.

This highly individualist orientation is best illustrated in the most popular movie review called "Waiting is the beginning of getting old in our life." This article was viewed 50,759 times on Rear Window and received 474 replies as of July 10, 2014, although the readership was definitely much larger because many copies of the article had circulated widely on the Chinese Internet. This 14,584 character long article was posted on December 11, 2000, and according to Gu Xiaobai, the author of this most viewed and replied movie review on Rear Window, he typed 1,000 characters a day for about 10 days to document the Hong Kong movies that had left marks on his life. Gu attributed the popularity of this article to his style:

> The reason why this post was so popular is that I wrote down the memory of youth for all of us. I used a relatively new angle to put together many things, a bit nostalgic, a bit inspirational, and at the same time a bit lost. Therefore, it can elicit a relatively strong feeling of reflection. And after all, it is an article easy to read.
>
> (December 30, 2011)

Another popular writer during the golden age of Rear Window, Tengjin Shu, also mentioned the topic of style. If her style has any similarities to Gu's, it is the individualism embraced in her writing. She was a college student when she started publishing movie reviews on Rear Window and her girly personal style received many critiques from male users. She said:

> At the end of my articles, I always finish with a sentence, "thanks for reading my words." I sincerely thought these were just words written by an individual and never really considered them movie reviews or even articles. I was indeed only a student at that time and that is why I never thought I am an authority in talking about movies, not even now. ... It was a style of female writers, very personalized and experiential.
>
> (December 27, 2011)

Although the actual writing styles performed in these movie reviews were idiosyncratic, appealing to common experiences and shared feelings through personal stories was from the beginning the stylistic element adopted by many folk movie reviewers. This style was further promoted when some of these people became professionals. Bonnie was among the last few folk movie reviewers who had made their names known through Rear Window. As a student studying at an art college, Bonnie was dedicated to creating her own art. However, different from many artists trained inside the official institution, Bonnie kept herself open to her readers. She interacted constantly with readers through the Internet and shared her private stories with many. After she became a playwright, she tried to mingle the details of personal life with the stories she was writing. Her view of movies was heavily influenced by her days on Rear Window, instead of the official training she received at the art college. She described:

> Movies are never what are happening on the screen. Movies are what happened between the movie screen and the audiences. Movies are private memories. What I learned in school was an academic view that the movies themselves are more meaningful and personal feelings about the movies do not really have anything to do with the movies. I don't think so now. Again, movies are not what is happening on the screen. Movies do not exist until audiences have emotional responses to them.
>
> (December 31, 2011)

The same point was made by Beitaixi, who became an independent film director after graduating from Beijing Film Academy and working for the commercial movie industry for a few years. Beitaixi started posting his reviews on Rear Window when he was a student. He was soon invited by the mass media to write regularly about movies, including personal columns on the topic. He described his standards of quality movies in a language that is almost identical to the other three interviewees quoted above:

A good movie has to be relevant to personal feelings about this world and this era. Maybe a background is this society in this particular age but everything has to go back to one's heart and mind and everything has to be expressed with sincerity. A good movie is not for others or for some institutions. It has to be about the feelings of a person.

(December 31, 2011)

The quotes by these reviewer-turned-movie makers suggest that the fan object that fascinated them has always been connected to their life experiences. An emphasis on personal histories and individual feelings was shared regardless of the differing writing styles. This orientation towards individualism, however, should not be misunderstood as an individualist culture, which is often in contrast to a collectivist culture claimed to be dominant in Asian societies (e.g., Yum, 1988). These folk movie reviewers started from personal experience but never ended in being selfish, isolated, or narcissistic. Instead, sharing with others has always driven their writings, and mutual understanding was what excited these writers when they found Rear Window. Therefore, what was behind such individualist orientation is the bigger reality that these individuals were no longer alone thanks to the Internet. In other words, all kinds of individualism resonated because the individuals were now networked. Networked individualism, according to Rainie and Wellman (2012, p. 12), means that people rely less on permanent memberships in settled groups (e.g., families, neighborhoods, or work units) but more on sparsely knit and diverse networks. The reason why these people can insist an individualist definition of quality movies is precisely because they can remain themselves without submitting to the norms of settled groups. When they transformed themselves from reviewers to playwrights or directors, their standards of quality movies were no longer just articulated in reviews but also presented in their creative works. When they tried to evoke the shared feeling of as many audiences as possible, they indeed pushed movies or, more precisely, their standards of quality movies into the public arena. The following section will exercise the technological centralism discussed in Chapter 2 to describe how web 2.0 technologies made this transition possible.

The mediation of web 2.0

The transformation of Rear Window users within the last decade took the same journey that the Chinese Internet has travelled. The golden age of Rear Window overlapped with the golden age of Chinese discussion forums (or in technical terms, Bulletin Board Systems, BBS for short). In addition to online community websites, such as xici.net or tianya.com, discussion forums were so common that almost each university had its own internal BBS and every portal site managed its own collection of BBSs. Discussion forums even became basic components of official websites such as e-government websites and the online versions of mainstream media (e.g., the Strengthen the Nation forum on people.com.cn, the official website of the *People's Daily*). Although Rear Window was one of the pioneering discussion forums for ordinary Chinese movie fans, other influential forums included movie-focused BBSs hosted on Sina and Netease, BBSs supported by websites specializing in cultural topics (e.g., Night Ferries of Movies), as well as other discussion boards under xici. net (e.g., Yellow Pavilion Movies). Around 2003–2004, these discussion forums started to decline for various reasons. Rear Window to Movies was said (Zhang, 2011) to have declined due to the heated yet deconstructive debate on whether Chinese movies were a kind of politics in 2003 (more evidence to show that Rear Window was not a Habermasian public sphere). Night Ferries of Movies, a forum that focuses on independent and artistic movies, was shut down in 2003, due to its inability to make money for the company behind it. Those BBSs on portal websites such as Netease were not able to be sustained due to both internal conflicts (a user from Hong Kong became the board manager and many users disliked him) and external challenges (Netease updated its server and interface, which caused lots of posts to be lost overnight) during 2005–2007.

Meanwhile, these online movie fans found a new playground where they could enjoy themselves and this new playground was blogs. It was not a coincidence that these online movie fans did not migrate to a new discussion forum to continue their communities. What distracted them was blogs, which became popular in China around 2004. Blogs had entered China as early as in 2000, but as we know now, due to the extreme popularity of discussion forums, blogs did not have much influence on the Chinese Internet in the first few years and even portal sites were hesitant to develop their blogging services. It was when one blogger, Muzimei, made her fame through publishing her diary about casual sex with many men, including one famous rock musician. The huge amount of attention Muzimei attracted not only invited many copycats to promote themselves through blogging private matters (e.g., posting nude pictures of themselves) but also inspired Internet companies to commercialize blogging services by making stars who attracted public attention. Sina was most successful in promoting its blogging service through a marketing strategy it still uses a lot when promoting new digital commodities such as microblogs. This marketing strategy shifts the focus of the Chinese Internet from ordinary users to outstanding celebrities. In order to compete against other companies that also provided blogs (e.g., blogcn.com, blogbus.com), Sina sent out numerous invitations to celebrities to open a blog with them and helped make the first ever queen of Chinese blogs, Xu Jinglei. Xu's blog has received 3 billion visits as of July 11, 2014, making her one of the most popular bloggers in the world.

The commercial promotion of blogs, I argue, was the real reason why discussion forums were not able to keep their users. Many Rear Window users who had earned some popularity during the BBS years became bloggers, an identity that is vastly different from being an author on a discussion board. Almost all of the 15 interviewees I met in 2011 had their own blogs. Some of them, such as Tengjin Shu, reached new heights of fame through effectively managing her blog and her image. On her blog, she no longer just talked about movies. Instead, she shared her personal life with her readers, mostly young female urbanites, by writing witty posts about her love life, and later marriage, and other personal issues. Bonnie's blog was also very popular, to the extent that she was able to publish a book out of her blog posts, and the book became a best-seller. Even Beitaixi, the independent film director, enjoyed sufficient visibility through blogging. His personal blog once attracted over 700,000 visits. The blogging wave turned these Rear Window alumni into small stars. Huang Xiaoxie, the girl who went to the USA to become a PhD in cinema study, commented on this transition:

> The age of blogs was even more personalized. Discussion forums are like classrooms, where all kinds of users speak out in the same space. In the age of blogs, everyone has his/her own small room to express him/herself. The center is the blogger and the readers can make a bit of comments. There is a little interaction. But basically it is not a platform for shared discussions.
>
> (December 6, 2011)

The golden age of blogs peaked around 2010, when almost one out of every three Chinese Internet users had his or her own blog (CNNIC, 2011). The blogging wave was ended by the new wave of social networking sites (SNSs), especially microblogging. Two leading SNSs in China, renren.com and kaixin001.com, both launched their open-to-all registration in 2008. Before that, there were literally no such Facebook sites in China because of an official ban. What played a significant role for online movie fans to gather together when star making via blogs dominated the Internet was an interest-oriented SNS, douban.com. Chapter 7 will discuss this SNS in detail. Douban functioned as a shared virtual space for online movie fans to discuss the movies they watched, through a unique network that connected both users and objects. A few new folk movie reviewers emerged from douban.com, including Muweier, one of the two said-to-be professional movie reviewers who can make a living out of writing movie reviews in China. Some Rear Window alumni also cross-posted their movie reviews on douban.com but their energy was mainly spent on managing their own blogs.

The real game changer did not appear among the SNSs though, and what effectively killed blogs was the Chinese version of the microblogging service, Weibo by Sina.com. Sina continued its celebrity-focused marketing strategy when promoting its microblogging service. They made a first-ever queen of the Chinese microblog, Yao Chen. Star bloggers, big or small, since then have abandoned their blogs to acquire Weibo accounts in order to keep the attention of their readers, or followers, to use a microblogging term. So did the Rear Window alumni. When checking the blogs by these Rear Window users on July 11, 2014, most of them have not been updated since 2009 and some blogs do not exist anymore. Apart from a few Rear Window alumni who became passive in the network, I managed to contact the majority of my 15 interviewees via Weibo private messages at the end of 2011. Weixidi, the founder of Rear Window, talked about this new format of mediation by Weibo:

> The age of blogs made ordinary Chinese into stars. This could be considered a kind of segregation. The years of BBSs were an age of integration but blogs were one person's private garden without many discussions. The age of Weibo is a correction to the age of blogs. It again enables interpersonal relationships to develop and conversations to happen. ... However, Weibo is too fast. Both posters and followers have no patience. ... Similar to BBSs, there are networks formed on Weibo. For example, celebrities only interact with celebrities. But such interaction is too fast and quickly buried by newer information. In Rear Window, there were alerts popped out if someone replied your post. But on Weibo, tweets are very easy to be missed.
>
> (December 26, 2011)

The Web 2.0 technologies, including blogs, SNSs, and microblogs, have mediated the transition of Rear Window users from a subaltern public to a regular public. If BBSs allowed the formation of a community of online movie fans, blogs turned some of the most active and prominent users into opinion leaders, or minor celebrities that attract public attention. Surprisingly, Facebook-type SNSs did not seem to play a big role in this transition, although an interest-oriented SNS, douban.com, took over the function of shared discussions that BBSs used to have when blogging was dominant among Internet users. The transition leapt through the SNS wave and went directly into a microblogging age. Weibo was able to keep the celebrity-centered network logic but allow more instant although less thoughtful interactions among users. The shared discussion function was restored a little bit on Weibo but still not up to the bar set by the BBS years. A new technology that became popular among Internet users after Weibo had gone through several rounds of political cleansing (e.g., real name policy and new interpretation of rumor dissemination) was Wechat, a private version of microblogging. This new Web 2.0 technology further limited shared discussion to known contacts. Although some affordances of Wechat such as public accounts allow users to subscribe to open channels and receive pushed messages, the dominant way of using Wechat is still within a private circle of known friends.

The mediation of ICTs in the transition of the Rear Window public is central to the process, as seen in how Rear Window users acquired new identities (e.g., celebrities) and new interaction modes (e.g., quick but superficial interactions on Weibo) when the dominant technologies on the Chinese Internet changed. However, these technologies are not merely programming codes. In other words, the technological affordances are consequences of commercial and political influence. The marketing strategy adopted by leading Internet companies such as Sina profoundly defined blogs and microblogs in China, rendering these two technologies being used in very different ways compared to their counterparts in other countries. Meanwhile, political forces have also significantly shaped the technologies: the banning of Facebook delayed the development of relationship-oriented SNSs in China for several years and the political clampdown of the big Vs (Weibo celebrities with verified accounts) forced some users into the private and safe space of Wechat. The mediation of ICTs was never just about technologies because technologies themselves were plugged into the network of heterogeneous actors that tried to use their own powers to define the network. The technological centralism exercised in the current section invites us to further investigate how technologies, along with human actors and deeper powers, constitute the network, which will be the focus of next section.

A networked regular public

Motivated by cinephilia, ordinary movies fans, most of whom never thought that they would become part of their dreams one day, came together to talk about their favorite movies on Rear Window. This coming-together was the first step leading to a networked subaltern public, when this public's visibility was limited and its discourse marginal. The mediation of ICTs enables the transition from a subaltern public to a regular public through social networking, or net-working among human actors. The majority of online movie reviewers were not in the profession of movie review or movie making when they started. Instead, they came from all walks of life, ranging from engineers to insurance agents. They met, became acquainted, developed friendships (romance some-times), and collectively re-identified themselves during the interactive process of exchanging their life experiences expressed in the form of movie reviews. Some of them quitted their jobs and became free-lancers (e.g., Weixidi). Some went into the mass media industry to make their own film magazines (e.g., 101) or became reporters or editors (e.g., Tengjin Shu). Still others took one step further to be key players in movie making (e.g., Gu Xiaobai, Bonnie, and Beitaixi). These changes of life paths were not possible without the social connections they managed to build through the Internet and, especially, online communities such as Rear Window.

If we borrow an over-used term social capital (Putnam, 1995), we can say that the reason why this subaltern public became regular was because of the accumulated social capital through active networking. For instance, Bonnie was successfully transferred to Beijing Film Academy after she became famous on Rear Window and received assistance from the professors working there. Wei Junzi, the former manager of the movie discussion board on Netease, eventually became an employee of Sina, in charge of its entertainment content. Gu Xiaobai was able to write his first play for a famous Chinese director, Li Shaohong, through the recommendation of friends. In the preface Li (2005, p. 2) wrote for Gu's book, Li mentioned Rear Window a few times:

Until one day I found a tool book titled "Movies+2002" (edited by Weixidi, added by author) and other books such as "Screaming for Hitchcock" (one of the editors was a former manager of Rear Window, added by author) and "Rear Window to Movies" (a collection of movie reviews posted on Rear Window, added by author) in SDX Bookstore, I found that I was wrong about my perception of these publications being merely movie catalogs. The level of expertise made me feel that I cannot ignore their existence. Well-known online communities such as Rear Window became the battle front for the new generation of movie reviewers. ... I found a new attitude in Rear Window where Xiaobai once to be the manager of and other relevant books. The sharpness and sensitivity of Xiaobai are juxtaposed with his easiness, just like the way he lives, completely void of an attitude of authorities. This made me look at Xiaobai in a different light.

Not all Rear Window users were able to strengthen their connections through networking with fellow users. There are also instances in which active members or even former managers became distant from the network, and even disappeared. A few famous nicknames and their disappearance puzzled many of my interviewees. Nobody seemed to know where they had gone to. One interviewee who used to write movie reviews for many mass media outlets admitted that he did not network that much with other users and, therefore, did not join the movement to change professions. He is currently an insurance agent and has not written about movies for a long while. The last manager of Rear Window was also not that into movies any more. During our interview, he seemed to be more passionate about the plants he was selling on the Internet than talking about movies and Rear Window. These examples show that the network logic gives individuals more freedom to either connect or disconnect, a convenient switch that can be turned on and off depending on the person's preference.

Although the social network facilitated by the mediation of ICTs is most obvious, what has been connected is more than human actors. In other words, what is behind the networking practices among individuals is the more hidden structure of a network of powers. The emergence of the Rear Window public has obtained support from commercial forces such as pirate movie industry and bars. The transition to a regular public had much to do with the further marketization of the Chinese economy and the diversity different commercial forces bring to the Chinese society. When the folk movie reviewers entered the movie industry, they often took the path of commercial movies because of their online popularity. In other words, they were offered the opportunity to become key players of movie making precisely because their works had proved to be popular among Internet users, who could become the buyers of tickets for the movies they took part in. Other folk movie reviewers who became mass media employees were also kept busy because of the proliferation of Chinese movie production since the open-up policy issued in 2003.

They often became part of the promotion campaign for these movies to gain attention and, more importantly, ticket sales. Such collaboration with the movie industry was not without risks, similar to the collaboration with mass media 10 years ago. Huang Xiaoxie commented on the risk of losing independence due to these ICT-mediated social networks:

> The tradition of Chinese society is to save face for people who are in your social circles. This applies to me too. Since I know some directors personally, I cannot criticize their works too harshly even if I have many reservations about heir works. I cannot offend them because we are for sure going to meet again. This is not good.
>
> (December 6, 2011)

In addition, the fact that many folk movie reviewers were recruited to take part in commercial movie making means only a few got involved in making independent movies. One of the exceptions was Beitaixi, who graduated from an official film institute, worked for the commercial movie industry for a while, and finally started making independent documentaries. Since independent movies are made out of the official institution, they are forbidden to circulate or release via official channels. Beitaixi told me that his documentaries cannot be found on the Internet because firstly, they would be deleted sooner or later and secondly, he wants to protect the privacy of those who are featured in the documentaries. For Beitaixi, the main platform to show his works is through film festivals. The China Independent Film Festival (www.chinaiff.org) was one of the most influential platforms and except for the first year, the other six years of this festival were hosted in Nanjing, the city where Rear Window was founded. The festivals were led by a group of academics from Beijing, who became connected to the folk movie reviewers through online movie fan communities such as Rear Window. The folk movie reviewers in Nanjing have played a significant supporting role during the festivals. For instance, Weixidi was one of the co-organizers and sat in the film selection committee. He explained how these independent film festivals can survive:

> At first the festival was supported by a gallery, out of commercial purposes. It was because independent movie makers have connections with the artists' circle. At first the movies were mainly experimental and therefore, it was hard to say whether they are ideological or not. However, they definitely are artistic and thus, can attract some celebrities to endorse. ... The gallery stopped its sponsorship after the economic crisis [in 2008, added by author]. Economically speaking, the entire modern art market in China was shrinking after that. The finance now is supported by an independent fund, owned by a successful businessman. A boss who aspires or who still has passion. This guy was a passionate youth before 1989 and after that, he became a businessman.
>
> (December 26, 2011)

Although the support for independent film festivals can be termed commercial as well, the market forces behind them were certainly different from a mass-oriented movie industry. When Bourdieu (1993) made his analysis about the artistic field, he pointed out that the market value of these artistic products lies precisely in their restricted production and, thus, restricted consumption. In other words, the fact that these independent movies cannot be accessed via other means adds to their market value in the artistic field. This is why an art business such as a gallery would have been interested in sponsoring an independent film festival. This commercial force, however, surely differs from a mass-produced, mass-consumed business model like a popular movie. The latter sponsor, a successful businessman who pursued his passion in his younger years through an independent film festival, illustrates how complicated powers can be. While support was made in a commercial means, the motivation behind the support is hardly commercial or money-driven. One can argue that it is at most out of the desire of exchanging economic capital for cultural capital, which had to be abandoned due to political reasons. The various commercial forces and their connections with the Rear Window public help to keep the visibility of this public and its appeals in front of the larger society. The networked regular public reveals the most recent historical transformation in China's social morphology: The diversification of social forces via the emergence of commercial powers. Next chapter will further discuss the complicated relationship between commercial powers and social forces through examining online translation communities.

Bibliography

Bourdieu, P. (1993). The market of symbolic goods, in *The field of cultural production: Essays on art and literature*, ed. R. Johnson, Columbia University Press, New York, pp. 1–34.

Chinese Internet Network Information Center (CNNIC). (2011). *The annual report of Internet development in China*. Retrieved from www.cnnic.cn/research/bgxz/tjbg/201101/P020110221534255749405.pdf.

Li, S. (2005). Preface: My rear window, in *Waiting is the beginning of getting gold in our life: Essays about movies*, ed. X. Gu, Guwuxuan Publishing House, Suzhou, China, pp. 1–3.

Putnam, R. D. (1995). Bowling alone: America's declining social capital. *Journal of Democracy*, 6, 68.

Yum, J. O. (1988). The impact of Confucianism on interpersonal relationships and communication patterns in East Asia. *Communications Monographs*, 55(4), 374–388.

Zhang, X. (2011). The days wasted in discussion forums. *Cinema World*, 9. Retrieved from http://site.douban.com/107846/widget/notes/131812/note/173653179/.

5 Online translation communities
From consumers to prod-users

The expansion of cultural industry in China and the advance of Internet technologies give rise to a growing body of fandom residing in Chinese cyberspace. The massive production of popular culture in the form of media outputs and consumer goods has cultivated a great number of loyal and active fans who tend to share their affections on a certain fan object with peers. The online space supported by Web 2.0 technologies not only provides a locale for those fans to gather and interact, but also in turn facilitates new ways to conduct the activities that fans enjoy doing together. China has witnessed a rapid proliferation of online fan communities that offered numerous channels and various platforms for Chinese netizens to participate in cultural practices in pursuit of all kinds of fan objects, not limited to movies. Among them, online translation communities have been quite a prominent phenomenon in the past years. When Rear Window users had to rely on pirate VCDs and DVDs to enjoy foreign movies, the quality of translation of the foreign language content was a challenging issue. The challenge became even more severe when the online fandom expanded from movies to foreign entertainment content such as games, TV dramas, and reality shows and the video streaming services made the access to such content even more effortless.

The online translation communities were initiated by groups of Chinese fans who love watching foreign entertainment content that is not provided in Chinese official outlets but are accessible from the Internet. They came together to translate the subtitles in foreign languages for better enjoyment, and to publish them on the Internet to share with fellow fans. It can be said that anyone in China who has ever consumed a foreign entertainment product acquired from an unofficial channel, such as a Hollywood movie not released publicly in China, must have benefited from their effort. Their success has inspired other kinds of online translation communities to emerge. These late-comers focus on translating news articles, commentaries, and speeches that are delivered in foreign languages. These translation communities are built on the spirit of sharing, volunteerism, and do-it-yourself, for they never charge for their work, which itself has entailed certain civic values. In addition, online activities have been moving toward the more civic side of the spectrum with the recent change in the content they translate—from pleasure-seeking entertainment to the content of educational and social value, such as open courses provided by world-famous universities.

As Henry Jenkins (2006a) argues in *Convergence Culture*, "(p)opular culture may be preparing the way for a more meaningful public culture," the question to be asked is whether these online translation communities in China can act as an embodiment of such transfer from cultural sphere to civic sphere, especially in view of Chinese government's strict control over citizens' political participation. Whereas a transition from a subaltern public to a regular public has been described in the previous two chapters, this chapter provides a different angle to look at the transition process through utilizing the concept of transfer. In order to address this issue, this chapter starts with a review of studies to show the fine line between fandom and activism. Analyses of the online translation communities' background, contributors' motivation to such volunteerism, and the procedure of the transfer are made based on participant observation and in-depth interviews with 20 community members. A discussion on the potential transfer between fan activism, civic engagement and political participation in the context of China is provided at the end of this chapter.

Fandom and fan activism

Fans used to be represented by the mass media as obsessed, deviant, and dangerous fanatics. In particular, the news media have cultivated a notion of fans as psychologically defunct. For example, crazy fans once caused the death of 35 Italian soccer fans following crowd disturbances at a European Cup Final in Brussels in 1985 (Sandvoss, 2005). Jenson (1992) noted that there are tendencies to pathologize fans both in early mass communication scholarship and in official high culture. Compared to popular representations of fandom, the portrayal of fandom in early academic approaches was rooted in an almost exclusive emphasis on structure. Fandom was interpreted as a consequence of mass culture in need of compensation for lack of intimacy, community, and identity. If in mass-mediated representation the fan is predominantly the perpetrator, then in academic analysis he or she is first and foremost the passive victim. A thread of academic thought treats engaging fans as immaterial labor. For instance, Terranova (2000) pointed out that online activity such as building virtual communities signifies free labor on the Net, which is simultaneously voluntarily given and unwaged, enjoyed, and exploited. Furthermore, Andrejevic (2008) argued that participants in online fan sites serve as value-enhancing labor for television producers. Similarly, Cote and Pybus (2007) proposed that the recent wave of SNSs (e.g., MySpace) contains a dynamic new source of creative power, the so-called immaterial labor 2.0.

This depiction of fandom as a consequence of psychological dysfunction or further development of capitalism constitutes the background against which fans first attracted attention from media and cultural studies scholars in the 1980s. According to Gray, Sandvoss, and Harrington (2007) in *Fandom:*

Identities and Communities in a Mediated World, the study of fandom can be contextualized across three distinct waves since the 1980s.

The first wave of fan studies was inspired by Michel de Certeau's (1988) notion of the tactics taken by the disempowered. John Fiske's work on popular culture and fandom (1989a,b, 1992) provided a useful starting point and an overall paradigm. Fiske's emphasis is on resistant readings and construction of the popular from the grassroots, and audiences' guerilla-style tactics of constructing meanings, fan communities, and thus sub-cultural resistance to the dominant culture. This is the celebratory phase, in which "fandom is beautiful," as the editors phrase it. The early phase of fan studies "constituted a purposeful political intervention that sided with the tactics of an audience in their evasion of dominant ideologies, and that set out to rigorously defend fan communities against their ridicule in the mass media and by nonfans" (Gray, Sandvoss, and Harrington, 2007, p. 2). The first wave of fan scholars attempted to take what used to be viewed as a derogatory practice and status and to turn it into a positive one (Costello and Moore, 2007).

The second phase was a response to the widespread new media and new forms of fan culture in the 1990s, in which fan communities proliferated endlessly, mostly fuelled by the Internet. Fandom seems to have become a common and ordinary aspect of everyday life in the industrialized world that is actively fostered and utilized in industry marketing strategies (Jones, 2003). From Fiske (1989a, 1989b, 1992) to Jenkins (1991, 1992), the increasingly ethnographic studies revealed a more complex relationship between fans as agents and the structural confines of popular culture in which they operate, for this relationship cannot be reduced to one being simply a consequence of the other. Further, in this phase, scholars often focused on the fans' construction of identities through their insertion into fan communities (Grossberg, 1992; Harris and Alexander, 1998). Through their identification with fan objects, people helped to define themselves. And fandom appeared more positively in the cultural industries themselves, which helped to nourish their fan communities in a highly competitive market (Kellner and Collette-VanDeraa, 2008).

A third phase of fan studies has emerged, claimed by the editors of *Fandom*, in which studies of fans and fan objects expands from looking at individual tastes and participation and examination of fan objects to "investigation of fandom as part of the fabric of our everyday lives" in which fan studies aim "to capture fundamental insights into modern life" (Gray, Sandvoss, and Harrington, 2007, p. 9). Studies have thus broadened the analytic scope to a wide range of different audiences reflecting fandom's growing cultural currency (Sandvoss, 2003, 2007; Hills, 2002, 2007; Scodari, 2004).

Fan activism, as a more specific subject under fan studies, however, has rarely been explored in terms of how its conceptualization evolves over these three waves. For many years, according to Rowe and his colleagues, "fan activism was regularly read as grass-roots resistance to cultural capitalism and its colonization of the life worlds of those whose authentic relationship to their cultural forms, identities and practices cannot be reduced to disciplined, obedient consumption" (2010, p. 299). For example, there were challenges from the Internet-based fan community against the narrative construction of the romantic relationship between Michael Schofield and Sara Tancredi in TV drama *Prison Break* (Knaggs, 2010). However, in comparison to social movements seeking political democracy or the rights and dignity of disadvantaged groups, fan activism embodied as complaints and outrage might appear as little more than a celebration of hobbyist trivia (Rowe, Ruddock, and Hutchins, 2010) or immaterial labor serving the global capitals (Andrejevic, 2008).

It is Henry Jenkins who raises fan activism out of the consumerist or cultural domains and lays out the ways in which fan activities start to change politics. Set against the backdrop of media convergence, fans as consumers of media content are offered different technologies to bring the flow of media under their control and to interact with other fans. A participatory culture, in contrast to the older notion of passive media culture, emerges out of a new mode of consumption as a networked practice as well as collective intelligence. Fan communities become knowledge communities that creatively appropriate and transform materials borrowed from mass culture, which empowers these communities in their relationship with corporate media. This new power is so far seen to be inserted into the entertainment system. However, whether it can be inserted into the political process is only a potential.

The gap between participatory media culture and participatory political culture is not a small one. How can activism in cultural forms be translated and transferred into activism in politics? Jenkins suggests that citizens started to apply what they learned as consumers of popular culture toward political activism. For instance, election-related video clips on Youtube show how participants applied their skills learnt from making amateur fan movies to political discourse making. Another transferrable between fan and political activism is agency: games like *the Sims Online* cultivate a sense of agency among players and encourage them to participate in civic engagement. In addition, fan communities provide a space or structure, which could be used to support political activities. This structure provides mechanisms of collaboration that fosters expertise other than official sources, of production that challenges corporatized or politically controlled discourses, of circulation that invites diverse responses. These fan spaces are not overtly political and thus, have lower stakes to bring politics closer to the everyday experience of citizens, as well as are less policed by ideological powers. In short, Jenkins sees the potential of skills, sense of agency, mindset of collaboration, structures supported by technologies (which in total is named participatory culture) being transferrable from cultural consumption to political engagement.

As entertainment and popular culture proliferate across Chinese media landscape, fandom has become a quite relevant and prevalent phenomenon in contemporary China, with fan objects ranging from popular singers, movie stars, sportsmen to teleplay, film franchise, and video games. Fans exist anywhere possible—in online clubs, forums, or at the scene of concert and other events. On one hand, these fans are active consumers constantly engaged in material consumption activities connected to direct products (music albums, DVDs, concert tickets, etc.) and derivative commodities (tie-in commercial goods, star-represented brands, etc.). On the other hand, they are dedicated to what Fung (2009) called "immaterial labors," in which they collectively participate in public activities supporting their idol, and establish their rapport and mutual identification through sharing and communicating informational content or affective expression. To certain extents, fans begin to assume an "intriguing new role of prosumers that integrates fan production, fan promotion and fan consumption all in one" (Yang, 2009).

Overall, Chinese government has been adopting a fairly tolerant attitude towards fan activities. As long as everything is kept at the material consumption level and within the party line, the authority will not interfere so much, for people's preoccupation with consumption and obsession with idols is "likely to divert them from the critical discourse of civic engagement that could undermine state legitimacy" (Fung, 2009, p. 297). However, if not by direct banning, the party-state still tries to exert its control in roundabout ways. In case the counter-forces of popular culture were upgraded to an uncontrollable level, the state has tried to co-opt them actively into its propaganda machine (Fung, 2009). For example, as a gesture to accommodate the expressive individuals of the new generation, the state held its own music award or reality show to keep fans within control, or to cultivate its own fans, so that it could spot immediately any organized collective activity that may threaten the "harmonious society."

The optimistic prediction from Henry Jenkins regarding fan activism, therefore, seems to be doubtful in the Chinese context. Are Chinese fans only entertainment seekers? Is their enthusiasm for cultural products purely driven by pleasure-seeking? What are the motivations that drive fans to participate in cultural production? How do the restrictions imposed by both political and commercial powers impact fans who want to spend their energy on causes beyond entertainment? Do new media provide any possibility for fans who actively participate in cultural prosumption to become political activists? The rest of this chapter will answer these questions using empirical evidence gathered through virtual ethnography.

From fans to online translation communities

As the influx of foreign cultural products becomes evident in the 2000s, Chinese consumers' need for both information and entertainment produced out of China become acute. Unfortunately, the policy infrastructure does not allow a free flow of foreign cultural products. On one hand, the import of such products is highly limited to a few institutions (e.g., Chinese Central Television) as well as a small number (e.g., 20 foreign movies per year) under the claim of protecting local cultural industry. On the other hand, the imported cultural products are often censored and edited to remove the politically sensitive content. Chinese audiences are thus left with no choice but looking for the complete versions of foreign games, movies, and TV dramas by themselves.

The emergence of broadband Internet in the 2000s opens the possibility of obtaining such products without going through the official venues such as TV channels, movie theaters, and DVD retailers. Fans residing in the market where access to one cultural product is guaranteed (e.g., American fans of *Prison Break*) upload it to the Internet to share with their fellow fans, but, apparently, the product is still in its original language. As most Chinese do not master English, translating such foreign entertainment content becomes necessary in order for Chinese fans to fully enjoy them. Therefore, fans come together and build communities to collaborate on translation tasks. The earliest translation communities were made around 2001–2002 by fans of Japanese comics and computer games. Shortly after, fans of foreign movies and TV dramas started to build their own communities. These movie or TV drama fan communities are often called Zimuzu (literally meaning subtitle groups) as what they do is essentially to provide subtitles in Chinese. The popularity of American TV dramas such as *Friends* and *Prison Break* has brought subtitle groups a great amount of online visibility. By 2007, the most well-known groups were Yidianyuan (Garden of Eden, YDY for short), FengRuan (Wind Soft, FR for short), and Renren Yingshi (Everyone's Video, YYeTs for short). The former two communities have about 400 regular translators and the third one has about 200 translators. These three communities, along with numerous smaller ones, have become an influential force in producing and disseminating translated foreign entertainment content in China (see Hu, 2012 for a more complete list of subtitle groups).

The evolution of Chinese online translation communities does not stop at subtitle groups. The format of distributed and collaborative projects is carried on to translation tasks of a different nature. Chinese netizens who are attracted by foreign mass media content start to join web 2.0 communities to translate news, analyses, talks and speeches conveyed in foreign languages. Yeeyan is the pioneer in this domain through signing agreements with foreign mass media such as Guardian and Forbes on translating their content into Chinese. Different from the grassroots nature of subtitle groups, Yeeyan is an Internet start-up founded by returnees from the Silicon Valley. Interviews with its founders Mr. Zhao Jiamin show that Yeeyan was aimed at profit-making from the first day of its inception.[1] Its commercial model cashes on a "hierarchical crowdsourcing" approach as subtitle groups have taken. In his email reply to our interview questions, Mr. Zhao explained that a hierarchy is necessary for controlling the quality of translation whereas the majority of contribution comes from the crowd.

Both subtitle groups and Yeeyan-type of web 2.0 sites cannot be imagined without the infrastructure provided by the Internet. Various technologies are used to facilitate the hierarchical crowdsourcing mode of collaboration. Taking American TV dramas as an example, an episode is first recorded and shared on a BitTorrent (BT) site located in Europe or the USA. A group of transportation editors put it on a Korean or Japanese server as Chinese Internet connects to these two countries much faster than to Europe or the

USA. At the same time, overseas members who live in the foreign countries record and upload subtitle files in English. Source editors are responsible for downloading these source files and put them up to Chinese servers. One episode is broken into multiple sections and multiple translators download their parts. One proofreader is responsible for checking all the translations. When proofreading is finished, all the segments will be put back together into one episode by timeline editors, who also check the correspondence between subtitles and scenes. The final products are then sent to dissemination websites such as shooter.com (for downloads of subtitles), verycd.com (BT seeds-sharing website) and the Chinese Youtube sites such as tudou.com or youku.com. The whole procedure takes only five hours to complete. For information-oriented translation sites, like Yeeyan and Dongxi, there are article databases categorized under different topics, from which the translator can "claim" the article he/she is interested in translating. After proofread by the site editors (mainly for a quick filtering of sensitive or obscene words), the translation will be posted on the website. In some cases, the editors may assign articles to some capable translators. The site may hold projects for special occasion, for example, translating a book on earthquake knowledge one year after the Wenchuan Earthquake. Then editors will recruit project managers and translators from the site for that specific project. The candidates will first finish a trial translation and send it back for editor evaluation. If the translation quality is good enough, the candidate will be assigned part of the book to translate, the amount of which depends on the pre-negotiated work schedule of each translator. After all parts are done, the project manager or site editor will get down to proofreading for grammar and style before all parts are combined into a complete whole. These virtual structures prove to be highly efficient in any kinds of translation tasks, regardless of their content.

Whereas subtitle groups seem to focus on entertainment, the Yeeyan-type of websites show an emphasis on information. This division becomes seriously blurred when translating open courses catches the attention of both parties. Since prestigious universities such as MIT and Harvard provide videos of their courses to the public for free, members of Chinese translation communities show great interest in such content. YYeTs, TLF, and Yeeyan have become the three major players in translating open courses. The same virtual structure that was used to translate *Prison Break* is applied on open course projects with only one significant difference: the translators must have some knowledge regarding the topics. As the open course content does not have serious copyright issues, mainstream portal websites such as Netease and Sohu join to be the dissemination websites. Each of them establishes its own open course page by collecting courses translated by various communities. Netease also provides its own translation by hiring freelance translators, who are said to be from both the Yeeyan-type of websites and college students majoring in English. From November, 2010 when Netease first officially presented the videos of open courses of world-famous universities, to August, 2011, the translated open courses posted on the Netease platform added up to 6,000 episodes (about 9,000 hours). In late 2011, the amount of courses translated reached 200 hours per month. The content of these open courses covers everything from arts, humanity, social sciences, to computing, and all kinds of natural sciences. The open course project has been well received by both traditional media and the general public (including non-netizens).

A dynamic Chinese online translation sphere is formed through the collective effort of translating open courses since 2010. Fans' volunteered contributions to open courses show that these fans are not just entertainment seekers trying to maximize their pleasure. If pleasure-seeking is not the only motive that drives fans to contribute, what are the fulfillments and satisfactions these fans-translators are trying to get? How do these motivations connect to who they are and what they do in their everyday life? The next section will address questions like these.

From personal interest to public good

The strongest force that drives fans to join and keep working in these groups is claimed to be interest and hobby. When asked why they are doing this, all our interviewees had used at least one of the following statements, "I am interested in...," "for personal hobby," "it's my interest," "I just like it." Most of these voluntary translators are young people in their twenties or thirties, and thus they are either employed or studying in colleges. Although their activities require professional skills in translating from a foreign language to Chinese, only a small number of them once specialized in a foreign language major. They rarely expect any material profit from these activities, like extra money, but simply consider them a good way to spend their leisure time.

The interest in the source texts plays an important motivating role, especially in terms of choosing what to translate. Yeeyan has its own original article database from which translators can select articles to work on, but translators tend to choose articles from sources other than the database, because they want to translate what appeals to them, and what they think is of good quality, no matter how many clicks or views they would get. For example, one respondent says, "I saw an article, and I liked it so much that I cannot help it, so I translate it." It also has something to do with what the translator is good at. For instance, one interviewee specializes in Information Technology (IT). When he sees an English piece about IT, he translates it because he loves it and thinks he can come up with a professional translation. And this "interest principle" also applies to open course translation, which is initiated by someone who is interested in the topic before he/she can recruit a team of others who are also interested.

These translators are also interested in language learning or translation *per se*, which helps to maintain their proficiency in the language. In the process of doing various translation works, their skills are greatly improved, from which they harvest ever increasing confidence, passion, and enjoyment. Now in China, English skills are considered a crucial qualification for job hunting.

Actually a lot of college students or working people take great pains in learning English by attending specially designed training courses, so that they can obtain the various English proficiency certificates which are to be presented as a competitive advantage in job hunting. But when asked if they want to acquire any credentials from what they do, the interviewees usually say, "Well, no such plan ... It really doesn't matter. It's only a hobby."

When the translated content bears on social, political, or educational meanings, like the open courses from prestigious universities, or news articles from Western media that provide views about China which are different from local mainstream voices, these translators seem to take on a great civic responsibility to open up people's minds, to broaden their horizons, and to offer them different kinds of knowledge. They think that what they communicate to the public is of great significance, and can bring various benefits to the receivers. However, when asked "which is the stronger motivation, for yourself, or for the public?," they actually tend to put their volunteerism into the personal category, while a few consider the two as not conflicting but complementary.

One respondent says his activities in Yeeyan is purely out of personal hobby and interest, "As one's ideal way of living is to fulfill each passing whim, I am actually making my whim come true." A highly active TLF member, who is also an open course team supervisor, says bluntly, "Actually, I think all my translation activities are for myself, 'I want to help netizens to learn English better, so I want to translate the subtitles?' no one thinks like that ... it is the same for open course, I like it, so I do it. It's like Adam Smith's theory – we promote the public interests while we are pursuing our own interests." Therefore, it all comes back to the process of self-fulfillment and self-improvement. Another contributor from TLF, who quit his job in real life and set up an independent open course Zimuzu website, spoke in the same vein, "My job is boring and meaningless ... I just want to live the way I want ... there are more personal elements involved. People always speak highly of me, but I am really not that great." But he does think public good is important, but not the first priority for him to start up. Although the translators believe it is necessary and important to let the public know alternative views, they do not hold the unrealistic hope that a couple of articles would exert great influence. What they can try their best to do is only to translate; drawing audience is quite another business. As one interviewee says, "Those who are interested will come to read on their own, those who are not will not read anything even if we send articles to them. I will not impose my views on others. As long as I know, nothing matters."

Although their primary motivation to do such voluntary work is not specifically for enlightening the public, when they receive feedback and appreciation from the readers/viewers and fellow translators, they do feel more motivated to continue or to excel in their work. They acquire a sense of distinction from the recognition that they are unique and extraordinary. As one subtitle translator says, "sometimes when I chatted with people and mentioned that I am a Zimuzu contributor, they would say, 'Really? that's cool!', and then I feel quite good about myself. It's like 'Wow, I am awesome!' ... it's not purely about my English skills, but about that the subtitle of this movie is done by me, and what I have done can be seen by other people. It feels awesome."

Whereas the motivation of participating in media production (translation in particular) is fairly fandom-like, the effects of such self-interested actions can be spilled out of the realm of fan culture. How does fan activism transfer from media production into civic engagement? What are transferrable and how are they transferred? The following section will address questions like such.

From participatory media culture to participatory civic culture

The case of open course translation indicates a turn of fan communities from entertainment seeking to knowledge sharing, an activity that could be considered as part of civic education. Although the evidence is not strong enough to say that this phenomenon is representative of the entire cyber sphere in China, the cases cited below suggest that there is a possibility to see components in supporting fan activities being transferred to civic activities. A good example is that one of the most popular courses is called "Justice" from Harvard University. If a topic like justice does not directly mobilize Chinese people to change their political situation, it at least serves the purpose of educating Chinese people what this civic value is about. The fact that this is the second best received course[2] till now suggests that the knowledge shared through translated open courses is definitely not just instrumental (e.g., how to make iPhone applications) and oftentimes, the values and principles entailed in the courses are what attract both the translators and the audiences.

However, the transfer from translating entertainment content to open courses is not a simple one. According to Jenkins, what can be transferred are basically four things: skills, sense of agency, mindset of collaboration, structures supported by technologies. What is evidently transferrable is the collaboration mechanism, the virtual structure that has been used in translating movies and TV dramas. However, the biggest challenge is the expertise required. Although expertise plays a role in translating entertainment content (e.g., dramas about doctors require medical expertise), the depth of knowledge needed to translate university-level specialized courses is far more demanding. One solution is to include translators who have the background in the specialty. As many translation community members are college students, it is not impossible to include at least one translator who has similar background in one project team.

There are still times when no one is a real expert in the highly specialized field. Translating "Astrophysics" from Yale University is one such case. The leader of this project is a girl who majored in economics. She had no knowledge in astrophysics before she decided to take on the responsibility of supervising this project. However, lack of expertise is not a barrier to her as the mindset of collaboration makes her believe that problems can be solved through collective efforts. She explained how collaborative mechanisms helped her: first, she relies a lot on online information from Google, Wikipedia, and so on, to educate herself during the procedure of translation. Second, her team members debate on the translation whenever there are confusions. Finally, when knowledgeable audiences send back comments, she immediately updates the translations.

As most of the translators are not foreign language majors, they have improved and maintained their language sufficiency through regularly translating foreign content. However, the skills transferred into open course translation are not just about the language. The astrophysics example shows that the skills of learning by oneself, peer-learning, as well as new media literacy such as crowdsourcing and searching, are transferred into the success of open course translation. "Astrophysics courses mentioned the big bang. Then I looked through all the material I can find about big bang theory, and then there was the Hubble theory, there were stars, etc. I searched for tons of material about each subject. I even studied logarithm again. So I don't know about the audience, but I do learn a lot myself," says the project leader of the astrophysics course.

What is also transferred is the sense that "I should be the person who does it" (i.e., sense of agency). When average Internet users wait for others (e.g., cultural industry) to produce the content they want, this group of fans has a high self-efficacy in creating content they like. They consider themselves not only capable but also responsible for translating the content they are interested in. One interviewee describes it well: "Frankly speaking, I am afraid other people would ruin the subtitle (bad translation). I don't want to see that, so I do it myself."

With this last piece of empirical note, it has to be clarified why participatory media culture is not likely to be transferred to participatory political culture in China for the time being. This has to be explained through the relationships between online translation communities and the government(s) at various levels. As content providers, these translation communities confronted the government(s) because of the information contained in the translated materials. At the end of 2009, Yeeyan was found to be down with a notice posted on its front page saying "(d)ue to our errors in handling some of the articles on the website, we went against the relevant regulations; therefore Yeeyan has to temporarily shut off its server, and adjust the relevant content." Interviewees from Yeeyan confirmed that after this close-down, stricter self-censorship was employed, such as the deletion of published articles that contain sensitive content and longer waiting time to be approved for publication. Copyright appears to be the battle ground where subtitle groups have to fight against commercial interests equipped with governmental assistance. In August 2010, YYeTs.com, one of the leading subtitle groups, announced its close-down as well as the confiscation of its server. The announcement stated that "we are trying our best to coordinate with relevant government agencies while raising funds from community members to buy new servers. We will also thoroughly clean out the content on our website." It was reported that this shut-down was caused by YYeTs' release of BT seeds for a local blockbuster. The two examples here illustrate how the government can pressure or even make such communities dysfunctional. With such density of surveillance and control, the transfer to translating political content seems to be unlikely, if not completely impossible.[3]

Identity: from consumers to prod-users

The fans gathered in Chinese online translation communities are very different from the image of obsessed, deviant, and dangerous fanatic often portrayed in traditional mass media. Instead, the fandom of foreign information and entertainment is practiced through calculated actions and efficient collaboration supported by the Internet technologies. In order to realize the goal of enjoying foreign content, the virtual structure that is built involves a hierarchical crowdsourcing procedure that cannot be completed without close collaboration among multiple parties. Therefore, the first conclusion is that the fan activism observed in Chinese online translation communities is driven by the fans' own deliberate choice.

The motivations that have driven fans to contribute are mainly interest based. The primary interest is on the content itself, being entertainment or information. These fans also hold an interest in learning or improving their language skills. After the fan communities were fostered online, being part of the communities gives the fans a sense of belonging which helps to sustain their contribution. Although distinction coming from outside of the communities serves as extra rewards, these fans–translators consider the social impacts of their efforts a byproduct of pursuing their personal interest. It is thus concluded that the translation communities found on the Chinese Internet were embarked around fan objects, although their implications enlarged as their activities entered into new realms such as civic education content.

Translating inaccessible foreign content voluntarily can be read as grassroots resistance to "a market economy with Chinese characteristics," which means everything within the party line is free to be commercialized. Although commercialization invades almost every corner of the cultural field that is allowed to enter, current legal and policy constraints forbid the Chinese cultural industry from freely supplying foreign cultural goods to the local market. It is in between the flooding of Chinese cultural commodities and the suppression of foreign content where the strategic prosumption emerges. On one hand, these fans take advantage of the Internet technologies to access the content unavailable in the local legal market, which could be considered as resistance to state dominance on information flow. On the other hand, we have to be cautious that although fans are not evidently subject to capitalist exploitation (e.g., working as free immaterial labor) because foreign cultural industry cannot fully capitalize on such labor yet, the exploitation could easily happen when the constraints withdraw, thanks to the readiness cultivated by these communities.

In addition, it was a concern that if fan culture dwells on hobbyist objects, fan activism is diverged from "more important struggles" (Rowe, Ruddock, and Hutchins, 2010) such as political progress. Jenkins (2006a) has shown that the fans' energy is not limited to the cultural realm and when conditions permit, fans seamlessly transform into political activists, in the context of the USA. The circumstances in China are quite different as political participation is heavily controlled by the government and a fine line is drawn between everyday life and political life for ordinary citizens. The findings show that most Chinese fans are aware of this boundary and their activism is consciously limited to fan objects that are not apparently political. From self-censorship to overt censorship, we are yet to see political content produced by foreign media becoming a regular component seen in these communities. However, it does not mean that fan activism seen in these communities has nothing to do with the "more important struggles." The open course program indicates that fan activism could be transferred from entertainment seeking to knowledge sharing, an activity that entails civic values if not political values. We see a possibility for a participatory civic culture to grow out of the collaborations done during the translation of entertainment content. The collaboration mechanism, including both the virtual structure and the mindset of working together, is easily transferred into translating civic education content. In addition, the collaboration experience cultivates a spirit of volunteering and sharing in the fans who are involved. The individual contributors are empowered by the successful collaborations in the sense that they perceive themselves as the agents of actions, without hoping that others will make changes for them.

This chapter concludes that the fan activism seen in Chinese online translation communities is sustained primarily through the spirit of volunteerism and the sense of agency it engenders, which constitute an identity that goes beyond enthusiastic fans. Its sustainability, however, is constantly challenged by censorship, copyright, and commercialization. The more-for-profit members such as Yeeyan have to conform to censorship requirements if they want to keep their business legal in China. Copyright also prevents commercial players such as portal websites from disseminating foreign movies and TV dramas. If the Chinese government decides to enforce strict copyright protection, the visibility of subtitle groups has to be seriously compromised, as we can predict. The volunteer-based communities such as subtitle groups are threatened by commercial forces as they try to commodify translation and devalue the spirit of volunteerism. These challenges make the sphere of online translation more dynamic rather than less, as different forces trying to define this newly emerging phenomenon with their own logic.

This chapter focuses on how fan activism is sustained and challenged in the context of Chinese online translation communities through constructing an identity of being prod-users. It is argued that a participatory civic culture is emerging through the collaboration between fans on translating foreign entertainment and information precisely because these fans have taken a different identity that cannot be found in popular discourses regarding fandom. This identity distinguishes fans from the passively receiving audiences. Instead, fans actively select which content they want to consume despite the structural constraints, be it censorship or commercialization. In addition, fans become producers when foreign content is recorded, transcribed, translated, and disseminated through an Internet-supported infrastructure. This identity is an embodiment of the value of volunteerism, the DIY (do it yourself) spirit, as well as the habits of sharing and collaborating.

Constructing new identities has been a consistent theme seen in online fan communities, which deserves more discussion now. The online movie fans described in Chapter 3 acquired an identity of reviewers who are capable of making judgments through their subaltern discourse. Later on, this self-identity became real through acquiring positions in the movie-related professions as we read in Chapter 4. An identity of opinion leaders or celebrities was introduced to these folk movie reviewers by Internet companies when they were trying to sell their blogging services. Those who eventually marched into the movie-making scene took the identity of film makers. What differentiates the identities evolved in the Rear Window community and those found in the online translation communities is that members of the latter fan community seemed to dwell on this hybridity of producers and users without the intention of becoming professionals. This difference has to be understood with foregrounding technology in the formation and maintenance of such fan communities. The identity emerging out of the hierarchal crowdsourcing supported by Web 2.0 technologies cannot be as individual-centered as the Rear Window style because none of the individuals would be able to accomplish the translation tasks by themselves. It now becomes clear that during the formation of a public, the identity acquired by that public has to be understood in relation to the fan objects (e.g., independent Chinese movies or foreign TV dramas), the technologies used to support the formation (e.g., BBSs or blogs or crowdsourcing sites), the diverse commercial powers (e.g., pirate movie industry or arts galleries or global cultural industry), and the ever-changing political powers. The next chapter will zoom in on one of the many relational dilemmas, namely the conflicts of cultural identities through consuming foreign TV dramas.

Notes

1 See an interview with Mr. Zhao Jiamin by *Programmer*, a magazine. Retrieved from: www.programmer.com.cn/4813/.
2 Second to a course about happiness from Harvard University, according to a Netease survey. Retrieved from: http://v.163.com/special/endclass/endclass1.html.
3 Translators who insist on uncensored information left Yeeyan to build Yizhe, a blog located outside of the Great Fire Wall. Yizhe regularly publishes translated foreign news and analyses that are obviously critical of Chinese government.

Bibliography

Andrejevic, M. (2008). Watching television without pity: The productivity of online fans. *Television & New Media*, 9, 24–46.
Certeau, de M. (1988). *The practice of everyday life*, University of California Press, Berkeley, CA.

Costello, V. and Moore, B. (2007). Cultural outlaws: An examination of audience activity and online television fandom. *Television & New Media*, 8, 124–143.

Cote, M. and Pybus, J. (2007). Learning to immaterial labour 2.0: MySpace and social networks. *Ephemera: theory and politics in organization*, 7(1), 88–106.

Fiske, J. (1989a). *Reading the popular*, Unwin Hyman, Boston, MA.

Fiske, J. (1989b). *Understanding popular culture*, Unwin Hyman, Boston, MA.

Fiske, J. (1992). The cultural economy of fandom, in *The adoring audience: Fan culture and popular media*, ed. L. A. Lewis, Routledge, London, pp. 30–49.

Fung, A. (2009). Fandom, youth and consumption in China. *European Journal of Cultural Studies*, 12, 285–303.

Gray, J., Sandvoss, C., and Harrington, C. L. (eds) (2007). *Fandom: Identities and communities in a mediated world*, New York University Press, New York.

Grossberg, L. (1992). Is there a fan in the house? The affective sensibility of fandom, in *The adoring audience: Fan culture and popular media*, ed. L. A. Lewis, Routledge, London, pp. 50–69.

Harris, C. and Alexander, A. (1998). *Theorizing fandom: Fans, subculture, and identity*, Hampton Press, Cresskill, NJ.

Hills, M. (2002). *Fan cultures*, Routledge, New York.

Hills, M. (2007). Media academics as media audiences: Aesthetic judgments in media and cultural studies, in *Fandom: Identities and communities in a mediated world*, eds J. Gray, C. Sandvoss, and C. L. Harrington, New York University Press, New York, pp. 33–47.

Hu, K. (2012). Chinese subtitle groups and neoliberal work ethic, in *Popular culture, co-productions and collaborations in East and Southeast Asia*, eds N. Otmazgin and E. Ben-Ari, NUS Press, Singapore, pp. 207–232.

Jenkins, H. (1991). Star Trek rerun, reread, rewritten: fan writing as textual poaching, in *Close encounters: Film, feminism and science fiction*, eds C. Penley *et al.*, University of Minnesota Press, Minneapolis, MN, pp. 171–204.

Jenkins, H. (1992). *Textual poachers: Television fans and participatory culture*, Routledge, New York.

Jenkins, H. (2006a). *Convergence culture: Where old and new media collide*, New York University, New York.

Jenkins, H. (2006b). *Fans, bloggers, and gamers: Exploring participatory culture*, New York University, New York.

Jenson, J. (1992). Fandom as pathology: The consequences of characterization, in *The adoring audience: Fan culture and popular media*, ed. L. A. Lewis, Routledge, London, pp. 9–29.

Jones, S. G. (2003). Web wars: Resistance, online fandom, and studio censorship, in *Quality popular television*, eds M. Jancovich and J. Lyons, British Film Institute, London, pp. 163–180.

Knaggs, A. (2010). Prison Break general gabbery: Extra-hyperdiegetic spaces, power, and identity in Prison Break. *Television & New Media*, 23, 1–17.

Rowe, D., Ruddock, A., and Hutchins, B. (2010). Cultures of complaint: Online fan message boards and networked digital media sport communities. *Convergence: The International Journal of Research into New Media Technologies*, 16, 298–315.

Sandvoss, C. (2005). *Fans: The mirror of consumption*, Polity, Oxford.

Terranova, T. (2000). Free labor: Producing culture for the digital economy. *Social Text*, 18(2), 33–58.

Yang, L. (2009). All for love: The corn of fandom, prosumers, and the Chinese way of creating a superstar. *International Journal of Cultural Studies*, 12, 527–543.

6 *House of cards*

From entertainment to politics

My Love from the Star is a South Korean TV series aired around late 2013 and early 2014 in the entire Asian region. The fantasy romance talks about an alien who landed on Earth in the Joseon Dynasty and, 400 years later, fell in love with a top diva in the modern era. The show received high ratings in and out of South Korea, with a 20% viewing rate recorded in the Philippines.[1] The TV series also became extremely popular in China when it was aired solely online through video streaming websites (Lin, 2014). The TV series has been watched 26.42 billion times on iqiyi.com, one of the many online streaming sites, as of July 27, 2014. The soap opera has taken the country by storm and everything featured in the show has sold like hot cakes, from the clothes, accessories, and makeup products, to the Korean style fried chicken and beer favored by the female protagonist. The *Washington Post* (Wan, 2014) reported that in March 2014, the Korean drama was discussed at China's National People's Congress, particularly in a committee of the political advisory body, the Chinese People's Political Consultative Conference (CPPCC), in order to understand why Chinese producers cannot make such a popular show. The move from entertainment to politics is made explicit when a picture widely circulated online positioned a young Xi Jinping, the current national leader, alongside Kim Soo-hyun, the male protagonist, and claimed that they look alike.

Popular entertainment is never void of political significance and so is its reception. If political reading can emerge out of an apolitical show such as *My Love from the Star*, it is not hard to believe that audiences definitely read politics out of entertainment content that relies on political topics to attract attention and to provide pleasure. As a special case of online foreign content, political TV dramas represent a genre of fan objects that issues a political invitation to its consumers. This chapter focuses on foreign media content and, more importantly, Chinese fans' interpretation of such content, which has been deliberately ignored in previous chapters. Whereas publics can form around any issue, those that form around foreign TV content such as political dramas have unique features, such as being prompted to embrace certain political values that might be alien to the social realities the fans live in.

This chapter starts from a political economic review of transcultural TV in China, followed by a structural analysis of the online sphere of transcultural TV fandom. Through a textual analysis of posts on the Baidu post bar for fans, this chapter shows how Chinese fans have interpreted one recent American political TV drama, *House of Cards*, according to two themes of contradiction: authentic/unauthentic and foreign/indigenous. When interpreting the depiction of American politics in the show as authentic, the fans did not hesitate to say that the depiction of Chinese politics was unauthentic. By contrasting the "real" American politics depicted in the show and the "real" Chinese politics based on personal experience, the identity struggle of being Chinese in the contemporary conditions of a network society is explored in the fans' interpretations.

The political economy of transcultural TV

The introduction of television into Chinese families was said to be the most important cultural and political development since the end of the Cultural Revolution (Lull, 1992, p. 59). In the early years of Chinese television (i.e., between 1958 and 1978), the medium was mainly used to showcase the success of the "Great Leap Forward" and functioned as a tool for intra-party power warfare (Huang and Yu, 1997). The first ever Chinese TV drama produced in 1958, *A Bite of the Cabbage Cake*, symbolizes how television was used to indoctrinate ideological control during this historical period. In order to compensate for the paucity of TV programs, imported foreign content became a regular occurrence during Chinese TV air time. Huang and Yu (1997) reported that in 1959 alone, China imported about 1,000 TV programs, 459 of which were from Hungary, while there were 349 from the former Soviet Union. It is thus worth emphasizing that the format and content of Chinese TV programs were from the very beginning heavily influenced by foreign imports. Although the stories and narratives depicted in the imported TV content might be foreign to the Chinese audiences, their understanding of television was nevertheless shaped by the content, which defined what television means to Chinese audiences. In other words, one can argue that the birth of Chinese TV and the invention of Chinese TV audiences were at the beginning transcultural. Without the two Chinese students who were sent overseas to learn about television, Chinese TV would not have been born (Huang and Yu, 1997). From day one, without the imported content that included news and dramas, Chinese TV would not have been able to show much to its audiences.

Transcultural TV in this chapter refers to TV programs that have originated from a culture other than that of contemporary mainland China since 1949. The word "transnational" is not used because some of the "foreign" content comes from regions that are not necessarily considered nations in a political sense. For instance, regions such as Hong Kong and Taiwan have long been seen as distinctive cultures different from the mainland's but not fully independent nations. The political economy of transcultual TV in the early years of Chinese television was rather simple: the state offered financial support to purchase foreign content from countries that were part of the Soviet bloc in order to ensure the correctness of ideological doctrine. The development of Chinese television encountered a significant setback during the Cultural Revolution (Zhao and Guo, 2005). Beijing Television, the first television station in China, was shut down for a month upon the launch of the Cultural Revolution and provincial stations were suspended indefinitely. Other than functioning as a tool of factional political struggles, Chinese television curtailed its other functions, including obtaining and showing content from other countries during those years.

After the introduction of the open-door policy in 1978, state-controlled TV broadcasters resumed the import of foreign TV content in order to deal with the challenges coming along with marketization. TV stations, like many other state-owned media outlets, were expected to survive financially on their own without governmental subsidies. Advertising was introduced to Chinese television in 1979 (Zhao and Guo, 2005) and the entertainment content increased tremendously to attract attention. Much of the entertainment content was imported from other countries, no longer just those that belonged to the Soviet bloc. Wang and Tsang (1996) found that, until the 1990s, the so-called capitalist countries were the major suppliers of foreign TV content. The older generation of Chinese TV audience has shown great enthusiasm towards these overseas TV programs. The most popular TV dramas during the 1980s were mostly imported ones from Japan, Hong Kong, Taiwan, and even Mexico and Brazil (Zhu, Keane, and Bai, 2008). In the early 1990s, American shows such as *Baywatch* and *Dynasty* drew three times more viewers than local shows (Hays, 2008).

By the end of the 1990s, Chinese TV industry has successfully transformed itself into a full-fledged entertainment business through structurally establishing provincial level broadcasting conglomerates and ideologically turning away from any significant intellectual debates (Zhao and Guo, 2005). In addition to extensively airing foreign entertainment, Chinese TV stations were able to imitate foreign TV content to produce their own popular hits. For instance, Beijing TV (later named CCTV) claimed the national record for viewing numbers with a soap opera called *Yearning* (*Kewang* in Chinese). The soap opera was said to imitate a style of melodrama popularized by the Japanese, Taiwanese, and Latin American TV dramas shown on Chinese TV channels (Zhong, 2012). Another popular TV drama, *Public Relation Girls* (*Gongguan Xiaojie* in Chinese), was shown around the same time but was made by a provincial TV station, Guangzhou TV. As Guangzhou is geographically and linguistically proximate to Hong Kong, this TV drama was modeled after popular Hong Kongese TV dramas and met with high viewership around the whole country.

Imitating or adapting foreign TV content can be said to be the driving inspiration for Chinese local producers. Starting from the 2000s, structurally strengthened broadcasting conglomerates (Zhao and Guo, 2005) and independent TV content providers (Liu, 2010) made a Chinese version of almost every popular TV show that could be found in the world. Take Hunan TV, one of the most influential provincial level broadcasting conglomerates, as an example. In addition to TV dramas, its variety shows, dating games, reality shows, law and order series, and even news programs, actively took in the components found in their foreign counterparts (Pu, 2013). For instance, *Dating with Roses* in 1990 was a copy of a Taiwanese dating show *About Romance* and the later banned *Super Girl* in 2005 was exactly modeled on *American Idol*. The most recent hit, first shown in 2013, was *Where are We Going, Dad*, a father–kids interaction reality show copied from South Korea. Whereas the earlier copycats were criticized for unauthorized usage of foreign content, the recent ones all obtained legal authorization from the original producers. The easiness of copyright purchase, along with cultural proximity, may explain why Asian shows such as those from South Korea, Hong Kong, and Taiwan have been dominant in such adaptation.

The online sphere of transcultural TV fandom

During the pre-Internet period, the format of transcultural TV fandom expression was supported by offline mechanisms such as fan clubs and print publications. The pirate VCD industry, similar to its significance in the case of foreign movies (see Chapter 3), played a pivotal role in disseminating transcultural TV content that was not available through the official TV channels. Nakano (2002) observed that the diffusion of many Japanese TV programs in China was actively initiated by the ordinary Chinese audiences, "(f)ar from being cultural imperialism pushed from the economic center." Starting from the late 1990s and early 2000s when the Internet was first introduced to the Chinese society, fan websites, modeled on offline fan clubs, were established to support particular stars. For example, Ailinquan was built in 2000 as the first fan website in mainland China to support the popular Taiwanese actress Lin Qingxia (Tieba.com, 2006). However, the influence of these fan websites was very limited due to the low Internet penetration rate and the website technology at that time.

The introduction of broadband Internet in the 2000s has made the transcultural consumption of overseas entertainment content available at he click of a finger. Meanwhile, the conglomeration of Chinese TV industry further limited the choices for Chinese audiences and forced those who are Internet savvy to search for their preferences on the Web. For instance, the fans of Japanese TV dramas, once satisfied by pirate VCDs, now turned to file-sharing sites and online fan clubs for their fan objects (Hu, 2005). Various online translation communities were built to break down the language barriers that most Chinese transcultural content fans face (see Chapter 5). The popularity of American TV dramas such as *Friends* and *Prison Break* has brought some subtitle groups a great deal of online visibility (e.g., YDY, FR, and YYeTs). Meanwhile, websites supporting online discussions about these TV shows mushroomed. Discussions of foreign TV shows were first scattered in various online forums, such as BBSs associated with subtitle groups, forums hosted by major web portals, and independent online forums. Around the early 2000s, BBSs connected with the subtitle group YDY were the largest and most influential forums for fans to discuss foreign TV shows. Discussion boards devoted to a particular show could be found in these large subtitle groups BBSs. All these communities opened up new areas for Chinese fans to express their enthusiasm and articulate their alternative cultural interests in foreign TV shows.

However, the wave of BBSs didn't last long as blogs took over the spotlight (see Chapter 4). While prominent BBS users became small celebrities through blogging, the majority of fans turned to a new online space, Baidu Post Bar, for interaction. The history of Baidu Post Bar dates back to 2003, three years after the establishment of Baidu. From around 2005, fans of foreign TV shows scattered in various BBSs began to gradually migrate to Baidu Post Bar. By the year of 2009, Baidu Post Bar defeated all its competitors and became the most popular space for fans of foreign TV shows to gather and share. At the end of 2012, Baidu Post Bar hosted 600 million registered users and over four million bars (163.com, 2012). One possible reason for the rise of Baidu lies in the fact that Baidu Post Bar is tightly connected with the Chinese search engine Baidu, which is currently dominant in Chinese online search market. When users search for a foreign show on Baidu, Baidu top lists the corresponding post bar on the result page, which is meant to attract new users to post bars.

Besides that, the popularity of the 2005 *Super Girl* (the Chinese version of *American Idol*) brought its post bar a huge number of clicks, other Internet events such as the Internet Crusade against some fans of Korean popular culture also helped Baidu Post Bar gain more visibility. The TVXQ Chinese fan incident of 2008 started from news spreading on the Internet that a TVXQ (a Korean pop group) member was in a physical confrontation with a pregnant Chinese woman who was a fan of the group. Chinese netizens were enraged by the TVXQ Chinese fans' defense of the group member and organized the destruction of the TVXQ post bar (Baoba in Chinese). The bar was made dysfunctional by robots posting thousands of empty posts in a short period of time. A similar incident happened again in 2010, when a concert by another Korean pop group, *Super Junior*, did not issue enough tickets to Chinese fans resulting in turmoil. Again, other Chinese netizens were enraged by the behavior of the Chinese fans and organized another round of bar bursting (also called the June 9th Crusade).

Although Baidu Post Bar is user-focused, the role of Baidu cannot be reduced to a carefree host who only provides a platform. Firstly, Baidu undertakes part of the state-delegated responsibility for Internet censorship. Creation of any new bars must be examined and verified by Baidu to assure that politically sensitive or pornographic bars cannot be founded. Baidu also strengthens its delegated control over speeches in post bars during sensitive times. For example, in May 2009, one month before the twentieth anniversary of the Tiananmen Square protest that ended on June 4, Baidu temporarily shut down the post and comment function in post bars associated with Chinese universities. Secondly, every bar can have up to three managers and 10 assistant managers, and application for the position of managers must be approved by Baidu on the basis of the applicant's activeness. Baidu can also terminate any managers who are considered as not working to the standards. Thirdly, Baidu takes the role of mediator to settle online disputes, and to manage appeals and complaints from users. However, Baidu fails to perform these responsibilities well, as post bar members and managers always complain about Baidu's managerial inaction. Whereas censorship and political control are directly and indirectly enacted by Baidu, fans' unauthorized circulation and consumption of foreign content has not been forbidden. Instead, Baidu Post Bar has been the most important source for many Chinese fans to find free access to foreign TV shows.

A large variety of post bars, covering almost every topic in the world, can be found in Baidu: from daily life to national events, from China to other countries, and from popular issues to marginalized interests. More than half of the top 500 bars, according to Baidu's ranking system, are entertainment focused. Bars for foreign entertainment also differ in media types, such as TV dramas, reality shows, documentary series, movies, music, and games. For foreign TV shows, post bars are further categorized by the original country of the show (e.g., the USA, the UK, and South Korea), the genre of the show (e.g., dramas, reality shows, variety shows, sports shows, etc.), and particular shows (e.g., *House of Cards*, *Friends*, etc.). According to the Baidu rank within the genre of TV dramas (as of July 17, 2014), the top 10 bars were almost all dedicated to foreign dramas with only two exceptions. The majority of these foreign TV dramas are from South Korea or the USA. The foundation time of post bars ranges from 2005 to 2013, and bars of Korean shows are generally newer than those of American or Japanese shows.

Baidu Post Bar has become the meeting point for most of fans of foreign TV shows, nowadays leaving only a very small number of people to use BBSs associated with subtitle groups. However, the interaction between post bars and subtitle groups is still evident. Members of subtitle groups could also be active users of post bars. Some post bars were initiated by subtitle groups, such as the *Kpop Star* bar. Recognizing the contribution of subtitle groups to making foreign content enjoyable to Chinese audiences, many bar managers also expressed their dissatisfaction with the speed and quality of translation, and that they dreamed of having their own translation team exclusively for their bars. With the increasing popularity of Weibo in recent years, bar managers with ambition and foresight have set up their official Weibo accounts as the second site to enhance the visibility of shows and bars. Compared to post bars, messages on Weibo could be spread more quickly and extensively through the functions of re-posting and tagging. For bar managers, Weibo is mainly used for diffusing information in the format of images, music, and video files, serving as an enriched channel to complement post bars where text is the dominant format of expression. In addition, chat groups built on instant messaging tools (e.g., QQ) by post bar members also extend the discussion and relationship among fans. Some of the bar members become close friends in real life through inter-acting via the intimate channel of QQ (the Chinese version of ICQ). A dynamic online sphere of transcultural fandom on foreign TV shows has been formed and maintained predominantly based on Baidu Post Bar and supplemented by other online spaces such as the subtitle groups, Weibo and QQ.

Reading politics out of political TV dramas

House of Cards is an American political TV drama produced by the online streaming service Netflix. The TV series centers on Frank Underwood, a Democrat congressman who gets himself into a position of power through ruthless manipulation and power games. Two seasons of the show were produced in 2013 and 2014 and a third season has been commissioned by Netflix. The show has received multiple Primetime Emmy Award nominations since its first season. Different from other popular American political TV dramas such as *The West Wing*, this TV series depicted American politics in a highly cynical and dark way. The dissemination of this TV drama in China was initiated by Sohu's online video channel in 2014, when Sohu streamed Season 2 simulta-neously with Netflix. Although the second season included sensitive topics such as the trading conflicts between China and the USA, the land dispute between China and Japan, and the corruption of Chinese government officials, Sohu managed to show all the 13 episodes after some cuts and edits. It was said that Wang Qishan, a high-ranking governmental official, recommended this show to his colleagues (ifeng.com, 2014).

The popularity of this show in China can be seen in the numbers of views on Sohu. The first season of the TV drama has been viewed 94 million times and the second season 92 million times. Various other video streaming websites such as QQ video channel have also provided free access to the show. Although only in its third season, the post bar of this show has already attracted over 36,000 users and the number of posts reached 126,546 as of July 17, 2014. In contrast, the nine-season classic *The West Wing* has a post bar of merely 472 users and 1,405 posts. We have to admit that *House of Cards* is not the American TV drama that attracts the most amount of attention from Chinese netizens. However, it is a unique instance that explicitly talks about politics and issues an obvious invitation to the audiences to focus on the political meanings of the show. The show not only covers American politics but also refers to Chinese politics when representing the international relationships among powerful nations. The murders, sex, corruption, and violence conveyed in the show make it very exciting to watch. The abrupt twists of plots both puzzled and amazed Chinese audiences. All of these made great topics of discussions and fueled the heated debates in the post bar.

The posts one can find in the post bar are generally four types: firstly, resource posts are those that include videos, pictures, music, e-books, quotes, news, and even ringtones relevant to the series. Secondly, discussion posts about the show are centered on the characters, the plots, the lifestyles, and the context shown in the series. For instance, many hot posts were about whether one character is likeable or not and why. Fans who cannot catch up with certain plot twists also posted their questions and they gave each other answers. Discussions about the show even extended to the lifestyle elements found in the show. For instance, one hot post discussed the recipe of making BBQ ribs as shown in one episode. What made the discussions about the show unique were those talking about the context of the show. As *House of Cards* is a political TV drama, basic understanding about the political structure and culture in the USA is necessary for the fans to fully enjoy the show. However, Chinese audiences often do not have such knowledge. There are thus many posts devoted to explaining the political context, ranging from the fundamental principle of division of powers to the nitty-gritty details such as the style of a party whip's shirt collar. Interesting discussions emerged from such posts when fans tried to use their own life experience in China to understand the political context in the USA. Thirdly, and most importantly, extended discussions often go beyond the show to talk about the comparisons between Chinese and American politics as well as the comparisons between American TV dramas and Chinese or Korean TV dramas. Finally, miscellaneous posts include management posts that state the rules of posting and replying, announcement posts that invite fans to join offline activities, survey posts that gauge the age, gender, geographical location, and even horoscope of the fan users, as well as irrelevant posts.[2]

The textual analysis in this chapter took advantage of posts that mostly fall into the second and the third category, with a selection criterion set at 100 replies and above. Survey posts were also consulted to understand the demographics of the fan users, who have been shown to be young (aged between 15 and early 30s) and live all over the country including cosmopolitan cities and recently urbanized towns. Both genders were present among the fan users although those who posted sounded more likely to be male. For example, one post, apparently written by a female college student, complained that her roommates had no interest in talking about politics with her. The majority of replies were sexist by saying that women are by nature apolitical and urged the author to find male friends for a chat.

The reality of American politics is explained in the knowledge posts that tried to help fans to fully enjoy the show. These posts went into detail when explaining a large variety of political issues in the USA. For instance, one post, claimed to be written by a student who had studied public administration in the USA, invited fellow fans to post any questions about the political system in the USA. The questions included basic ones such as how to differentiate the left and the right in the American context, and what the role of the vice-president is compared with the president, as well as advanced ones such as what confidentiality waiver means, and what a party whip does. Another post listed terminology that had appeared in the show and provided explanations. The post started with very basic terms such as the *Washington Herald* and evolved into a discussion about the lobbyist institution. A debate emerged out of the discussion of lobbyism: some thought that this was no different from bribing while others believed that lobbyists could contribute to the balance of power. Another interesting case was a discussion about the wealth of American politicians. One episode showed the house owned by a billionaire who had tried to influence politics. Another post, which received over 600 replies, was titled "Impossible to understand: Why are the politicians in the show so poor?" The author listed a few details to make the point, including one significant plot in which the female protagonist betrayed her husband for sponsorship worth 200,000 dollars. The answers focused on two aspects: one said the purchase power of American dollars is pretty high so even a small number can afford many things; and the other answer tried to use statistics to prove that American politicians receive little salary and have to openly declare their properties so they are indeed poor. Regardless of the issues being explained and discussed, the fans seemed to trust the authenticity of the show and often used historical events (e.g., Watergate) and real examples (e.g., the salary of Obama) to prove that the show was honestly depicting the reality of American politics.

However, when it comes to the depiction of China and Chinese politics, the fans did not have that much trust. A regular topic in the post bar was to question the authenticity of the depiction of China in the show. One widely mentioned detail was a map shown in the TV series, in which Taiwan was not a part of China. Another episode showed how Chinese hackers hacked American websites. Quite a few posts pointed these details out and interpreted them as either a way to distort reality in order to make China the villain or a political tool to distract Americans' attention from their internal conflicts, both of which are meant to make the show more exciting. As one reply said, "it is just for fun." Another detail was about the negotiation team sent by China, which was made up of a group of young nationalists. Some replies interpreted this as there are not many senior Asian actors in the USA. Although the interpretations were not uniform and some fans did believe that the depiction of China was real, the fact that there were significant disagreements among the fans regarding the authenticity of such details indicates the double standards many fans used when evaluating the realness of this show.

The reason why these Chinese fans had different evaluations of the depictions of China vs. the USA is because most of them have first-hand living experience in China whereas only mediated experience about the USA. The issue of authenticity thus becomes a matter of personal experience. To be fair, most of the fans would not have had the opportunity to witness the local politics depicted in the show, such as meeting the negotiation team from China or knowing high-profile businessmen who may have a voice in Washington. Nevertheless, these fans believed that their understanding of the local culture and their direct experience of everyday politics may grant them some authority in judging the authenticity of Chinese politics shown in the TV series. Such assumptions of knowing our own politics are critical when fans try to collectively make sense of their personal experience through referencing the show. The comparisons to American politics depicted in the show ultimately serve the goal of finding out what it means to be a Chinese in the contemporary conditions of a network society.

Identity: being Chinese in a network society

A persistent question in research of transcutlural flow of information is to ask how the consumption of foreign cultural goods would influence consumers' identification with the indigenous culture. A critical tradition that prognosticates cultural imperialism was so prominent (Wang, 2009) that even Chinese state ideology taps into the power of the terminology to resist so called "Westernization." Since it is impossible that "today a country or region could isolate or de-link itself from the global networks of power" (Hardt and Negri, 2000, p. 284), cultural imperialism is argued to be inevitable when those with more power force their cultural products to those with less power, which results in homogenization of various cultures, deprivation of indigenous identification, and denial of local autonomy. One thread of empirical research focuses on how exposure to foreign media may weaken identification with indigenous cultural values. For instance, Zhang and Harwood (2010) found that viewing imported TV programs was negatively associated with viewers' endorsement of interpersonal harmony values, which were claimed to be a key component of Chinese traditional values.

On the other hand, the active audience perspective (Fiske, 1989; Hall, 1980; Morley, 1993) suggests that audiences, as located in communities and histories, are actively negotiating, if not subverting, the meanings conveyed in the cultural products. For instance, Radway (1984) found that romance readers form "interpretative communities" to collectively make sense of the texts. Ang (1985) observed the cultural differences in reading *Dallas* among audiences who come from different countries that vary in their histories, values, and traditions. Tan (2011) found that Chinese viewers of *Friends* demonstrated varying degrees of affective impact, which did not escape the culturally coded constraints. Hu (2008) argued that the narrative reflexivity planted in Japanese TV dramas drew Chinese audiences to engage in reflexive thinking and implicit therapy on themselves. The "foreignness" found in these transcultural media content, as argued by Chua (2008), is a source of viewing pleasure when audiences practice both identification with and distancing from the characters and actions on screen.

In order to manifest the contradiction of foreign vs. indigenous, this section turns its focus on the comparisons between American politics as imagined through the TV show and Chinese politics as experienced by the Chinese fans. Actually, such comparisons are so regular in the post bar that they became the most frequently posted topic and received the most replies. One post, titled "Speaking of being strategic, Americans are far behind Chinese," resulted in more than 1,000 replies, making it the second most replied post following a survey post asking for fans' geographical locations. A similar post was titled "Frank is a joke, his level could only be laughed at was he in CCP." Another post had a title of "Chinese politics is totally different from American politics." These posts seemed to practice distancing from the American politics depicted in the show. The "foreignness" of doing politics in the USA indeed became a source of viewing pleasure for the fans when these posts listed point by point how the ways of doing politics in the USA would fail in China. For instance, one plot depicted that the male protagonist, Frank Underwood, killed two people with his own hands. This was seen by the Chinese fans as unimaginable in China, and even a low-caste official would not have done it. However, the discussions following such comparisons often ended with contrasting conclusions. Some fans concluded that Chinese politics is better than American politics and they often faced harsh critiques or vulgar personal attacks from the opposite view holders, who thought Chinese politics is much worse than American politics. A significant amount of fans seemed to position themselves in the middle, emphasizing that both the Chinese tradition and the development stage China is in necessitate the way in which Chinese politics is done now, as well as denying that the future of Chinese politics would be to become American politics.

Surprisingly, a small number of posts tried to identify the Chinese fans with the foreign show and became popular among the fans too. One post was titled "I am a loser – From Frank to Freddy," in which the author confessed that he had started from dreaming of becoming someone like Frank and now only wanted to make a living as Freddy, the owner of the BBQ restaurant, does. The post received 234 replies that were different from those posts that involved harsh critiques; the majority of replies tried to help the author by encouraging him to pursue his dreams. One reply even used Frank as a role model, stating that Frank had been stumbling in his career when he was younger, which is not actually mentioned in the show. Another post was titled "Let us discuss, what an ordinary Chinese civil servant can learn from *House of Cards.*" Although some replies immediately pointed out that American politics is so different that there is almost nothing Chinese civil servants could learn, other replies thought that there were still things that could be learned such as following the right boss and being resourceful. The practice of identification with the characters and actions on screen hinges upon self-reflection on one's own life experience, which goes beyond simply seeking pleasure from "foreignness."

The textual analysis of the comparison posts shows that the collective interpretation elicited by viewing this American political TV drama defines being Chinese through first making explicit what a Chinese political reality is, and then figuring out how to survive in such a reality. Being Chinese, rather than carrying out certain values and cultural conventions, is identified as having to live in the Chinese reality. This identification process is pragmatic compared to a cultural identity that assumes some continuations of tradition or a value-oriented identity that assigns some beliefs moral preferences. The "here and now" way of identifying being Chinese shows the embeddedness of many Chinese in this new era of a network society. They become Chinese because they see through the TV show that they are not able or even willing to break away from the network they are now embedded in, although this network presents tremendous challenges for them to survive. The authentic/unauthentic and foreign/indigenous contradictions manifested in the interpretations of the show are moments of discovery that reveal the reality of contemporary China, which is not that optimistic. When the identities of movie reviewers, online celebrities, movie makers, and online prod-users introduced new possibilities into the fans' lives, the identity of being Chinese forged through the fans' reading of *House of Cards* is rather limiting, giving the sense of agency up to the over-determinism of structured powers. This finding confirms again that during the formation of a public, the identity acquired by that public has to be understood in relation to the fan objects (e.g., an American political TV drama), the technologies used to support the formation (e.g., online discussion forums), the diverse commercial powers, and the ever-changing political powers.

Notes

1 Retrieved from AGB Nielsen Philippines' Facebook update at www.facebook.com/a gbnielsen.philippines/posts/809273412425009.
2 They are also called "water posts" since the BBS era because these discussions are often random and have nothing to do with the fan object. However, the random discussions help improve the interpersonal interactions among the users and thus, become a regular category of posts one can find in online discussion forums.

Bibliography

Chua, B. H. (2008). Structure of identification and distancing in watching East Asian television drama. *East Asian pop culture: Analysing the Korean wave*, 1, 73–90.

Fiske, J. (1989). *Understanding popular culture*, Unwin Hyman, Boston, MA.

Hall, S. (1980). Encoding/decoding, in *Culture, media, language*, eds S. Hall, D. Hobson, A. Lowe, and P. Willis, Hutchinson, London, pp. 128–138.

Hardt, M. and Negri, A. (2000). *Empire*, Harvard University Press, Cambridge, MA.

Hong, J. (1998). *The internationalization of television in China: The evolution of ideology, society, and media since the reform*, Greenwood Publishing Group, Santa Barbara, CA.

Hu, K. (2005). The power of circulation: Digital technologies and the online Chinese fans of Japanese TV drama. *Inter-Asia Cultural Studies*, 6(2), 171–186.

Hu, K. (2008). Discovering Japanese TV dramas through online Chinese fans, in *Media Consumption and Everyday Life in Asia*, ed. Y. Kim, Routledge, New York.

Huang, Y. and Yu, X. (1997). Broadcasting and politics: Chinese television in the Mao Era, 1958–1976. *Historical Journal of Film, Radio and Television*, 17(4), 563–574.

ifeng.com (2014). *Everyone loves House of Cards?* Retrieved from http://news.ifeng. com/opinion/special/houseofcards/.

Jiang, Q. and Leung, L. (2012). Lifestyles, gratifications sought, and narrative appeal: American and Korean TV drama viewing among Internet users in urban China. *International Communication Gazette*, 74(2), 159–180.

Kim, S. (2009). Interpreting transnational cultural practices: social discourses on a Korean drama in Japan, Hong Kong, and China. *Cultural Studies*, 23(5–6), 736–755.

Leung, L. (2008). Mediating nationalism and modernity: The transnationalization of Korean dramas on Chinese (satellite) TV. *East Asian Pop Culture: Analyzing the Korean Wave*, 53–69.

Li, S. (2010). The online public space and popular ethos in China. *Media, Culture & Society*, 32, 63–83.

Lin, L. (2014). Korean TV Show Sparks Chicken and Beer Craze in China. *The Wall Street Journal*, 26 February. Retrieved from http://blogs.wsj.com/chinarealtime/ 2014/02/26/korean-tv-show-sparks-chicken-and-beer-craze-in-china/.

Liu, B. R. (2010). Chinese TV changes face: The rise of independents. *Westminster Papers in Communication and Culture*, 7(1), 73–90.

Lu, S. H. (2000). Soap opera in China: the transnational politics of visuality, sexuality, and masculinity. *Cinema Journal*, 40(1), 25–47.

Morley, D. (1993). Active audience theory: Pendulum and pitfalls. *Journal of Communication*, 43(4): 13–19.

Nakano, Y. (2002). Who initiates a global flow? Japanese popular culture in Asia. *Visual Communication*, 1(2), 229–253.

Pu, L. (2013). A longitudinal study of the foreign TV programming pattern of China Chongqing TV, 1981–2010. *Intercultural Communications Studies*, XXII(3), 1–17.

Song, G. (2010). Chinese masculinities revisited: Male images in contemporary television drama serials. *Modern China*, 36(4), 404–434.

Tan, S. K. (2011). Global Hollywood, narrative transparency, and Chinese media poachers: Narrating cross-cultural negotiations of Friends in South China. *Television and New Media*, 12, 207–227.

Wan, W. (2014). Chinese officials debate why China can't make a soap opera as good as South Korea's, *The Washington Post*, 7 March. Retrieve from www.washingtonpost. com/world/asia_pacific/chinese-officials-debate-why-china-cant-make-a-soap-opera-as-good-as-south-koreas/2014/03/07/94b86678-a5f3-11e3-84d4-e59b1709222c_story. html.

Wang, G. (2009). Going beyond the dualistic view of culture and market economy: Learning from the localization of reality television in Greater China. *Chinese Journal of Communication*, 2(2), 127–139.

Wang, J. and Chang, T. K. (1996). From class ideologue to state manager: TV programming and foreign imports in China, 1970–1990. *Journal of Broadcasting & Electronic Media*, 40(2), 196–207.

Weber, I. (2002). Reconfiguring Chinese propaganda and control modalities: A case study of Shanghai's television system. *Journal of Contemporary China*, 11(30), 53–75.

Yang, J. (2012). The Korean wave (Hallyu) in East Asia: A comparison of Chinese, Japanese, and Taiwanese audiences who watch Korean TV dramas. *Development and Society*, 41(1), 103–147.

Zhang, Y. B. and Harwood, J. (2002). Television viewing and perceptions of traditional Chinese values among Chinese college students. *Journal of Broadcasting & Electronic Media*, 46(2), 245–264.

Zhao, Y. and Guo, Z. (2005). Television in China: History, political economy, and ideology. *A Companion to Television*, 28, 521–539.

7 Douban versus Renren
Fan objects as network nodes

This chapter makes a more profound effort to discover and describe the network logic. This network logic, which resonates with Castells' argument (2006), can be viewed as firstly the formative principle of a network society. The network logic is also the dominant cultural logic in Kazys Varnelis' concept of networked publics, a concept that emphasizes connections or "links between people, between machines, and between machines and people" (2012). This chapter tries to illustrate the network logic by distinguishing two different kinds of network structure, namely interest-oriented versus relationship-oriented SNSs. While the former links people to people, the latter connects both humans and things. Given that networks are the foundation of collective action, the transformed relationships logically have the chance to change the outlook and essence of contemporary collective action in an emerging Chinese civil society. From the focus on primary groups (e.g., extended family, friends and colleagues) to the booming of interest groups (e.g., the hiking club), the Internet plays a significant role in transforming social relations in China. In addition, from common social contacts to shared fan objects, Chinese people now initiate and maintain relationships via brand new means.

As social network sites (SNSs) have become extremely popular among Internet users in recent years, research attention has been drawn to an array of websites such as Instagram, Google+, Facebook, Twitter, YouTube, LinkedIn, MySpace, and many others. The focus has often been on contemplating the public/private nature of these sites (e.g., Boyd, 2007), identifying the needs and gratifications associated with the usage of SNSs (e.g., Bumgarner, 2007; Joinson, 2008), discussing the risks of using SNSs (e.g., Ibrahim, 2008; Livingstone, 2008), and evaluating the contribution of SNSs to social capitals (e.g., Ellison, Steinfield, and Lampe, 2007) and political participation (e.g., Skoric, Ying, and Ng, 2009). SNSs as a genre of websites have been well clarified but the diversity within SNSs has yet to be fully acknowledged and studied. A pioneering attempt was made by Papacharissi (2009), when she compared the underlying structures of three different SNSs and analyzed how their structures influence user interactions. This lack of evidence hinders our understanding of the complexity of SNSs because the phenomenon is simplified to a handful of successful cases such as Facebook. Moreover, the lack of in-depth investigation of SNSs prevents us to see how the web 2.0 technologies go beyond replicating our existing social networks, and create a new logic of networking through their digital capacities.

This chapter starts with a review of theoretical thinking on collective action and its social network foundation. The diversity of the Chinese SNS scene provides the context in which my investigation of the network logic has been conducted. The data sources in this chapter come from Douban, a SNS that connects users not only through social ties but also via fan objects such as books, movies, and music albums, and a Facebook-type SNS, Renren. Relying on a structural analysis of the websites, the network structure in Douban is presented in contrast to the network structure in Renren. In addition, it is crucial to learn about how the networks behave. An online survey of the members of the social networks is used to examine how individuals use the two networks in distinctive ways and, thus, form and maintain different kinds of social relationships on the two SNSs.

Collective action and social network sites

Collective action, as defined by Bimber and colleagues (2006), refers to a set of communication processes involving the crossing of boundaries between private and public life. Social network theories are used to explain collective action because the crossing of boundaries is a social behavior. Ties with different strengths in social networks have different influences on collective action. Strong ties seem to be particularly effective in nurturing social trust and fostering social capital (Putnam, 2000). However, there are also weaknesses in strong ties. Macy and colleagues (1997) argued that strong ties may discourage the use of peer pressure to sanction free-riding behaviors. Moreover, Gargiulo and Benassi (1998) found that cohesive ties function as a source of rigidity that hinders the coordination of complex organizational tasks. Strong ties may not be as flexible as weak ties with regard to the accommodation of change.

In addition, Granovetter (1981) argued that weak ties have their respective strengths—weak ties that bridge different social networks are particularly efficient in organizing collective action that involves novelty or controversies. Empirical findings show that when the calls for collective action are new or controversial, groups formed on the basis of weak ties compared to groups based on strong ties are more successful in recruiting members and mobilizing resources (Steinberg, 1980). Weak ties perform better in such a situation because they are more likely to introduce diverse information (Hansen, 1999) and bring different network segments together (Granovetter, 1981).

Coleman (1990) argued that opportunities for collective action were threatened by the decay of a wide range of traditional civic associations that were once to be the social network sites of face-to-face engagement. Putnam (2000) found that these *relationship-oriented* groups, many of which were dated from the American industrial revolution and Progressive eras, have suffered nearly universal declines in membership (often declining 50% from peak twentieth-century levels). In contrast, the anonymous *interest-oriented* groups have grown rapidly. These groups typically involve a shared interest, anonymous membership, the exchange of some kind of value such as dues for political representation or information and newsletters, but no personal interaction or accountability among members. This chapter distinguishes relationship-oriented networks from interest-oriented networks by looking at the organizational principle of the networks. In relationship-oriented networks, the principle is to establish and maintain strong social relations. For instance, members of a bowling club may share an interest in bowling, but the way in which they find out about each other is through existing social contacts (neighbors, friends of friends, etc.) and the way in which they maintain their relationship is through regular personal interactions (going bowling together every week). In contrast, in interest-oriented networks, strangers get together because of the shared interest(s). They find each other through their shared interest(s) (e.g., subscribing to the same newsletter) without having known each other before-hand. They maintain a lukewarm relationship without intensive personal interactions. Nevertheless, they can work together for collective action such as signing a petition, donating to a cause, and so on.

Most studies on SNSs focus on relationship-oriented sites such as Facebook and MySpace.[1] Although the functions such as search can facilitate the forma-tion of new ties (Ellison *et al.*, 2007), these relationship-oriented sites are found to be mainly used to develop strong ties among existing social contacts (Boyd and Ellison, 2007). Users of relationship-oriented SNSs regularly interact with only a sub-portion of their listed contacts (e.g., friends on twitter) and their levels of involvement (e.g., number of tweets) are correlated with the number of this sub-portion rather than the total number of contacts (Huberman, Romero, and Wu, 2008). Gilbert and Karahlios (2009) found that the intensity of interaction (e.g., number of words exchanged in wall posts on Facebook) serves as the best predictor of the perceived strength of ties. Analyzed together, the two studies suggest that users of relationship-oriented SNSs only interact with their strong ties on a regular basis. One problem with strong ties is that they tend to be homogeneous (Flanagin, Stoh, and Bimber, 2006). Homogeneity or homophily in social networks may discourage tolerance and encourage the enclaving of small groups, which is argued to be unhealthy for democracy (Sunstein, 2007). If we define collective action as crossing boundaries between public and private life, homogeneous networks seem to reinforce the connections in private life but demonstrates no particular strength in turning private activities into public ones. In other words, homogeneity of the network puts constraints on the scale and the type of collective action that may take place.

SNSs seem to encourage homogeneity if we only examine the relationship-oriented sites (Thelwall, 2008; Vie, 2007). Liu and colleagues (2006) suggested that the profiles on relationship-oriented sites imply deeper patterns of culture and taste. But this fabric of taste, as described by the authors, is only a latent one. This means that private interests such as music, books, films, and food revealed in user profiles are not the primary organizational principle of the social networks afforded by these sites. Offline pre-existing contacts dominate the formation of ties on such sites. Our investigation of the phenomenon of SNSs is limited by the focus on the relationship-oriented sites. The interest-oriented sites that privilege the formation of new ties among strangers who share some common interests and keep such connections as weak yet bridging ties may provide distinct implications regarding collective action.

Social network sites in China

SNSs in China have gone through a rapid development within the last decade, although the speed of growth has been slowed down recently. The percentage of Internet users who use SNSs increased from 19% in 2006 (CNNIC, 2006) to 61% in 2013 (CNNIC, 2013). Among these Chinese SNSs, the majority are the Facebook type of relationship-oriented sites such as Renren, Kaixin, and Pengyou. There are also websites that successfully revamped itself and rebranded as SNSs (e.g., Q-zone). Two SNSs have used a different marketing strategy by focusing on certain genres of fan objects: 51.com is an online gaming community by connecting gamers through games; Douban covers a broad range of cultural products such as books, movies, and music albums.

Douban.com was launched on March 6, 2004, before the wave of SNSs had reached the mainland. Initially, this site focused on books and invited members to post book reviews. In May and July 2005, Douban added movie and music applications respectively. A recommendation system was created to boost sharing behaviors among members. People can rate books, movies and music albums, publish reviews, and discuss with other users through a discussion board attached to every single fan object. As SNSs became trendy in China, Douban strengthened the social networking functions by giving each user a profile page (i.e., my douban) and developed some in-site communication tools such as a microblogging application. Along the years, Douban has experimented with many other functions such as a blog aggregation service (9.douban), an online radio system (douban.fm), an e-book system (read. douban), and an e-commerce service (dongxi.douban). The most recent technological development is the mobile application of Douban, which attempts to include the large range of functions in one. The number of Douban users has increased steadily over years, with the first one million registered users reached in November 2007. In November 2014, Douban announced that there were 75 million registered users, 16.7 million book entries, 1.1 million music album entries, and 3.2 billion movie reviews.[2]

Renren.com was established in December 2005 with a different name, Xiaonei (literally meaning on campus), because of its restriction of users to college students. The initial function of Xiaonei was to invite student members to communicate with friends by updating them on their current status. Zheng and Lin (2008) found that homogeneity of members is one of the characteristics of Xiaonei. Xiaonei continued to expand its scope and opened up to the high school and young professional markets at the end of 2007. Xiaonei finally extended its access to everybody by August 2009 and changed its domain name into Renren (literally meaning everybody). Both the interface and the functions on Renren are highly similar to Facebook, to the extent that controversies over copyright were raised. Renren went for Initial Public Offering (IPO) in mid-2011 and the most recent finance report (released in November 2014)[3] indicates that there were 44 million active users who logged in to the website monthly during the second and third quarter of the year. Figure 7.1 shows the daily reach of both sites during July to December, 2014. Douban is clearly more popular than Renren, a pattern that was reversed from four years ago, when the daily reach of both websites was recorded by the author. The Alexa data showed that during November 2009 and April 2010, Renren's daily reach was around 8,000 to 10,000 per million users whereas Douban's was below 6,000. The numbers indicate that Douban's popularity remained relatively the same over the years but Renren's popularity has largely decreased, partially due to the emergence of Weibo and Wechat.

Methods

This chapter attempts to examine two aspects of networks[4] that are afforded in interest-oriented and relationship-oriented SNSs. The first aspect is the network structure, which focuses on the structural features of the networks and often presents itself in a graphic way. A structural analysis of the two websites examines the components or functions that are used to support network building and maintenance. Examples are used to illustrate the different designs of two digital platforms and how they lead to different network structures. The second aspect of networks is the network behavior, which focuses on the

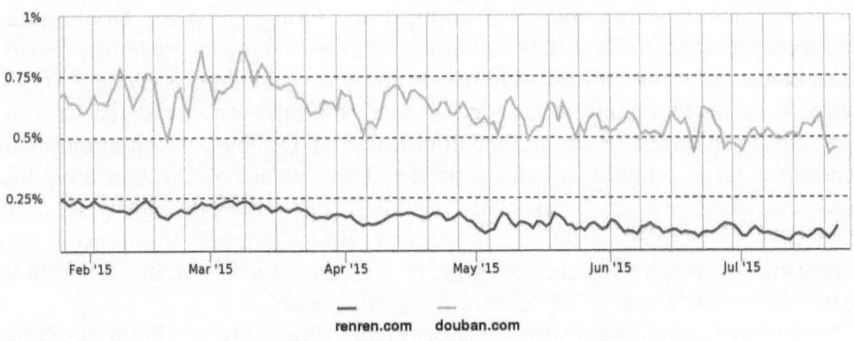

Figure 7.1 Historical traffic trends: reach percent
Source: www.alexa.com.

dynamics of aggregate behavior in a network. Not only the network behavior has direct consequences compared to pure structures, but also although the structural features of the websites can suggest certain usages, users may or may not follow these suggestions and behave as suggested. A second method, an online survey of members of a purposive sample (i.e., four social networks recruited from the websites, two each site), is operated in order to provide data that tell us how members of networks actually use the websites.

Structural analysis

Taking advantage of the registered status in both websites, the functions and components afforded by the websites were fully explored and examined by the author. The focus of the structural analysis is on the possibilities enabled by the available options rather than a systematic content analysis of any of the options, such as what has been presented in profiles. However, in the course of the analysis, more than 200 profiles from Douban and approximately 300 profiles from Renren were encountered. In addition, sub-sites, forums, groups, and various applications were studied, as well as site documents (FAQs, privacy statements, help, terms of use, etc.) and relevant news reports. After clarifying the network features of the two websites, a network graph was generated based on data obtained through a crawler, SocSciBot.[5]

Survey

As both an addition to and a verification of the structural analysis, an online survey was conducted on a purposive sample of the networks formed within the websites.[6] Networks, rather than individual users, were sampled because our research is more interested in the differences between networks formed on the two websites. Two networks were selected from each site. One network belongs to an experienced user (defined as using the website regularly for more than one year) and the other belongs to a new user (defined as using the website regularly for less than one year). Invitations to join the survey were sent out to the contacts of these two users. The response rates to individual invitations were around 30% on both sites. The total sample size was 186, in which 94 were Renren users and 92 were Douban users. The survey responses were collected during March and April, 2009.

The sample presented an average age of 23 and an average education of 16 years, which equals to a college degree in China. About 54% of them were female. Over 70% of the respondents were relatively experienced users who had been using the two sites for more than one year. The daily usage was evenly distributed from 30 minutes to 1 hour (27%), 1 hour to 2 hours (23%), and 2 hours to 3 hours (27%).[7] Most respondents got to know about these sites through their friends or colleagues (65%). However, if we break the data into two websites, it shows that Renren users almost exclusively relied on existing social contacts (94%), whereas only 36% of Douban users became aware of Douban through old ties. A significant portion (27%) of Douban users found Douban through search engines.

New versus old ties

The question was phrased as "among your Renren/Douban friends, how many are friends or acquaintances that you already know in your offline life?" 5 refers to "almost none", 4 to "between 20% and 50%", 3 to "between 50% and 80%", 2 to "more than 80% but less than 100%", and 1 refers to "all of them."

Bridging social capital

Ellison and colleagues (2007) developed indices to measure different types of social capitals. We used a shortened version of measures of both bridging and boding social capital. Bridging social capital included seven items: (1) Interacting with my friends makes me want to try new things; (2) Interacting with my friends makes me interested in what people unlike me are thinking; (3) Talking with my friends makes me curious about other places in the world; (4) Interacting with my friends makes me feel like part of a larger community; (5) Interacting with my friends makes me feel connected to the bigger picture; (6) Interacting with my friends reminds me that everyone in the world is connected; (7) Interacting with my friends gives me new people to talk to. A five-point Likert scale was used, with 1 meaning "totally disagree", to 5 meaning "totally agree." Cronbach's alpha is 0.90 for the entire scale. Therefore, a variable that averages through the seven items was created to represent bridging capital.

Bonding social capital

The index included five items: (1) There are several people I trust to solve my problems; (2) The people I interact with would put their reputation on the line for me; (3) There is someone in my group friends I can turn to for advice about making very important decisions; (4) The friends I interact with would be good job references for me; (5) When I feel lonely, there are several people I can talk to. The same five-point Likert scale was used. Cronbach's alpha is 0.82 for the entire scale. A variable that averages through the five items was created to represent bonding capital.

Self-reported usage

The usage was classified into five categories: (1) I have used Renren/Douban to check out someone I met socially; (2) I use Renren/Douban to learn more about my classmates/colleagues; (3) I use Renren/Douban to learn more about other people living near me; (4) I use Renren/Douban to keep in touch with my old friends; (5) I use Renren/Douban to meet new people. Again, the five-point Likert scale was used for each measure.

Results

The boundaries between the private and the public

When defining collective action as crossing the boundaries between private and public life, it becomes necessary to first identify what the boundaries are. Papacharissi (2009) argued that there are three levels of boundaries in social network sites. At a preliminary level, the boundary refers to criteria for membership; at a secondary level, the boundary means protocols for access to private information; and at a tertiary level, the boundary is the ability to control your own surroundings.

Using the same hierarchy of boundaries, how Renren and Douban define their public and private arenas was examined through a scrutiny of the functions they provide, along with the survey data about actual usage behaviors. At the first level, both websites are currently open to everyone. An easy registration will grant users the access to the websites. Renren requires more personal information than Douban. Whereas Douban only asks for e-mail, password, a username, and a location, Renren requires users to disclose their real names and gender in addition to e-mail and password. This very first step of registration reveals that Renren desires or encourages a membership that directly links to an individual's offline identity. In contrast, Douban's criteria for membership are looser. Our survey asked whether respondents used their real names as user names. The results confirm that almost all Renren users registered with their real names, whereas only 8% of Douban users chose their real names as usernames.

At the second level, the distinction between the private and the public is set up via access to member profiles. Renren allows different privacy settings to control who can access an individual's profile. Profiles can be completely public and visible to anybody. They can be visible to friends only, and a real name, a snapshot and a fraction of the friends list are visible to visitors. They can even be invisible to anybody, including the user himself. Douban users, in contrast, are offered a limited range of controls over access to their profiles. Douban profiles are public, without an option to hide the front page. Anybody can click on a username and see this person's front page. Users are only allowed to choose not to be searchable by username and e-mail address. When users add in movies/books/music albums, they can check the option of "do not let others know." As a consequence, the entry will not show up in the public profile. The user can also choose to make a blog entry visible only to himself or participate in a private group that is visible only to the group members. However, the access to information about friends, group memberships, activities, and status updates is not allowed to be blocked. The information has to be part of a user's profile and visible to all visitors. Therefore, the boundary at the second level is more controlled by individual users on Renren than on Douban.

At the third level, both websites allow users to customize the functions and components they use. Douban offers their users the freedom to arrange the layout of their front page and decide what is broadcasted. Broadcasting is a function similar to the status updates on Facebook. It posts a short sentence describing any moves a user has made, including adding a movie/book/music album, adding a friend, joining a group, writing a blog entry, uploading a picture, recommending and sharing, and participating in an activity. Douban allows users to set who is able to see these updates, ranging from nobody to anybody. Moreover, Douban utilizes web 2.0 technologies to aggregate individual user data and reflect the aggregation on their web pages through ratings and rankings.[8] This means that a user's private actions, such as rating a movie, become one piece of contribution to public knowledge, even if the user decides to hide this rating from others. The anonymous aggregation of private data fundamentally changes our presumption of a natural division between the public and the private. In this sense, Douban users cannot opt out of the aggregative modeling used by Douban designers and thus a part of their surrounding (i.e., the recommendation system) is out of their control. Renren, in contrast, allows users to control the visibility of their own activities and their friends'. Renren users are able to not only set who can see their updates but also decide whose updates they want to see. For example, they may choose not to see the updates about pictures-posting. Therefore, at the tertiary level, Renren provides users with stronger control over their own surroundings than Douban.

In summary, the boundaries between the private and the public are more up to the users' control on Renren than on Douban, probably because Renren profiles are directly linked to offline identities. For Renren users who set the boundaries clear, they are not readily available to be mobilized into collective action unless the action is already salient within their networks. For Douban users, they are automatically, to a certain degree, present in the public arena by being forced to keep some of their profile information publicly accessible (e.g., groups and friends). They are also forced to be exposed to friends' status updates, which raises the chances of encountering requests for collective action. In addition, the aggregation design of Douban results in users' behaviors, regardless of whether they are visible to other users or not, becoming contributions to a public recommendation system. We may summarize that the mobilization of collective action is more dependent on users' offline contacts on Renren, whereas unintentional or spontaneous exposure to requests of collective action holds a better chance on Douban.

The features of social networks

How difficult it is to cross the boundaries is only one side of the story. The other side of the story talks about the motivations and perceptions of potential participants. These motivations and perceptions are individual, but still subject to the influence of social ties. Social network theories come into play by suggesting that the characteristics of social networks influence people's involvement in collective action. Previous research (Siegel, 2009) shows that the following characteristics of social networks have been found to be influential when explaining collective action: (1) the network structure, (2) the size of the network, (3) the prevalence of weak ties, and (4) the individual motivations for getting involved in these networks.

The structures of the two types of networks supported by the sites can be first examined through looking at the ways of relationship formation. Renren is a Facebook-type SNS which runs on the premise that people use their real identities to establish online ties. Therefore, the formation of a relationship is predominantly based on offline ties such as family members, schoolmates, colleagues, and neighbors. The network structure basically shows that users often belong to multiple clusters of social contacts at the same time. Only a few contacts are able to bridge different networks. Thus, a user has to go through these nodes (i.e., people) to get in touch with other people in other networks. This mode of relationship formation constrains the type of new ties a user can forge due to the limited number of bridging nodes (i.e., people).

The purpose of Figure 7.2 is to present the network structure of Douban, which shows a distinct pattern of relationship formation through objects rather than social contacts. The darkest dots represent objects, referring to three things: movies, books, and music albums. The second darkest dots represent the user and the user's contacts. The lightest dots represent groups, activities, and other links.[9] Douban allows users to connect to each other through both friends and objects. In this type of network, the nodes are not just people. Objects function as nodes that may link other objects and other people. A user can link to another user through a book, a movie, or a music album. For example, there are only two people who have seen the same movie and they do not know each other. The linkage between them is that Douban lists their names together under the category "who watched the movie." A user may go to the homepage of that movie and find this other user by looking at the list. This mode of connecting is confirmed to be popular among Douban users by survey data. Our Douban respondents indicated that they found new friends by first reading their comments to an object (66%); second, by going through existing friends (56%); third, by joining the same group (52%); fourth, by looking through the list of "who watched the movie/read the book/listened to the music album" (34%); and fifth, by participating in the same activity (24%).

One major difference between the network structures of Renren and Douban is their different approaches to relationship formation. The approach of Renren is user-centric, whereas the approach of Douban is object-centric. According to Li and colleagues (2008), the user-centric approach discovers new ties based on the social connections among users. In contrast, the object-centric approach does so based on the common objects fetched by users in an

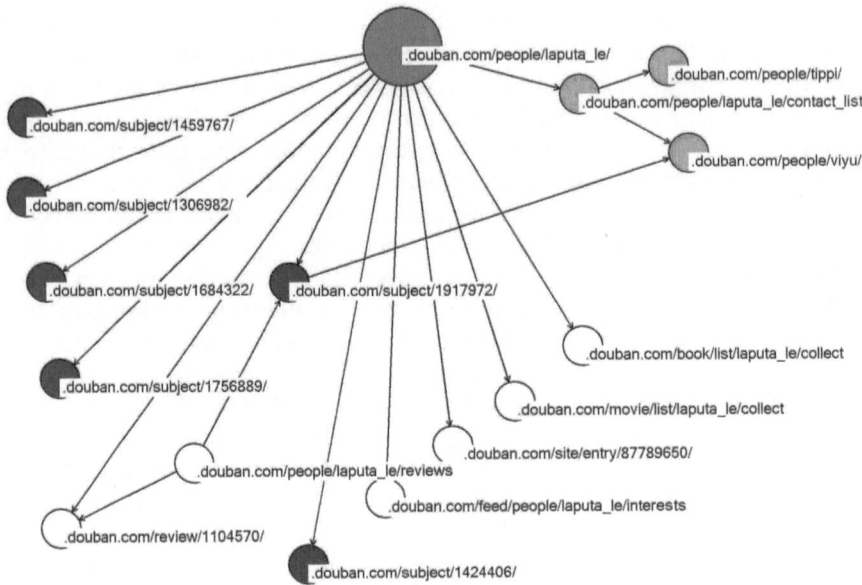

Figure 7.2 The network structure of Douban

online community. Studies have found that this object-oriented approach can efficiently identify trends and types of interest as well as expertise in the online communities (Kelkar *et al.*, 2007). Similarly, Sripanidkulchai and colleagues (2003) took advantage of the interest-based shortcuts to efficiently locate content in decentralized peer-to-peer systems. Interest-based shortcuts work well because a peer who has a particular piece of content that one is interested in is very likely to have other items that one is interested in as well. As an object-centric network, Douban offers an efficient means to locate users that may have similar interests, which suggests a different mechanism of mobilization and organization when coming to collective action.

The sizes of network on the two sites are not very different. The survey data show that Renren users had an average of 172 contacts and Douban users had 102 contacts. From a collective action point of view, the scope of the social capital we need depends on the scale of the problems we face. Therefore, size itself cannot tell us much about whether a network is more ready for collective action than another one. However, weak ties, especially bridging weak ties, are considered as crucial for collection actions, especially those involving novelty and controversies (Granovetter, 1981). Weak ties between newly acquainted users were found to be more prevalent on Douban than on Renren. Over 90% of Renren friends were users' offline contacts. A majority of Douban users (71%) indicated that less than half of their friends were offline contacts. In addition, Douban offers a "friending" option which is not reciprocal, meaning that a user can add a person to the list of "people whom I care about" (similar to the "following" list on twitter) without getting this person's approval of being listed. A list of "people who care about me" (similar to the "follower" list on twitter) is generated if any users add you as "people whom I care about." Most Douban users (82% when asking about "people whom I care about" and 72% when asking about "people who care about me") reported that people listed under these one-way friending categories were almost all new ties. Moreover, our respondents slightly agreed that the new ties on Douban were weak[10] (M = 3.13).

The strengths of weak ties lie in the possibility that they can bridge different networks. As Granovetter (1981) emphasized, only weak ties that bridge are important for collective action. We thus asked our respondents how the social ties formed on the two websites help them to bridge different social networks. Using the indices created by Ellison and colleagues (2007), we measured users' perception of bridging and bonding social capitals supported by Renren versus Douban. The data show that Douban users perceived more bridging capitals than Renren users. For example, Douban users agreed that interacting with friends made them become interested in what people who are unlike them are thinking (M = 3.67) whereas Renren users slightly agreed to the same statement (M = 3.04). The difference is statistically significant (t = −4.44, p < 0.001). A full report of such findings is listed in Table 7.1. The table essentially shows that on all the measures of perceived bridging social capital, Douban users rated higher than Renren users. In contrast, Douban users rated either lower or almost the same as Renren users on all the bonding social capital measures. For instance, the classic measure of job reference shows that Renren friends served a stronger function of bonding ties (M = 3.00) than Douban friends (M = 2.58, t = 3.01, p < 0.01). The perceptions were consistent with the self-reported usages of the two sites. Table 7.1 shows that Renren users mainly used the website to develop strong ties among existing contacts, including friends, classmates/colleagues, people living nearby, and offline acquaintances. Douban users, however, used Douban predominantly for the purpose of forming new ties.

In summary, the network structure of Douban compared with that of Renren allows a different way to form new ties—through common interests (i.e., objects) rather than existing social contacts. This mechanism of connection encourages users to meet new people. As a consequence, Douban users tend to have more new ties than Renren users. As expected, these new ties are mostly weak ties. Users also agree that these weak ties help them to establish bridging social capital. It is argued that bridging social capitals can efficiently mobilize people into collective actions that involve novel and controversial issues (Granovetter, 1981). Therefore, it is concluded that the Douban networks provide a better chance for mobilizing novel and controversial collective action than the Renren networks.

The network logic, collective action, and Chinese civil society

This section examines the differences between an interest-oriented SNS, Douban.com and a relationship-oriented SNS, Renren.com, in terms of their

Table 7.1 Bridging and bonding social capitals perceived by Renren versus Douban users

	Renren users	Douban users
Bridging social capital	3.15***	3.65
Interacting with my friends makes me want to try new things.	3.04***	3.82
Interacting with my friends makes me interested in what people unlike me are thinking.	3.04***	3.67
Talking with my friends makes me curious about other places in the world.	3.21***	3,71
Interacting with my friends makes me feel like part of a larger community.	3.16*	3.54
Interacting with my friends makes me feel connected to the bigger picture.	3.24***	3.77
Interacting with my friends reminds me that everyone in the world is connected.	3.34	3.46
Interacting with my friends gives me new people to talk to.	3.03***	3.57
Bonding social capital	3.11*	2.87
There are several people I trust to solve my problems.	3.13	3.18
The people I interact with would put their reputation on the line for me.	3.13***	2.42
There is someone of my friends I can turn to for advice about making very important decisions.	3.19*	2.87
The friends I interact with would be good job references for me.	3.00**	2.58
When I feel lonely, there are several people I can talk to.	3.12	3.28
Self-reported usages		
I have used Xiaonei/Douban to check out someone I met socially.	3.05***	2.28
I use Xiaonei/Douban to learn more about my classmates/colleagues.	3.35***	2.37
I use Xiaonei/Douban to learn more about other people living near me.	3.26***	2.20
I use Xiaonei/Douban to keep in touch with my old friends.	3.64***	2.40
I use Xiaonei/Douban to meet new people.	2.80+	3.10

Note: Independent samples t-tests were run for each of the measures. ***$p<0.001$, **$p<0.01$, *$p<0.05$, +$p<0.10$.

structural features that enable different social networks and networking behaviors to emerge. The data show that Douban makes the boundaries between public and private life very vague and even dissolves such boundaries through the aggregation mechanisms. As a result, Douban networks encourage the formation of new ties among strangers through shared interests such as books and movies. Moreover, these new ties often develop into bridging ties that connect distinct social networks. Renren, in contrast, provides effective means to users to control the boundaries between the private and the public. Therefore, strong ties among existing social contacts are fostered on Renren.

A social network that connects strangers via common interests and maintains such bridging weak ties has its significant contribution to collective action. One difficulty associated with mobilizing people for collective action is locating the relevant individuals who are interested in the cause behind the action. An interest-oriented SNS like Douban provides efficient ways to locate the relevant individuals because of three factors—the visibility of users' interests, the connections between strangers, and the usage of interest-based shortcuts to form ties. For example, an online activity called Earth Hour 2010 attracted over 20,000 Douban users to participate. If a Renren user wants to recruit people to join an activity like this, he has to rely on his social network that is based on existing offline contacts. One problem with this type of recruitment is that a user's contacts may not be motivated to participate because the connections were not established based on the shared concern regarding environmental issues. A Douban user, for example, can go to the page of the movie *An Inconvenient Truth* and find the users who have rated this movie five-star and send an invitation to these users. The diverse ways of articulating and observing users' interests on Douban open up many channels to locate the relevant others. Moreover, because the majority of Douban contacts are strangers, the recruitment message is able to travel beyond a particular user's limited offline contacts, reach a broad social circle, and increase the probability of recruiting the right people. In addition, recruiting Douban friends is likely to be successful because ties that are connected by one common interest (e.g., *An Inconvenient Truth*) are likely to share more interests (e.g., Earth Hour).

Moreover, interest-oriented SNSs allow users to have personal interactions, which facilitate the maintenance of weak yet bridging ties. We can consider interest-oriented SNSs similar to the large-scale mail-list groups (Putnam, 2000) in terms of its ability to handle massive number of users who do not know each other. However, interest-oriented SNSs overcome one critical shortcoming of these mail-list groups—impersonal interaction—which may lead to lack of social trust among the group members. Personal and direct communications between Douban users are supported by in-site mails, wall posts, status updates, and many other tools. Personal interaction fosters a sense of bond between users, facilitates the diffusion of messages, and mobilizes collective action.

Regarding the development of Chinese civil society, how to mobilize collective action among Chinese citizens is an important issue. Observers (e.g., Yang,

2009) documented the creative acts of online activism in China and argued for a co-evolution of the Internet and Chinese civil society. Internet-based collective action is not only getting increasingly popular in China, but also contributing to the development of civil society. Civil society in China is still under-developed due to both the state control and the relatively recent modernization progress. Identifying and pursuing a common interest with strangers who do not belong to an individual's primary groups (e.g., an extended family) are still relatively new to the Chinese. SNSs in China, adding to discussion forums (e.g., tianya.com, mop.com) and blogosphere (e.g., blog.sina.com.cn, blogbus.com), provide another means to meet other fellow citizens and act in collective forms. Both old ties and new ties are now open to the possibilities of online mobilization. An interest-oriented SNS, compared with a relationship-oriented SNS, seems to be more open to collective action that centers on new and controversial social issues because such concerns may not be well shared among a person's primary groups.

However, a further question is what Zheng and Wu (2005) have asked: "[i]t is not a question of whether internet-based collective action is possible … the question is whether internet-based collective action can succeed in challenging the state." The new ties formed on Douban and the vague boundaries between public and private life cannot guarantee Chinese citizens the power to challenge the state. The reason is simple—all web applications are developed by human programmers. The programmers can use codes to encourage collective action and they can use the same codes to forbid collective action. A good example is the close-down of Douban groups in early 2009. Following the policy of "cleaning online content" issued by the central government, Douban was forced to examine all existing groups and delete those which contain "inappropriate content". After this wave of close-down, all new groups and activities are now subject to a censorship before they can be put into effect.

But it is a different claim to say that Chinese civil society is unable to develop if citizens cannot explicitly subvert the state domination. The state has overplayed civil society for a long time when almost every aspect of social life was closely controlled by the state apparatus. Along with the adoption of economic freedom, Chinese people and their lives are now less linked to the state and more connected to fellow citizens. To recognize the necessity to interact with other social members in civic ways is the first step to building a civil society. Chinese SNSs at their current stage may only be able to promote shared understanding and connections that serve as the foundation of trust and cooperation. Such trust and cooperation are especially valuable when they are among strangers, suggesting the unique contribution of interest-oriented SNSs to the formation of civil society. In addition, the state cannot be a system that is isolated all together from civil society. The state is also run by people, who inevitably belong to social networks. If one collective action is widespread in the social networks, we can expect state runners to be influenced by the collective action as well.

This chapter, therefore, contributes to our understanding of collective action and civil society in China by clarifying how publics can be formed through connections made possible by shared fan objects, which become highly visible and effective nodes in interest-oriented SNSs like Douban. Such a social-formative principle largely expands the options individuals have when trying to network with other social members. The social relationships formed following such a principle are primarily weak yet bridging ties, which allow innovative publics to come into being. However, linking users through objects is only one mechanism implied in the network logic.[11] If a mixed network of humans and things is at work, users should be able to link to objects unknown to them through other users too. This second mechanism of relationship formation will be explored and explained in the next chapter.

Notes

1 Some may argue that dating sites also attract strangers with similar interests (e.g., looking for a life partner). However, dating sites are still relationship-oriented, in terms that users want to establish and maintain strong social relations ultimately. Dating sites fit only one criterion of interest-oriented SNSs—users find each other through shared interests.

2 Andong, Douban announced that monthly visitors reached 2 billion, twice the number from last year. Retrieved from www.techweb.com.cn/internet/2013-11-13/1356287.shtml, November 13, 2013.

3 Chinanews, Renren's number of monthly active users stabilizes, showing the return to campus strategy effective. Retrieved from http://finance.chinanews.com/it/2014/11-21/6803054.shtml, November 21, 2014.

4 Easley and Kleinberg (2010) summarized that there are three aspects of networks that we can examine, namely, network structure, strategic behavior, and the feedback effects. This chapter only includes the former two aspects in its analysis.

5 Information about this software can be found at http://socscibot.wlv.ac.uk/.

6 The fact that only two SNSs were included and analyzed may bring up problems of the representativeness of the sample, the sources of the differences we have found, and the generalizability of our findings. Firstly, two websites are by no means representative of the entirety of SNSs in China. However, the key argument of this chapter focuses on the different structural features of two websites and their influence on social networking. It is ideal if we have included multiple sites that fit the classification of interest-oriented and relationship-oriented sites. But the two sites were the only two that can be found at that time. Now the gaming community 51.com could serve as an empirical test of the claims made in this chapter. Our future efforts should be made to locate and examine more SNSs that run along the line of interest-oriented networks in order to expand the generalizability of our findings. Secondly, the differences we observe here may actually be explained by other factors such as the different groups of users (e.g., Renren started with a target on college students while Douban has been open to all) rather than different structural features. However, our survey shows that there are no big disparities in basic demographics between the two sites' users. We tend to think that our findings reflect an interactive procedure between users and the structural features. The structures encourage certain usages and the users appropriate the features to meet their own needs. For instance, one user may choose Renren to maintain his offline

social contacts and use Douban to explore new relationships. The structural features of the two websites should be the foundation based on which such a perception was formulated.

7 This skewedness towards heavy users actually strengthens the validity of our study, as we are more interested in the possibilities enabled by different SNSs rather than a survey of all users' perceptions and behaviors.

8 The website aggregates individual data points and presents the results to users via many means, such as number of users who viewed the movie, number of users who rated the movie five-star, and tags applied by users to describe the movie. The website also recommends relevant objects to users based on the users' behaviors (similar to the recommendation system on amazon.com).

9 Douban users can create groups and any users who know this group can request to join. Each group has its own front page on which a discussion forum is available. Members of the groups are allowed to post and reply on the forum. Non-members are allowed to browse the posts if the group is set as pubic. Activities are similar to groups in terms of the technical functions, except that activities have a start and an end date. For example, "environmentalists" is a group and "Earth Hour 2010" is an activity. Groups are categorized under a series of themes such as arts, life, and hobbies. There are 147,352 groups on Douban as of 24 March 2010. Activities are differentiated by tags such as photography, charity, and design. The number of activities is too large to estimate.

10 The classic way to define relationship strength is to look at the frequencies of contact. If there are few exchanges of greetings between a pair of contacts, the relationship is considered to be weak. Here a different prompt of weakness was used by asking for users' perception. Respondents were explicitly asked to perceive whether new ties formed on Douban are weak to them by using a five-point Likert scale.

11 Theoretically speaking, there should be five mechanisms of relationship formation in a mixed network of humans and things: Firstly, users are linked to users through users (similar to the traditional relationship-oriented SNSs); secondly, users are linked to users through objects (focus of this chapter); thirdly, users are linked to objects through users (focus of next chapter); fourthly, objects are linked to objects through users; and fifthly, objects are linked to objects through objects.

Bibliography

Bimber, B., Flanagin. A. J., and Stohl, C. (2005). Reconceptualizing collective action in the contemporary media environment. *Communication Theory*, 15(4), 365–388.

Boyd, D. M. (2007) Social network sites: Public, private, or what? *Knowledge Tree*, 12. Retrieved from http://kt.flexiblelearning.net.au/tkt2007/?page_id=28, accessed 26 April 2009.

Boyd, D. M. and Ellison, N. B. (2007). Social network sites: Definition, history, and scholarship. *Journal of Computer-Mediated Communication*, 13(1). Retrieved from http://jcmc.indiana.edu/vol13/issue1/boyd.ellison.html, accessed 19 October, 2008.

Bumgarner, B. A. (2007). You have been poked: Exploring the uses and gratifications of Facebook among emerging adults. *First Monday*, 12(11) (November). Retrieved from www.uic.edu/htbin/cgiwrap/bin/ojs/index.php/fm/article/viewArticle/2026/1897, accessed 26 April, 2009.

CNNIC. (2009). *The 23rd Statistical Report on the Internet Development in China*, Retrieved from www.cnnic.cn/uploadfiles/pdf/2009/3/23/131303.pdf, accessed 21 July, 2009.

CNNIC. (2013). *The 2013 Research Report on User Behaviors in Chinese Social Networking Applications.* Retrieved from www.cnnic.net.cn/hlwfzyj/hlwxzbg/201409/P020140901333379491503.pdf, accessed 15 December, 2014.

Easley, D. and Kleinberg, J. (2010). *Networks, crowds, and markets: Reasoning about a highly connected world,* Cambridge University Press, Cambridge.

Coleman, J. S. (1990). *Foundations of social theory,* Harvard University Press, Cambridge, MA.

Ellison, N. B., Steinfield, C., and Lampe, C. (2007). The benefits of Facebook 'friends': Social capital and college students' use of online social network sites. *Journal of Computer-Mediated Communication,* 12(4). Retrieved from http://jcmc.indiana.edu/vol12/issue4/ellison.html, accessed 22 October, 2008.

Flache, A. and Macy, M. W. (1996). The weakness of strong ties: Collective action failure in a highly cohesive group. *Journal of Mathematical Sociology,* 21, 3–28

Flanagin, A. J., Stoh, C., and Bimber, B. (2006). Modeling the structure of collective action. *Communication Monographs,* 73(1), 29–54.

Gargiulo, M. and Benass, M. (1998). Trapped in your own net? Network cohesion, structural holes, and the adaptation of social capital. *Organization Science,* 11(2), 183–196.

Gilbert, E. and Karahlios, K. (2009). Predicting tie strength with social media. *Proceedings of CHI 2009,* Boston, MA.

Granovetter, M. S. (1981). The strength of weak ties: A network theory revisited. *Sociological Theory,* 1, 201–233.

Hansen, M. T. (1999). The search-transfer problem: The role of weak ties in sharing knowledge across organization subunits. *Administrative Science Quarterly,* 44(1), 82–111.

Huberman, B. A., Romero, D. M., and Wu, F. (2008). *Social networks that matter: Twitter under the microscope.* Retrieved from http://ssrn.com/abstract=1313405, accessed 15 March, 2010.

Ibrahim, Y. (2008). The new risk communities: Social networking sites and risk. *International Journal of Media and Cultural Politics,* 4(2) 245–253.

Joinson, A. N. (2008). 'Looking at', 'looking up' or 'keeping up with' people? Motives and uses of Facebook. *Proceedings of CHI 2008,* Florence, Italy.

Kelkar, S., John, A., and Seligmann, D. (2007). An activity-based perspective of collaborative tagging. *Proceedings of ICWSM,* Boulder, CO.

Kyung-Hee, K. and Haejin, Y. (2007). Cying for me, Cying for us: Relational dialectics in a Korean social network site. *Journal of Computer-Mediated Communication,* 13(1). Retrieved from http://jcmc.indiana.edu/vol13/issue1/kim.yun.html, accessed 26 April, 2009.

Li, X., Guo, L., and Zhao, Y. (2008). Tag-based social interest discover. *Proceedings of the International Word Wide Web Conference (WWW2008),* Beijing.

Liu, H., Maes, P., and Davenport, G. (2006). Unraveling the taste fabric of social networks. *International Journal on Semantic Web and Information Systems,* 2(1), 46–78.

Livingstone, S. (2008). Taking risky opportunities in youthful content creation: teenagers' use of social networking sites for intimacy, privacy and self-expression. *New Media and Society,* 10(3), 393–411.

Macy, M. W., Kitts, J. A., and Flache, A. (1997). The weakness of strong ties II: Collective action failure in a self-organizing social network. *Proceedings of the American Sociological Association Annual Meeting (SAS97),* Toronto.

Papacharissi, Z. (2009). The virtual geographies of social networks: A comparative analysis of facebook, linkedin and asmallworld. *New Media and Society*, 11(1–2), 199–220.

Putnam, R. D. (2000). *Bowling alone: The collapse and revival of American community*, Free Press, New York.

Siegel, D. A. (2009). Social networks and collective action. *American Journal of Political Science*, 53(1), 122–138.

Skoric, M. M., Ying, D., and Ng, Y. (2009). Bowling online, not alone: Online social capital and political participation in Singapore. *Journal of Computer-Mediated Communication*, 14(2), 414–433.

Sripanidkulchai, K., Maggs, B., and Zhang, H. (2003). Efficient content location using Interest-based locality in peer-to-peer systems. *Proceedings of IEEE-Infocomm Annual Conference*, San Francisco, CA.

Sunstein, C. R. (2007). *Republic.com 2.0*, Princeton University Press, Princeton, NJ.

Steinberg, L. (1980). *Preexisting Social Ties and Conflict Group Formation*. Paper presented at the 1980 meeting of the American Sociological Association, New York.

Thelwall, M. (2008). Homophily in MySpace. *Journal of the American Society for Information Science and Technology*, 60(2), 219–231

Vie, S. (2007). *Engaging others in online social networking sites: Rhetorical practices in MySpace and Facebook*. Unpublished Dissertation, The University of Arizona, Tuscon, AZ.

Yang, G. (2009). *The power of the Internet in China: Citizen activism online*, Columbia University Press, New York.

Zheng, Y. and Lin, L. (2008). When Campus SNS Sparks Reality – Xiaonei net's Computer- Mediated Interpersonal Communication. *Journal of Guangdong Polytechnic Normal University*, 3.

Zheng, Y. and Wu, G. (2005). Information technology, public space, and collective action in China. *Comparative Political Studies*, 38(5), 507–536.

8 Weibo publics
Celebrities as network nodes

Celebrity culture is an important component of contemporary popular culture. Although entertainment stars have always been influential in areas outside the entertainment industry, the prominence of celebrities in contemporary politics has reached new heights (West and Orman, 2003). While Arnold Schwartze-negger became governor of California, China now has a first lady who is formerly a popular singer. Research on celebrity activism showed that celebrities can enhance the visibility of social movement, attract audiences and supporters to donate to the causes, and grab the attention of policy makers (Meyer, 1995). Meanwhile, the fandom of these celebrities could also shape the supporters' values, attitudes, and behaviors (Schultz, 2001). Among the factors that accentuate celebrity politics is the profound role of the media (West, 2005). If visibility is inherent to the formation of publics, the media accelerate celebrity politics through constantly and repeatedly representing celebrities' performances on political issues. Rojek (2001) distinguishes among "ascribed celebrity," which concerns linkages such as family connections, "achieved celebrity," which is won by outstanding achievement in fields such as sports, and "attributed celebrity," which builds its fame on media representation (i.e., famous for being famous). The degree to which performance is mediated clearly differentiates the three types of celebrity. The attributed celebrity would not be able to exist without media representation. West (2005) points out that celebrities use social or political causes as a way to keep their names in news.

Regardless of the motives of celebrities getting involved in politics, political communication is being reshaped by celebrity culture. A debate on whether this means something good or bad for politics seems to neglect that politics itself has never been simply good or bad. Van Zoonen (2004) argues that we should examine how popular culture becomes relevant to political communication. Among the many ways that connect the two, Van Zoonen (2004) finds that both politicians and celebrities perform to create their own constituencies or audiences nowadays. They invite their supporters/audiences to make emotional investment in them through performing their personalized sides in various spheres. Corner (2003) identifies three such spheres in which politicians must perform: the private life, the sphere of political institutions and processes, and the sphere of the public and the popular that is fully mediated. The connection between political and celebrity culture is most evident in the third sphere, when the private sphere is brought into the public sphere in order to perform the "authentic self" (Van Zoonen, 2005, p. 75). Such performance is made with the purpose of reaching the widest circle of audiences and, thus, gathers a large number of onlookers. However, when information technologies allow the previously isolated mass audiences to see, interact, and connect to each other, what such celebrity performance gathers is no longer mere onlookers but a network of social members who are drawn to the same fan object, the celebrity him/herself. In addition, when this network of social members makes their engagement visible, primarily through the mediation of ICTs, they become a public.

This chapter focuses on Sina Weibo, a microblogging service that primarily relies on celebrity users to maintain its popularity. Situated in the recent development in China's celebrity culture, I will explore the phenomenon from the perspective of the celebrity–fans relationship as a new type of social relationship, which differs largely from the traditional Chinese term, *Guanxi*. After that, a review of empirical studies on Sina Weibo further clarifies how the concentration on celebrity users has shaped the communication patterns in this particular microblogging platform. The content analysis of selected celebrities' Weibo updates illustrates to what extent the entertainment-seeking followers may encounter socio-political issues such as the widely influential social concern, PM 2.5. More importantly, a Weibo public gathers around the celebrity and his/her performance on such social issues. The celebrity performance may have influences on how the gathered public understands, responds to the issue, and even joins the performance on the issue. The influence is gauged in two ways in this chapter: one is a social network analysis to show the network structure built on repost behaviors and the other is a content analysis of the correspondence between celebrity updates and user comments. This chapter concludes that celebrities can be seen as fan objects and connect their followers to unexpected or unknown social issues. The connectivity of such super-nodes is the backbone of the emergence of the "flash" issue publics that have been repeatedly formed on Sina Weibo. Both the strengths and weaknesses of such Weibo publics are discussed in the conclusion.

Celebrity culture in contemporary China

Celebrity culture isn't just an American or European phenomenon. As early as in the Communist years, the party-state has extensively used personals that conform to the dominant ideology as role models or national heroes (Edwards, 2010) to inspire, educate, and persuade ordinary Chinese (Jeffreys and Edwards, 2010). During the post-1978 reform days, all kinds of celebrities (e.g., movie stars, TV hosts, sportsmen, and self-made stars on the Internet) emerged out of the rapid economic growth and development of the local cultural industry. The fast development of a market economy has advanced the abundance of consumer and entertainment goods, of which celebrity performance and endorsement are at the core. Many entertainment stars become the cultural products themselves and are sold to their fans for their fun value (e.g., Furong Jiejie). "Achieved celebrity" emerges in large numbers as a free market economy gave birth to industry elites such as real estate developers, financial investors, and company CEOs (Davies, 2010). Meanwhile, professionalization in the literary, sports, and entertainment industries led to the emergence of the "attributed celebrity," who builds their fame on media representation through their performance in not only bestsellers, TV shows, and movies but also philanthropy (Hood, 2010) and public debate (Kong, 2010).

Academic research on the topic of celebrity culture in contemporary China is still scarce. Among the few pieces of such works, the focus is often put on exploring the alternative subjectivities introduced by the diverse range of Chinese celebrities (Lin, 2013), the media environment which gives prominence to such celebrity culture (Roberts, 2010), the dynamics between the market, the party-state and various celebrity figures (Kong, 2005), and the cultural distinctions of celebrity culture in China (Davies, 2010). I would rather take the perspective of social network to examine how the loosely defined fans engage in the relationship with celebrities, who are no more than familiar strangers to most ordinary Chinese. Although the Chinese have always been highly embedded in social networks, the Chinese counterpart of relationship, namely *Guanxi*, has a narrower boundary (Gold, Guthrie, and Wank, 2002, p. 6). Firstly, Guanxi has to be personal: one does not have Guanxi with a public figure such as a celebrity, unless they have some private interactions. Secondly, Guanxi has to be reciprocal: a fan who knows a celebrity, but not vice versa, is not qualified to claim a relationship with the celebrity. Thirdly, Guanxi often connotes an exchange of resources, including information, gifts, favors, social support, emotional commitment, and more. The traditional understanding of social relationship in China is pretty much limited by Guanxi, which is materialized in social connections such as kinship, neighbors, and fellows who share the same native place. It is only modern to Chinese when they are put into other types of relationships because of social institutions such as schools, working units (Danwei), neighborhood communities (Juweihui), and military units (Budui). Schools, Danwei, Juweihui, and Budui are all state-led social institutions started back in the Communist years and the relationships formed under such institutions are viewed by some scholars (Guthrie, 1998) as structurally shaped instead of culturally inherited. The marketization reform begun in the 1970s brought into existence new social institutions that are not under full control of the state, such as privately owned companies. However, new social relationships such as business partnership and employer–employee relationship seemed to continue the tradition of Guanxi, where social sentiment or human feeling is not separated from these economic relationships (Kipnis, 2002).

Against this backdrop of the evolving Guanxi, it is not hard to see how a relationship with a well known stranger, i.e., a celebrity, is unique to ordinary Chinese. We have to first admit that continuity with Guanxi exists in the emotional attachment between the fans and the celebrities. The celebrity–fan relationship involves not only an exchange of enjoyment and fame, but also human feeling that is emphasized in Guanxi. For instance, a commentator (Wang, 2014), who is also an insider of the music industry, invented a term, fans networking, and argued that one of the key features of fans networking is the intense emotional need. The emotional attachment from fans to celebrities is so strong that it almost equals a romantic relationship. Different from the exclusionary nature of a romantic relationship, fans do not mind showing off their affection in front of other fans. They interact with other individual fans not only to develop a fan–fan relationship but also to perform intimate communication in order to convert the observers into fans. Such performance is highly participatory and often self-organized. Celebrities function as fan objects to provide the focus of the performance by fans.

This relationship with celebrities, however, largely differs from Guanxi: it is not personal (as in not having regular private interaction), nor reciprocal (as in that the majority of fans are anonymous to the celebrities); the formation of such relationship is highly individualist and fluid, albeit the apparent influence of media institution. The mediation of ICTs has profoundly changed the interaction patterns within the celebrity–fans relationship. Previously, the interaction between celebrities and fans had to go through the mass media channels and were subject to the constraints of the gatekeepers such as journalists and editors. The interaction among fans was minimal, limited by one's own social network. Now, fans can have constant updates from the celebrities through following their Weibo accounts, and immediate interactions with other fans through commenting on each other's Weibo replies. The contradictions and consistencies between Guanxi and celebrity–fans relationships are further complicated by the mediation of Weibo, which refers to a range of microblogging services in China.

Microblogging in China

Although Sina Weibo is currently the most well-known microblogging service in China, it did not exist until the earliest Chinese microblogging websites, including Fanfou, Jiwai, and Digu, were forced to close down after a Xinjiang riot in July 2009. Sina took this opportunity to launch its own microblogging service in September 2009 and, since then, implemented a series of policies, including real name verification and active recruitment of celebrity users. Sina's practices have made Chinese microblogging services so different from Twitter that they have their own name, Weibo. Real name verification, which attaches a V symbol to a user name if the user has sent in identity documents to verify his/her real name, was introduced by the major Weibo providers in early 2012. Active recruitment of celebrity users was a continuation of Sina's marketing strategy during the blogging years. After making a blogger queen Xu Jinglei, Sina again utilized its commercial power to make a microblogger queen Yao Chen.[1] The emphasis on celebrity users of Sina Weibo has attracted millions of ordinary users to pay attention to what these big Vs have to say. Recent data (CNNIC, 2014) show that the overall penetration rate of Weibo services was 43.6% in China. Sina Weibo was the leading service provider with a rate of 28.4%, closely followed by Tencent Weibo (27.2%). The same report indicated that 50.8% of Weibo users have celebrities as contacts, the fourth popular category following real-life friends, classmates, and colleagues.

The prominence of celebrities on Sina Weibo has been confirmed in many academic studies. Among verified users, big Vs dominate the information dissemination process in terms of both potential influence and activeness (Wang, She, and Chen, 2014). Most of the big Vs or top influential users are entertainment stars or some kinds of celebrities. Multiple studies (e.g., Chen, *et al.*, 2012; Liao, *et al.*, 2013; Yu, Asur, and Huberman, 2011) confirmed that the top users, measured by trend-setting ability, number of comments, page views, or followers, are mostly celebrities. The networks of these top celebrity users tend to show a power law distribution, which indicates a small number of nodes that have higher in-degree, lower reciprocity, but a shorter path (Guo, *et al.*, 2011). Real name verification makes a significant contribution to the prominence of celebrity users, as Chinese Weibo users tend to follow people who have higher social status and number of followers than themselves (Chen, *et al.*, 2012). Real name verification also helps with faster and wider repost propagation (Huang, *et al.*, 2014; Huang and Sun, 2014) and stimulates active interaction and participation among the users (Chen and She, 2012). Although the above-mentioned studies mainly focused on Sina Weibo, at least one study (Li, *et al.*, 2012) demonstrated that Tencent Weibo is very similar in terms of the prominence of a small number of influential users.

Academic attention has also been paid to find out which topics become trendy or widespread on Weibo and how these topics become trendy. Scholars reported that trending topics on Sina Weibo are driven by a small number of users, who are opinion leaders/celebrities (Li, *et al.*, 2014), early adopters who have diverse networks (Bao, *et al.*, 2013), and accounts that have a large amount of ghost followers who frequently repost but never post original updates (Yu, Asur, and Huberman, 2012). The trending topics on Sina Weibo tend to be jokes, videos, and entertainment content, compared with the hot topics on Twitter (Yu, Asur, and Huberman, 2011), probably due to censorship of politically sensitive issues (Fu, Chan, and Chau, 2013; King, Pan, and Roberts, 2013). The contagious level of Sina Weibo is lower than that of Twitter, as the probability of a Weibo user to respond to an issue, given the number of this user's contacts who have already responded to the same issue, is significantly lower than that of a Twitter user (Shuai, *et al.*, 2014). Although Sina Weibo was also found to be used as a news platform (Wu, *et al.*, 2013) and a public administration tool (Liu and Zhou, 2011; Sullivan, 2013; Zhang and Negro, 2013), the leading role of celebrities in Weibo communication requires an examination of how celebrity users performed with regard to widespread social issues, and functioned as network nodes to gather and shape Weibo publics of such issues.

Methods

In this chapter, I have chosen to focus on one widely concerned social issue, PM 2.5. Weibo has been shown to be critical in dissemination of information about disasters, such as H1N1 influenza, earthquakes, train crashes, and many more (Wang and Bai, 2014). PM 2.5, or haze, is an interesting case as it has occurred in many Chinese cities and has a day-to-day effect on a large number of ordinary Chinese. Although the severity of the health consequences of PM 2.5 is not crystal clear, PM 2.5 has been one of the most important health concerns for many urban residents. At least one of the reasons can be attributed to the celebrity performance of this issue. Quite a few big Vs, including famous entrepreneurs, entertainment stars, celebrity journalists, and public intellectuals, have been active in propagating this issue. Therefore, this issue, compared with other more politically sensitive issues, serves as a good case by which we can examine the connection power of celebrities as network nodes. In order to identify celebrities who have talked about this issue, we used a keyword search (e.g., PM 2.5, haze, air pollution, fog, etc.) to search through the updates of the top 350 users according to Sina Weibo's own popularity rankings.[2] All the celebrity users who have mentioned the key words were classified into different categories, such as entertainment stars, entrepreneurs, journalists, intellectuals, and so on. In this chapter, I have decided to focus on four representatives of these celebrities, namely Pan Shiyi (entrepreneur), Yao Chen (actress), Xu Xiaonian (intellectual), and Li Kaifu (entrepreneur).

Social network analysis

The empirical analyses are made in two steps. A social network analysis was made based on repost behaviors. In other words, we used a program in Python through Weibo API to retrieve and record all reposts (including both pure reposts and comments) of the selected celebrities' Weibo updates that contain the key words. Then we merged the repost networks of each of the updates to form an overall repost network that includes all users who have reposted the selected updates. Finally, Ucinet was used to visualize the repost networks.

Content analysis

A content analysis was then made to analyze the correspondence between the celebrities' updates and the comments they received. We randomly selected 10 relevant updates from each of the four celebrities (and if there were less than 10 such updates, selected them all) and under each of the 10 updates, we randomly selected one page (i.e., 25) of comments. We coded the updates in terms of publication dates, number of reposts, number of comments, original or not, and picture or not. We then coded the comments in two dimensions, one is whether the comment is focused on the issue or the celebrity him/herself and the other is whether the comment is emotional or reasonable or both (see Van Zoonen, 2005 for a discussion on the significance of the two dimensions). Content is classified as issue-focused if it talks about the causes, severity, influences of PM 2.5 as well as government actions, policy debate, and social reactions. If the content aims at questioning the celebrity's motive, assessing the celebrity's performance, or asking the celebrity to make certain actions, the content is coded as celebrity-focused. Indicators of emotion include emoticons, usage of emotional words (e.g., angry, frustrated, etc.) and absence of substantial information and arguments. Indicators of reason refer to presence of substantial information and arguments such as statistics, explanations of causes, evaluation of different explanations, presentation of evidence, and more. Two coders have coded 20% of the content and calculated the inter-coder reliability. Percentages of consistency in non-continuous measures ranged from 60% to 100%. An average correlation between two coders' coding of continuous measures was 0.90. Both indicate a satisfactory to good inter-coder reliability.

Results

The search results show that although PM 2.5 is one of the few social issues celebrities tend to propagate, the actual volume of their updates on this issue was still low. Among the 350 accounts we crawled through, only 116 have ever mentioned the key words. Judging from the amount of relevant updates, one celebrity, Pan Shiyi, stood out with 166 updates, and 100 of them were his original writing. Pan is the CEO of SOHO (see Zha, 2013 for a more colorful description of him), a well-known real estate brand in China and famous for its modern style architecture. The company was selected by Forbes in 2006 and 2007 as one of the "most respected Chinese companies." The Weibo account of Pan enjoyed a steady position in the top 10 celebrities with the highest page views, and, oftentimes, was ranked top one among celebrity entrepreneurs. The total visits to his blog exceeded 70 million and the number of his Weibo followers reached 16 million. Owing to the particularly high number of updates written by Pan, his Weibo updates were used as a high threshold, to which other celebrities' performance can be benchmarked.

Other celebrities who have been talking about this issue only did so occasionally,and most of them posted fewer than 10 updates on the issue. The three representatives I chose fall into three categories: entrepreneur, entertainment star, and public intellectual. The descriptive statistics in Table 8.1 show that Yao, the famous actress and Weibo queen, attracted much more reposts and comments than Pan, Xu, and Li, despite that she only posted 13 PM 2.5-related updates over the years. Her updates were also more emotional than other celebrity updates, with 70% of her updates expressing her emotions towards the issue (see Table 8.2). Only Yao and Pan have ever shown

Table 8.1 Descriptive statistics of PM 2.5 updates by selected celebrities

Celebrities	Categories	# of PM2.5 updates	Original	Average # of reposts	Average # of comments
Pan Shiyi	Entrepreneurs	166	100	962	479
Yao Chen	Entertainment	13	8	5763	3122
Xu Xiaonian	Academic	7	3	691	273
Li Kaifu	Entrepreneurs	24	4	1822	744

emotional responses to other celebrities who posted relevant updates, almost all in the fashion of showing positive affections towards other celebrities. We used the same four codes to content analyze user comments under the PM 2.5 updates. A simple bivariate correlation analysis was run between celebrity updates and user comments. Table 8.3 shows the correlations and considering that comments can only occur after updates, my interpretation of the correlations here prefers tobe directional. Basically, we can see from the numbers that reasonable posts about both the issue and the celebrities led to reasonable comments about both the issue and the celebrities. Reasonable posts about the celebrities, however, reduced emotional comments about the celebrities. Emotional posts about the celebrities led to emotional comments addressed to the celebrities and reduced both reasonable and emotional comments on the issue. We can conclude that the style of celebrity performance on the issue has influences on the way their commentators voice their responses to the issue. When celebrities tried to take the limelight by turning the emotional focus to them, they discouraged their commentators to voice responses to the issue, either reasonably or emotionally.

The network analysis[3] was based on an aggregation of repost networks around relevant updates of the selected celebrities. Owing to the large number of reposters, the visualization of these networks in Figures 8.1, 8.2, and 8.3 only included the top 100 reposters, measured by their level of betweenness in the networks. Betweenness means the number of times a node acts as a bridge along the shortest path between two other nodes. The indicator identifies, although

Table 8.2 Results of content analysis of selected celebrities' PM 2.5 updates

	Reason-issue	Reason-celebrity	Emotion-issue	Emotion-celebrity
Pan Shiyi	90%	20%	20%	20%
Yao Chen	60%	0%	70%	20%
Xu Xiaonian	57%	14%	43%	0%
Li Kaifu	100%	0%	30%	0%

Note: The percentages here were calculated based on total number of PM 2.5 updates. The categories were not mutually exclusive. In other words, one update can be coded in all four categories.

Table 8.3 Significant simple bivariate correlations between user comments and celebrity updates

	User comments			
	Reason-issue (R-I)	Reason-celebrity (R-C)	Emotion-issue (E-I)	Emotion-celebrity (E-C)
Celebrity Updates R-I	.389*			
Celebrity Updates R-C		.551***	–.342*	
Celebrity Updates E-I				
Celebrity Updates E-C	–.629***		–.566***	.780***

Note: Only statistically significant correlations were presented in the table. ***p<.001, **p<.01, *p<.05, +p<.10.

arguably, the most influential nodes in a network. The size of the nodes in the graphs indicates the number of followers, as larger size refers to more followers. The distance between the nodes shows the length of path to connect the nodes, as longer distance refers to more connection steps. In order to show how these celebrities connect to their reposters and may provide opportunities for their reposters to connect to each other, another decentralization analysis was made by taking the celebrities out of their own repost networks and see what are left. In each of the graphs, the left part shows the top 100 betweenness network, and the right part shows the de-centralized network.

Both Xu and Li had relatively similar repost networks. They are nodes that add strength to the connectivity of their networks, but without them there are still significant sub-networks that would connect their reposters to each other. In other words, their presence strengthens the cohesion of their networks but does not mandate the existence of the networks. Interestingly, Yao's repost network is in vast contrast. She was the only center in her network and she connects to her reposters in a one-to-one way. The majority of her reposters do not connect to each other and there were no sub-networks left if she was taken out of her network. In other words, her network fully relied on her to hold different nodes together and if she disappears, the network collapses. Combining with the content analysis, we now have basic understanding about the networking power of entertainment stars such as Yao in gathering an issue public. In summary, compared with other kinds of celebrities, Yao was able to attract a large amount of attention from individuals who were mainly attached to her rather than the issue *per se*. The public gathered around Yao's PM 2.5 updates did not connect to each other and were largely influenced by Yao's style (i.e., emotion-rich) in performing this issue.

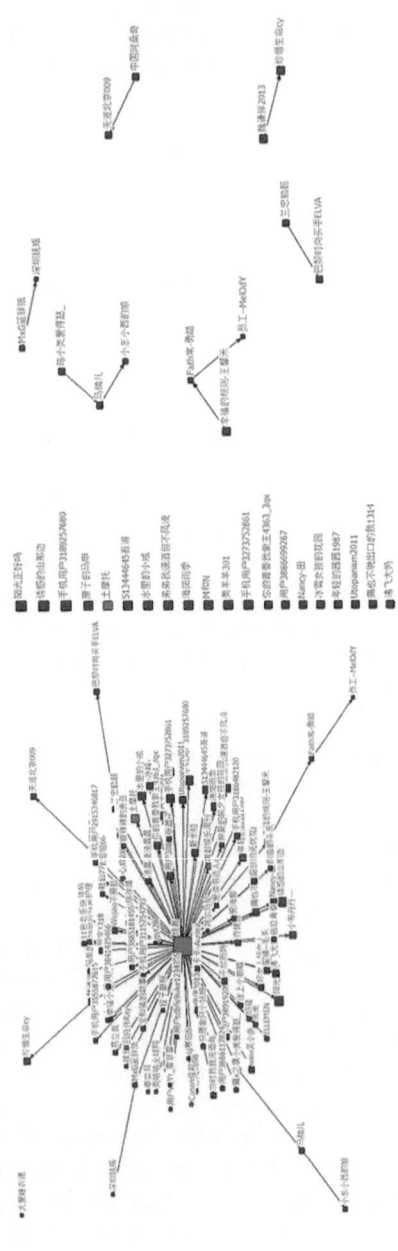

Figure 8.1 Yao Chen's Repost Network based on the Top 100 Reposters (Before and After De-centralization)
Note: The top 100 reposters were identified using their betweenness scores. Betweenness means the number of times a node acts as a bridge along the shortest path between two other nodes. The size of the nodes in the graphs indicates the number of followers, as larger size refers to more.

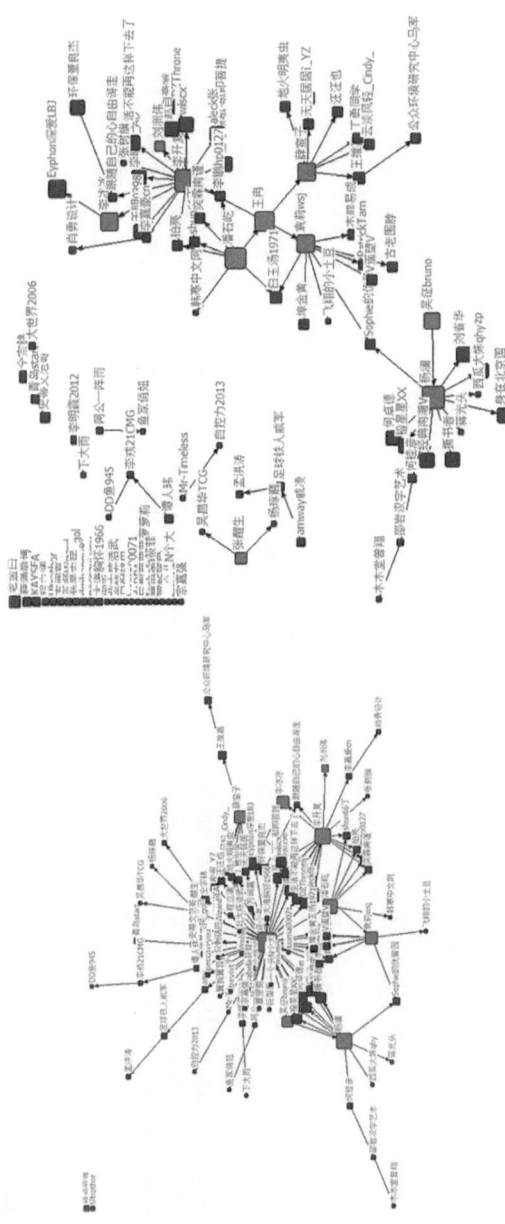

Figure 8.2 Xu Xiaonian's Repost Network based on the Top 100 Reposters (Before and After De-centralization)

Note: The top 100 reposters were identified using their betweenness scores. Betweenness means the number of times a node acts as a bridge along the shortest path between two other nodes. The size of the nodes in the graphs indicates the number of followers, as larger size refers to more.

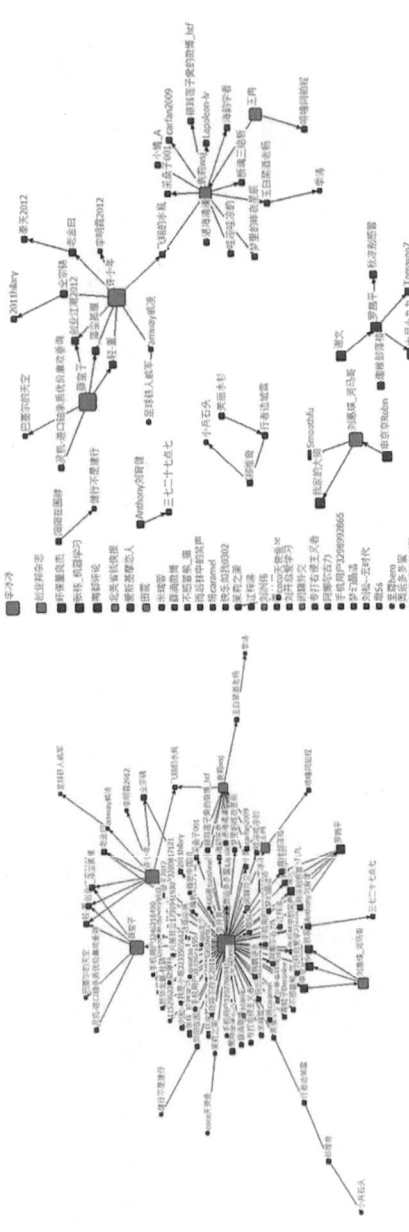

Figure 8.3 Li Kaifu's Repost Network based on the Top 100 Reposters (Before and After De-centralization)
Note: The top 100 reposters were identified using their betweenness scores. Betweenness means the number of times a node acts as a bridge along the shortest path between two other nodes. The size of the nodes in the graphs indicates the number of followers, as larger size refers to more.

The network logic, issue publics, and celebrities

In contemporary celebrity culture, what attracts the emotional investment of fans is often the celebrities themselves. Fan objects become celebrities, or, more precisely, the symbolic representation of these celebrities in various media channels. Technologies such as Weibo intensify the instant and constant interactions between fans and celebrities, creating a type of social relationship that is new to many ordinary Chinese. This new relationship is neither personal nor reciprocal but, nevertheless, affords the flow of information, sentiment, and emotion. What are transmitted in the fans–celebrity network are not just the celebrity performance and the fan reactions. Celebrities link their fans to various issues when they perform on such issues. Although PM 2.5 is a widespread social concern, we should not assume that the fans already know about the issue very well. Celebrity propagation of various aspects of the issue, including both reasonable statements and emotional expression, expose fans to such unexpected or unknown issues. If we consider both human beings and issues as network nodes capable of bringing more nodes into the network, we can see that Weibo celebrities successfully turned their fan publics into issue publics through performing on social issues and eliciting the fans' performance on the same issues.

Because such issue publics are gathered around celebrities and shaped by their performance style, Weibo publics tend to show a feature that resembles an emerging social phenomenon "flash mobs." These publics are flashy in the sense that their attention to and performance on the issues are kept through their linkage to a limited number of influential users. When the big Vs stop propagating such issues or turn to other issues, these publics quickly shift their attention from one issue to another as a response. This could explain why many Weibo incidents enjoy a large amount of attention, but only maintain the attention for a short time period. The vulnerability of such fans–celebrity networks is thus obvious: the super nodes (i.e., celebrities) can be taken out of Weibo networks and the networks around the super nodes subside and in the worst case, disappear. This has been the reality of Weibo during the wave of anti-rumor action in September 2013.[4] After big Vs being silenced and some eliminated, the public debate on Weibo has decreased significantly. This change more or less confirms that celebrities can function as network nodes to link their fans to issues. In the meantime, the weakness of such networks lies in the over-emphasis on the centrality of these celebrities.

The degree to which the networks around celebrity users is vulnerable, however, is not uniform across different celebrities. Another conclusion we can draw from the empirical findings is that different kinds of celebrities connect to Weibo publics in different ways. If we look at the other non-entertainment celebrities such as entrepreneurs and public intellectuals, they seem to first form alliances with other influential users through discussing the same issues. After the core of the network is in existence, they are able to augment each other's influence through tapping into their celebrity friends' networks. Unlike

Yao's network which focuses on her and resonates with her emotional expression, the lower centrality of non-entertainment celebrities in their networks allows more space for Weibo users to focus on the issue. One may even argue that users may pay attention to these non-entertainment celebrities for different reasons. The users may have less emotional attachment to these celebrities and their fan objects are less of the sentimental side of the celebrities but more of their views and opinions on social issues. The emergence of these non-traditional celebrities and their relationships with the general pubic are interesting research topics that deserve further academic examination.

The most recent development in China's microblogging sphere is the increasingly popular usage of Wechat,[5] the private chat application that incorporates both Facebook's status update within predefined social circles and Weibo's subscription to public accounts. Wechat was created by Tencent, the Internet company that built its market on the instant messaging tool QQ. It is not surprising that Tencent became a market leader again through capitalizing its strength in chat software. However, Wechat is no longer ruled by celebrity users as the subscription function it provides does not allow public accounts to push messages into users' status flow. Instead, the prominence of one piece of information is often seen in the number of friends (who tend to be real friends not virtual strangers) who have reposted that piece of information. Although it is still too early to draw any conclusions regarding Wechat's role in Chinese social formations, this most recent development suggests that network structure, as well as the characteristics of network nodes (especially the super nodes), has an undeniable impact on network behaviors.

Notes

1 http://ent.sina.com.cn/s/m/2011-07-19/18003363738.shtml.
2 The popularity rank of Sina Weibo changes constantly depending on an algorithm only known to Sina. Our search was conducted in early 2014. The rank can be found here: http://data.weibo.com/top/hot/all.
3 Due to the large scale of Pan Shiyi's repost network, it does not make mathematical sense to compare his network with other selected celebrities'.
4 *Southern Weekend, Big V is dying?* Retrieved from www.infzm.com/content/94222.
5 http://weixin.qq.com/.

Bibliography

Bao, P., Shen, H. W., Huang, J., and Cheng, X. Q. (2013). Popularity prediction in microblogging network: A case study on sina weibo, in *Proceedings of the 22nd international conference on World Wide Web companion*, International World Wide Web Conferences Steering Committee, pp. 177–178.

Chen, Z., Liu, P., Wang, X., and Gu, Y. (2012). Follow whom? Chinese users have different choice. arXiv:1212.0167.

Chen, J. and She, J. (2012). An analysis of verifications in microblogging social networks–Sina Weibo, in *32nd International Conference on Distributed Computing Systems Workshops (ICDCSW), 2012*, IEEE, Piscataway, NJ, pp. 147–154.

CNNIC (2014). *The 2014 Research Report on Usage Patterns of Chinese Social Networking Applications.* Retrieved from www.cnnic.net.cn/hlwfzyj/hlwxzbg/sqbg/201408/P020140822378154144978.pdf, accessed January 13, 2015

Corner, J. (2003). Mediated persona and political culture, in *Media and the Restyling of Politics: Consumerism, celebrity and cynicism,* eds J. Corner and D. Pels, Sage, London, pp. 67–84.

Dai, J. and Reese, S. D. (2007). Practicing public deliberation: the role of celebrity blogs and citizen-based blogs in China, in *Harmonious Society, Civil Society and the Media Conference,* Beijing, pp. 20–21.

Davies, D. (2010). China's celebrity entrepreneurs: business models for 'success', in *Celebrity in China,* eds L. Edwards and E. Jeffreys, Hong Kong University Press, Hong Kong, pp. 193–216.

Edwards, L. (2010). Military celebrity in China: The evolution of 'heroic and model servicemen', in *Celebrity in China,* eds L. Edwards and E. Jeffreys, Hong Kong University Press, Hong Kong pp. 21–45.

Fu, K. W., Chan, C. H., and Chau, M. (2013). Assessing censorship on microblogs in China: discriminatory keyword analysis and the real-name registration policy. *Internet Computing, IEEE,* 17(3), 42–50.

Gold, T., Guthrie, D., and Wank, D. (eds) (2002). *Social connections in China: Institutions, culture, and the changing nature of guanxi,* Cambridge University Press, Cambridge.

Guo, H., Lu, Y., Wang, Y., and Zhang, T. (2011). Measurement of the Weibo hall of fame network, in *Instrumentation, Measurement, Computer, Communication and Control, 2011 First International Conference on,* IEEE, Piscataway, NJ, pp. 192–195.

Guthrie, D. (1998). The declining significance of guanxi in China's economic transition, *The China Quarterly,* 154, 254–282.

Hood, J. (2010). Celebrity philanthropy: The cultivation of China's HIV/AIDS heroes, in *Celebrity in China,* eds L. Edwards and E. Jeffreys, Hong Kong University Press, Hong Kong, pp. 85–102.

Huang, X., Quan, C., Liu, S., and Man, Y. (2014). visualization and pattern discovery of social interactions and repost propagation in Sina Weibo, in *Neural Networks (IJCNN), 2014 International Joint Conference on,* July, IEEE, Piscataway, NJ, pp. 1401–1408.

Huang, R. and Sun, X. (2014). Weibo network, information diffusion and implications for collective action in China. *Information, Communication & Society,* 17(1), 86–104.

Jeffreys, E. and Edwards, L. (2010). Celebrity/China, in *Celebrity in China,* eds L. Edwards and E. Jeffreys, Hong Kong University Press, Hong Kong, pp. 1–20.

King, G., Pan, J., and Roberts, M. E. (2013). How censorship in China allows government criticism but silences collective expression. *American Political Science Review,* 107(2), 326–343.

Kipnis, A. (2002). Practices of guanxi production and practices of ganqing avoidance, in *Social connections in China: Institutions, culture, and the changing nature of guanxi,* eds T. Gold, D. Guthrie, and D. Wank, Cambridge University Press, Cambridge, pp. 21–34.

Kong, S. (2005). *Consuming literature: Best sellers and the commercialization of literary production in contemporary China,* Stanford University Press, Redwood City, CA.

Kong, S. (2010). Literary celebrity in China: From reformers to rebels, in *Celebrity in China,* eds L. Edwards and E. Jeffreys, Hong Kong University Press, Hong Kong pp. 125–144.

Li, D., Zhang, Y., Chen, X., Cao, L., and Zhou, C. (2014). Detecting hot topics in Sina Weibo Based on Opinion Leaders, in *2014 International Conference on Computer, Communications and Information Technology (CCIT 2014)*, Atlantis Press, Amsterdam.

Li, D., Zhang, J., Sun, G. G. Z., Tang, J., Ding, Y., and Luo, Z. (2012). What is the nature of Chinese MicroBlogging: Unveiling the unique features of Tencent Weibo. arXiv:1211.2197.

Liao, Q., Wang, W., Han, Y., and Zhang, Q. (n.d.). Analyzing the influential people in Sina Weibo Dataset, in *Proceedings of the Symposium on Selected Areas in Communications*, IEEE, Piscataway, NJ.

Lin, Zhongxuan. (2013). *China•internet•celebrity: Power and resistance of contentious society in miniature*. Retrieved from http://ssrn.com/abstract=2241887.

Liu, Y. and Zhou, Y. (2011). Social media in China: Rising Weibo in government, in *Digital Ecosystems and Technologies Conference (DEST), 2011 Proceedings of the 5th IEEE International Conference on*, IEEE, Piscataway, NJ, pp. 213–219.

Meyer, D. S. (1995). The challenge of cultural elites: Celebrities and social movements. *Sociological inquiry*, 65(2), 181–206.

Roberts, I. D. (2010). China's internet celebrity: Furong Jiejie, in *Celebrity in China*, eds L. Edwards and E. Jeffreys, Hong Kong University Press, Hong Kong pp. 217–236.

Rojek, C. (2001). *Celebrity*, Reaktion Books, London.

Shuai, X., Liu, X., Xia, T., Wu, Y., and Guo, C. (2014). Comparing the pulses of categorical hot events in Twitter and Weibo, in *Proceedings of the 25th ACM conference on Hypertext and social media*, ACM, New York, pp. 126–135.

Schultz, D. (2001). Celebrity politics in a postmodern era: The case of Jesse Ventura. *Public Integrity*, 4, 363–376.

Sullivan, J. (2014). China's Weibo: Is faster different? *New Media & Society*, 16(1), 24–37.

Van Zoonen, L. (2004). Imagining the fan democracy. *European Journal of Communication*, 19(1), 39–52.

Van Zoonen, L. (2005). *Entertaining the citizen: When politics and popular culture converge*, Rowman & Littlefield, Lanham, MD.

Wang, T. (2008). *"Let a Hundred Celebrities Blossom!": Does China Face a New Cultural Revolution? The Rise of Celebrity Culture in China*. Doctoral dissertation, University of Leeds, Institute of Communications Studies.

Wang, S. Y. and Bai, H. (2014). A case study on micro-blog communication characteristics related to haze during the Harbin haze disaster, in *Management Science & Engineering (ICMSE), 2014 International Conference on*, August, IEEE, Piscataway, NJ, pp. 120–125.

Wang, T. (2014). *Fans networking: The success/failure factor of the cultural entertainment industry in the future ten years*. Retrieved from http://mp.weixin.qq.com/s?__biz= MjAzNzMzNTkyMQ==&mid=203090644&idx=1&sn=2706fe7e10bc08516cbcbaf8fb eb1d49&scene=2&from=timeline&isappinstalled=0#rd.

Wang, N., She, J., and Chen, J. (2014). How big vs dominate Chinese microblog: a comparison of verified and unverified users on sina weibo, in *Proceedings of the 2014 ACM conference on Web science*, ACM, New York, pp. 182–186.

West, D. M. (2005). American politics in the age of celebrity. *Hedgehog Review*, 7(1), 59.

West, D. M. and Orman, J. M. (2003). *Celebrity politics*, Prentice Hall, Upper Saddle River, NJ.

Wu, Y., Atkin, D., Lau, T. Y., Lin, C., and Mou, Y. (2013). Agenda setting and micro-blog use: An analysis of the relationship between Sina Weibo and newspaper agendas in China. *The Journal of Social Media in Society*, 2(2).

Yu, L., Asur, S., and Huberman, B. A. (2011). What trends in Chinese social media. arXiv:1107.3522.

Yu, L., Asur, S., and Huberman, B. A. (2012). Artificial inflation: The true story of trends in Sina Weibo. arXiv:1202.0327.

Zha, J. (2013). *Tide players: The movers and shakers of a rising China*, The New Press, New York.

Zhang, Z. and Negro, G. (2013). Weibo in China: Understanding its development through communication analysis and cultural studies. *Communication, Politics & Culture*, 46.

9 Fandom publics
Social formation in the network society

Mediated publics, networked publics, and fandom publics

In the discipline of media and communications, a serious effort of defining "public" arose from the studies of public opinion (Price, 1992). Another recent endeavor to explicate "publics" was made in Livingstone's (2005) edited volume on audiences and publics. Both works essentially claim the same: the centrality of mediation in the formation and manifestation of the publics. Price's communicative model of public emphasizes that in a mass society, only mass media are able to afford the discussion and debate that constitute a public. Livingstone (2005, p. 26) coined the term "mediated publics," arguing that "one cannot now imagine how the public can be constituted, can express itself, can be seen to participate, can have an effect, without the mediation of various forms of mass communication." When the media mediate, "they select, prioritise, shape, and so on, in accordance with the institutions, technologies, and discursive conventions of the media industry." It is clear that mediation in Livingstone's work has a broader coverage than that in Price's work, without limiting media to mediating discussion and debate meanwhile with an acute awareness of the problematic role mass media play.

While mediated publics remains a compelling term, the logic and mechanism of mediation certainly have changed since the transformation from a mass media era to a new media era. Chadwick (2013, p. 4) refers to the co-existence of the older and newer media as "the hybrid media system," in which the logics, "defined as technologies, genres, norms, behaviors and organizational forms," of both older and newer media interact to define the information flow, although the interdependence is not symmetrical. The logic of newer media is not completely free from the co-option of the logic of older media, when professional news organizations take advantage of citizen journalism or grassroots activism to reinforce their elitist status. Moreover, the logic of newer media is not by itself non-problematic, no matter how much it takes disguise under invisible algorithms. Van Dijck (2013) pointed out that the ecosystem of social media is dominated by corporate forces that seek commercial interests, although the mediation of social media follows a different set of values, such as "popularity, hierarchical ranking, neutrality, quick growth, large traffic volumes, fast turnovers and personalized recommendations" (p. 154). What we see here is the emergence of another group of elitist actors, the major chains of platforms, including Facebook, Google, and Apple, serving the ideology of neoliberalism. Fuchs (2014) provided an even more radical critique by claiming that the logic of newer media is not much different from the Marxist understanding of capitalist exploitation of human labor initiated in the Industrial Revolution, if we truly understand the political economy of social media.

The logic of newer media and their mediation may be part and parcel of the larger social logic called the network logic. In fact, some scholars (Ito, 2008; Boyd, 2010) preferred networked publics over mediated publics, as the former seems to highlight the networking capacities enabled by new ICTs, which are not merely media in the traditional sense. The tenet of the argument is to say that technologies are constitutive of the publics. What separates networked publics from the more traditional notions of publics is how networked publics are "restructured by networked technologies" (Boyd, 2010, p. 39), which allow people to communicate through "complex networks that are bottom-up, top-down, as well as side-by-side" (Ito, 2008, p. 2). The structural affordances of networked technologies introduce new dynamics into shaping networked publics. The new dynamics, according to Boyd (2010), include invisible audiences, collapsed context, and the blurring of public and private, all of which render networked publics that are organized around attention. What seems to be contrasting is the newness in the discourse of networked publics versus the oldness in the discourse of the political economy of social media. Although how publics are formed seems to have distinct patterns now, the deeper logic of the political–economic forces does not change much. Then if the reason why we want to study the social formation of publics is primarily motivated by the political meaning of the publics, how do we reconcile the seemingly disparate implications drawn from the two threads of scholarship?

I argue that the network logic is the logic behind the networked capitalism, or the networked technologies, or the networked publics, although the implications of these networked entities may not be in harmony. So what is the network logic? I will attempt to clarify the answer with a review of three prominent network theories, namely Social Network Theory (SNT), the network society, and Actor Network Theory (ANT). Network in SNT is essentially social, in the sense that it exclusively focuses on humans or human entities (e.g., communities or organizations). Being human-centric does not mean being interpersonal, however. SNT concerns as much about interpersonal networks as inter-organizational or inter-national networks. The network logic in SNT is a logic that is *non-reductionist and relational*, turning our attention to describing the nodes, their relationships, and the structures and behaviors of the networks. Kadushin (2012) summarized 13 basic propositions under SNT and these propositions can be seen as the content of the network logic in SNT. It includes propositions such as "the greater the homophily the more likely two nodes will be connected" (p. 6) or "weak ties facilitate the flow of information from otherwise distant parts of a network" (p. 30) or "cores possess whatever attributes are most valued by the network" (p. 41). The network logic in SNT thus provides us basic understandings about how humans and entities consisting of humans connect to each other, without much emphasis on the new ICTs. In other words, SNT sees human societies as always in the structure of networks, whereas ICTs are just means through which humans are connected.

In contrast, the network society is first of all a historical phenomenon, developed in response to the historical emergence of new ICTs. Van Dijk (1999) claimed that "we may call the twenty-first century the age of networks" (p. 2) and the network society connects individuals, households, groups, and organizations through the communication networks powered by new ICTs. Castells (2006) went a step further to argue that technology is society, and the network society is the "social structure resulting from the interaction between the new technological paradigm and social organization at large" (p. 3). "Digital communication networks are the backbone of the network society, as power networks (meaning energy networks, added by the author) were the infrastructure on which the industrial society was built" (Castells, 2006, p. 4). These accounts of the network society clearly indicate that the network logic here is not an everlasting logic that can be used to describe any historical ages of the human society and instead, encompasses a set of different structure and principle compared to the previous historical ages, the most salient among which is the omnipresence of new ICTs.

The network logic of the network society specifies that networks as a type of social structure are not any kind of networks but those operated by ICTs (Castells, 2006). The content of this network logic is more far-reaching than what SNT has been talking about. According to Castells (2006), the network logic is configuring economics, politics, and sociability in today's world. What is particularly relevant to social formation is the idea of "networked individualism," which refers to "the mode of building sociability along self-selected communication networks, on or off depending on the needs and moods of each individual" (Castells, 2006, p. 12). Wellman (2005) used the same term, networked individualism, in the sense that the connectivity in the network society transits *from place-to-place to person-to-person*. Here individualism is not understood as in the dualism of individualist versus collectivist values but to emphasize that "(t)he person has become the portal" (Wellman, 2005, p. 15). Another emphasis shared in Castells' and Wellman's networked individualism is *the enhanced personal ability of self-selection* of social networks. Van Dijk (1999, p. 155) made the same point by saying that "(t)he technological capabilities of bridging space and time enable people to be more *selective* (emphasis added in the original text) in choosing coordinates of space and time than ever before in history." People are no longer confined by their geographical location and hence, the time frame associated with the space. Their capability of switching on and off different social networks they may claim a membership of is greatly enhanced by the new ICTs, which enable a new communication mode termed by Castells (2006, p. 13) as "self-directed mass communication," combining both interpersonal and mass communication in one.

Compared with the above two network theories, ANT has a very unique way to approach the network logic. ANT agrees with SNT that network is not something that becomes prevalent in response to an emerging historical context. Furthermore, ANT claims that "(n)etwork is a concept, not a thing out there" (Latour, 2005, p. 131) and "(i)t is a tool to help describe something, not what is being described." Therefore, the network logic in ANT is less about a type of social structure but more about an epistemological stance we can take to account for our social realities. As a methodology, ANT is thus not limited to describe one historical phase of human society, and not even human society itself. The network logic here should be appreciated in view of the basic ontological positions ANT embraces: the world is simultaneously natural and social. Therefore, any description of society cannot be complete without taking non-human entities into account. Instead of actors that often imply human agency, we have to study the relations among actants, which can be either human or non-human. As long as some actants are able to influence other actants, we should admit that these actants have agency. The definition of influence, and thus agency, in ANT is found in terms such as mediation and translation. Latour (2005, p. 40) made an effort to differentiate mediator from inter-mediary, the latter of which does not perform any work of transformation. When an actant is able to mediate or translate other actants, the network or the associations among the actants are (re)enacted into existence. Mediation, since now, is no longer an action that is only relevant to media (including both mass media and new media) but a metaphor of enacting agency by any actants (including those which do not have material forms such as ideas). The network logic in ANT is very much a logic of *tracing the actants and their moves*, without prescribing the boundary of the network, the features of the actants, or the nature of the inter-relations.

So what is the network logic in this book? Remember that my ambition is both larger and smaller than the above-mentioned three network theories. It is smaller because I am perplexed by one particular social formation that is of the publics, while I am not trying to bring in discussions about other social formations such as labor, families, or even communities. My ambition is larger than SNT because the scope of my description includes both human and non-human actors, especially fan objects and new ICTs, which make the network logic in this book hardly just "social." Meanwhile, my understanding of network is different from the network society tradition because I do not see networks as primarily technical networks or a seamless integration of the social and technical networks. Again, I learn from ANT that the network logic is an epistemological stance that we can take when studying the process of social formation. What should be foregrounded are those humans and things that can act to influence the process and, thus, leave traces. In other words, heterogeneous actors (or actants) that include individuals, groups, organizations, institutions, technologies, physical objects, biological species, and many more should be seen as related to each other and co-evolve over time.

Fandom publics are thus publics described following the network logic I just mentioned. Instead of attempting to stick some labels to a fixed category, my relational concept of fandom publics tries to describe the process or the movement of forming publics around fan objects through new ICTs. The effort really stops there, while any intention of making value judgment about the process resides outside the conceptualization. Fandom publics have been observed to, first, form with *the enhanced self-selection and self-organization of communication networks by individual fans.* Chapters 3 and 4 have provided a longitudinal account about how the individual fans of movies are able to recreate their lives via the social connections they made in the virtual fan space, Rear Window to Movies. Whereas various motivations may be relevant here, the initial drive for the early-generation fans was to share their love for movies. This love for movies was very self-centered considering how the social networks they were embedded in a decade ago had almost nothing to do with movies. However, during the process of constructing and disseminating their own discourses, the individual fans not only made visible their self-expressions, which collectively present a face of a subaltern public to the larger society, but also made possible the change of their identities in accordance to their preferred selves, such as shifting careers to the movie industry. This self-centered selection and organization of communication networks is also illustrated in individual fans who actually decided to break away from the fan network and became irrelevant. The first proposition about fandom publics may still sound too "social" to some, suggesting the human agency implied in the words such as self-selection and self-organization. I want to clarify that when I say self becomes the center of selection and organization of communication networks, it does not necessarily mean that they are entirely the individual's determination. It is because that self is not entirely determined by individuals (e.g., movies exist before movie fans), and that a large range of communication networks is available to the individuals that is not determined by individuals, either.

Hereby I introduce the second proposition under the concept of fandom publics: *the mediation of new ICTs, or the networking capacity afforded by newer media, is key to the formation of fandom publics.* So how key is key? Allow me to use the language of ANT again to say that these new ICTs are able to mediate other actants by "making others do things" (Latour, 2005, p. 107). Chapter 5 shows that media technologies, such as pirate VCDs and DVDs followed by broadband Internet, make foreign-language content easily accessible to Chinese fans and fans start to volunteer for collaborative translations because the ICT-based mechanism (i.e., hierarchical crowdsourcing) makes such collaboration possible. This mediation of new ICTs is especially evident when the majority of interviewees stated that their intention was not to have some social impact but very personally oriented towards the fan objects. To some extent, we may say that the "intent" of the technologies (e.g., data storage and data sharing) wins over the intent of individual fans (i.e., better enjoyment of the fan objects) and makes the fans do things that each of the individuals may not have envisioned. This is exactly how "key" new ICTs are to the formation of fandom publics.

Chapter 7 is a great illustration of how new ICTs not only make fans do things but also make fan objects "do" things. In the case of Douban, fan objects such as movies, books, and music albums are critical to the assembly of a network. These fan objects have been there for decades or even centuries and it is only when Douban technologies, such as user ratings and automated recommendations, translate these fan objects into their current digital life, these fan objects are able to start doing things that they cannot do before. One such thing is to connect human users, through being the common focus of attention and related performance. When human users form social relationships through these digitalized fan objects, their relationships also tend to be different from those social relationships that are aimed at accumulating social capitals. For instance, Douban friends may not be able to introduce job opportunities to each other but they can easily bring more fan objects to each other because of their already shared interests indicated in the formation of relationship via fan objects.

So far I have more or less dwelled on the formation of fandom publics and we have to be reminded that the formation is not just one historical moment. In order for a fandom public to exist, the fandom public has to continuously perform to achieve visibility in a digital world where attention becomes scarce resource. The third proposition is thus: the formation of fandom publics has to rely on *visibility achieved through the associational relationships among individuals and their constant performances*. If a fandom public stops performing and it cannot be visible to the larger society, the fandom public ceases to exist and the members of the fandom public go precisely to the opposite of public, private. From the subaltern discourses constructed in the Rear Window to Movies forum (Chapter 3), to the heated discussions on the Baidu Post Bar for *House of Cards* fans (Chapter 6), the performances made by the fandom publics take various formats and engage diverse claims. The understanding that their performance is mediated by new ICTs and fan objects urges us to seriously consider the concept of style. In which fashion do the fandom publics perform themselves into being? How do the other actants in the network, such as new ICTs and fan objects, mediate their performance to display some new styles? What would be the political implications of such publics performing stylistically on fan objects in front of the larger society?

Issue publics, affective publics, and fandom publics

As early as in the formative years of public opinion research, it has been recognized that not everyone in a given population (e.g., all citizens in one country) can be counted as member of a general public. Those individuals who are unorganized, disconnected, and invisible only possess mass opinions, if they have opinions at all (Price, 1992). Price's communicative model of public proposes that only if one individual is involved in discussion and debate on a collective issue, the person can be qualified to be a member of a public. With mass media being the space in which such discussion and debate happen, the involvement of members of a public can be found spreading along a spectrum of degree of activeness. The most active member may advocate for the issue using political participatory mechanisms such as shouting slogans in front of video cameras. The least active member may only get involved in terms of paying attention to news and stories about the issue. What is in common among all these members is this shared involvement in an issue. The concept of issue publics highlights the fact that people are not able to get involved in all collective issues and, instead, they can be attached to only a limited range of issues that affect them or interest them. Empirically, it is not likely to have a general public when each member gets involved in all collective issues. The implication of issue publics is that the size, composition, and organization of publics change according to different issues.

If issue publics suggest that the social formation of publics is driven by personal interest in issues, the concept of affective publics stipulates that the social formation of publics is driven by affects. Papacharissi (2014) defined affect as intensity of feeling (p. 135) and affective publics as "public formations that are textually rendered into being through emotive expressions that spread virally through networked crowds" (p. 133). While issues seem to provide a shared focus of attention, "an affect can be intense but abstract in its focus at the same time" (Papacharissi, 2014, p. 16). For instance, when a trending topic emerges on Twitter and the hashtag might seem to suggest shared attention, the driving force behind the popularity of that hashtag isn't really one commonly understood collective issue but is rather organized through "a repertoire of playful performance strategies that rethink the personal as political, and the political as that which is personally felt" (Papacharissi, 2014, p. 117). In other words, affective publics may or may not share basic understanding of the issues but the issues are often inspiring enough to activate and sustain "deliberatively improvised showing off of the self" (Papacharissi, 2014, p. 129), rather than the discussion and debate with other performers. I argue that "co-performance" is an apt word to capture how members of affective publics use issues as stages of performance and how they can be each other's audiences when they perform at the same time, largely thanks to the mediation of new ICTs such as social media. However, such co-performance does not necessarily lead to other involvements such as knowledge about the issues, or actions to make changes. The flowing energy that connects individual members of an affective public is the intensity of feeling, regardless whether the feeling is positive or negative, or whether the opinion regarding the issue is favorable or unfavorable.

Price (1992, p. 43) points out that within the attentive issue public, "we find the intermingling of mass and public." It is hard to tell whether a person is member of a public if only attention is attached to the issue and the attention is paid privately without any visibility to others. Therefore, my conceptualization of fandom publics emphasizes *visibility*, although the visibility can range from being visible to a few people, all the way to being visible to the entire society. In addition, the visibility is achieved through performance or more precisely, *co-performance* by connected individuals. This idea of co-performance includes a broad range of content, which can be emotive expression, rational discussions, or even just visible attention-paying (e.g., pure re-tweets). This co-performance also has its own style and aesthetics, which are highly personalized yet highly connected. On one hand, the style is very much self-selected and self-organized, to the extent that from the perspective of an individual, it is no more than a showing off of the self (Papacharissi, 2014), be it a sympathetic self or a reasonable self or an emotional self or a playful self. On the other hand, the individual performers are not completely isolated from and invisible to each other and instead, their performances resonate, add to, and remix with each other to form a flow of affect that is contagious. To paraphrase Papacharissi's (2014, p. 21) metaphor of affect as "the force that drives the unconscious tap of the foot to the music," the virality of such co-performance roots in the spontaneous and improvised style that one sees in multi-artists music jamming, which triggers the performance an isolated individual performer would not be able to make. I argue that the connections among members of fandom publics are less like the connections "formed between a performer and an ever-evolving, partially imagined, audience" (Papacharissi, 2014, p. 129), but rather the connections formed among co-performers who can be each other's imagined audience.

Let us now focus on which co-performance by fandom publics has been observed in this book, with an emphasis on three components: imagined audience, style, and aesthetics. In Chapter 3, I described how the fans that congregated on Rear Window to Movies performed through discursive formats such as sharing their personal reviews of banned or unavailable movies, as well as engaging in heated debate on quality movies. We should not ignore that even within this relatively small fan community, the co-performance is often more conflictual than consensual. When the fans resonate with each other's sentiments or furiously argue against each other, they are performing in front of multiple imagined audiences: the first imagined audience refers to other active fans, who are also co-performers; the second imagined audience is other passive fans, lurkers who pay attention but do not make their voices heard; and the third imagined audience is indefinite, whoever may come across their writings for various reasons. The co-performance is at least self-entertaining if it is kept within the active fans only. But more often than not, the co-performance is seen by unexpected audiences as well. These unexpected audiences occasionally become visible when, for instance, a private message sent from a magazine editor asks to re-print an article, or a website manager requires the discussion board manager to remove certain posts. Therefore, although the audience of such co-performance is imagined by the fans, it does not mean that such imagination is always baseless or illusory.

The co-performance moved out of the stage of Rear Window to Movies later, as evidenced in Chapter 4. Many fans have now become professional media writers or movie makers, who have visibility in other performing spaces such as mainstream mass media or movie theaters. Although the performance in traditional media outlets now is more individual than before in the format of one's creative works, a certain level of co-performance is still sustained thanks to the social connections that have been built among these fans. Their co-performance can still be observed in SNSs such as Weibo. A good example was the official crash down of an independent movie festival in Beijing in 2014. Many former Rear Window fans joined the online petition through re-tweeting the news on Weibo, regardless of their divergent views about independent movies in China. The idea of co-performance is best illustrated in Chapter 5, which centers on how fans of foreign-language content rely on hierarchical crowd sourcing to translate the content. For the online translation community, almost all of their performances are in the format of collaborative works. However, unlike carefully organized collective actions, this co-performance allows individuals to keep their own personal motivation and style without forcing them to conform to some collective identities in some formal structures. The individual effort needed in such collaborative works is relatively small and thus does not require the volunteers to change too much their existing motivation and style to adapt to the collective goal. In some sense, the collaborative outputs are like the byproducts of their personal activities, which are driven by individual enjoyment more than collective goals.

The style of fan publics' co-performance is thus both personal and mixed, as well as both ludic and contagious. From the perspective of an individual fan, he/she is only performing him/herself without considering too much how he/she should perform as member of a public, because the social category, public, is fluidly defined. From the perspective of an audience watching the co-performing public, it is a chaotic performance with a mixture of various styles but shares a flowing energy, which might be called affect. Corner and Pels (2003) noticed this seemingly self-conflicting political style that combines personalization and de-differentiation. When political identification becomes more personalized and less institutionalized, the logics of once-to-be distinct fields (e.g., politics versus economics) are increasingly getting non-distinguishable. Bennett and Segerberg (2010) proposed a term "connective action" to make a similar point that political actions are highly personalized yet organized in a network structure in which new ICTs play a central role. The network logic discussed in the last section is the underlying logic that leads to the visible style of the co-performance of fan publics. Corner and Pels (2003, p. 10) have put the style in vivid language: "the single God-like political leader who embodies a sacralised national unity is replaced by a whole firmament of little gods who rise and fall in a never-ending game of public reputation-making-and-breaking."

Finally, the aesthetics, or what is appreciated as good taste by the fandom publics, needs to be discussed. This question is far more complicated than the previous two because of the personalized yet mixed nature of co-performance. Hereby I attempt to answer the question with some initial pointers that are inspired by previous research such as that of Corner and Pels (2003). The chapter that best illuminates my understanding about aesthetics of politics in fandom publics is Chapter 6. The two themes, namely, authenticity and indigenousness, mark the kind of stylist co-performance valued by fandom publics. Being authentic literally means being original, and when it is used to evaluate fandom objects such as a political sit-com, the sit-com must be original without copying other shows. When being authentic is used to evaluate fans' personalized performance, the origin must be one's self instead of any imposed values from institutions. Fandom publics appreciate an authentic performance, despite of the content and format of the performance. This explains why personalization is a prominent style seen among the folk movie reviewers on Rear Window to Movies. This also explains why the *House of Cards* fans interpreted the parts regarding Chinese politics as lack of authenticity and missing original reading of the Chinese realities. Meanwhile, fandom publics dislike performance based on grand narratives that seem to be above the individuals. The interesting conflict over what is quality movie between the folk movie reviewers and the academics illustrates how fandom publics do not trust any overgeneralization of principles or values. Instead, they prefer believing in multiple individual stories, their rich details, and their open-ended interpretations. This preference of authenticity stemming from a true self (or multiple true selves) has to be understood along with the second theme on indigenousness. Being indigenous literally means occurring naturally in a particular place, and when it is used to evaluate a political sit-com, the sit-com must play stories that could naturally emerge in a particular context. That is why the *House of Cards* fans dislike the parts on Chinese politics because these are misunderstandings of the Chinese realities and would never actually happen in the current conditions of mainland China. When being indigenous is used to evaluate fans' personalized performance, the performance has to emerge out of the reality in which the self is shaped. However, we have to be reminded that the performance itself can be either a truthful reflection or an intentional distortion of the reality or most of time, something in between. For instance, in Chapter 8, I talked about how celebrities and fans co-perform on the issue of PM 2.5 and their co-performance is not always addressing the reality of the issue but often distracted to become a way to foster emotional attachment between the celebrity and his/her fans. However, this co-performance is very much indigenous because the trigger of this co-performance is the local reality that perpetrates majority of Chinese urbanites' everyday life. Another example could be Chai Jing's PM 2.5-focused documentary *Under the Dome*, which made waves on the Chinese Internet in early 2015. Her stylistic performance of celebrity activism is appreciated by many Chinese fans as indigenous because she addresses a truly local issue, although many of her statistics and evidence lack scientific rigor. One can imagine that Al Gore's *An Inconvenient Truth* would not have made such impact in China despite similar focus, precisely because the performance is not natural to the Chinese realities. If authenticity and indigenousness are the two aesthetic standards appreciated and enjoyed by fandom publics, what implications regarding power and politics can we draw from this always evolving social category? To make the question even broader, how do the network logic underlying fandom publics and the performativity of fandom publics bring new dynamics into the ever-changing power struggle and political balance?

Popular culture, politics, and power: a critique of fandom publics

Earlier, I admitted that my theoretical ambition in this book centers around the conceptualization of fandom publics and the definition itself does not really entail much value judgment about whether fandom publics are good or bad, or whether fandom publics empower the citizens or the existing powers such as an authoritarian government or multinational companies or the notorious West. In this last section, I focus on suggesting some answers to such calls for value judgment by trying to examine the implications of fandom publics through some prominent critical frames, namely democratization, post-Marxism, post-colonialism, and post-modernism. Critiques based on these four frames can be roughly translated into the following four questions: Are fandom publics bad for democracy? Are fandom publics free and immaterial labor? Do fandom publics reinforce the dominance of the West? Is the concept, fandom publics, a grand narrative; or, if not, does the concept suggest "anything goes"?

When it comes to academic works on contemporary China, a haunting spirit is democratization. Almost every single social change in China has been put under scrutiny from the lens of democratization. A latent criterion of value judgment is to say if this new phenomenon facilitates democratization, it is good; and if it does not, it is bad. Meng (2010) called this way of thinking "democratize or die" and argued that it is "an essentially Western-centric view that treats China as the inscrutable and inferior 'other' to be converted to 'one of us' ('us' as liberal democracies …)" (p. 502). Besides such post-colonial critique of democratization, I'd like to highlight the content of democratization. As a historically specific phenomenon in disguise of a universal value, contemporary liberal democracies emphasize political institutions such as elections, multi-party systems, separation of powers, rule of law, and a constitution that protects human rights, personal freedoms, and individual liberties. Democratization often means acquisition and practice of the above-mentioned political institutions. Therefore, if a new social phenomenon or social change does not contribute to building such institutions, it is considered by advocates for democratization as evil at worst, or irrelevant at best.

My understanding of fandom publics from the perspective of democratization has two facets: firstly, fandom publics do not regard democratization as their ultimate goal; secondly, fandom publics do not necessarily influence democratization only in one direction. Although the political implication of fandom publics is one important reason why this work has been written, democratization is not the political end fandom publics wish to reach. The politics of fandom publics is not a politics of democracy, but a politics of survival first, then a politics of recognition. A politics of survival indicates that not all social categories have to exist, just like not all TV shows have to be renewed. Fandom publics that gather around fan objects have to first of all ensure their existence, regardless whether their survival is achieved in a democratic or a totalitarian system. After gaining existence, fandom publics become public through playing a politics of recognition (Taylor, 1994), a politics that struggles for being recognized as existing. Such recognition may go all the way to be acknowledged in a constitution, which can be seen as a democratization effect. But most times, the recognition fandom publics try to achieve is much less monumental, manifested in their satisfaction in knowing that there exist other fans who share their passion. Does this politics of survival and recognition lead to democratization? The answer is perhaps not. We can observe that in certain circumstances such as banning of fan objects, fandom publics strive to protect their shared interest by making the banned objects available to each other and, in some sense, promote the freedom of information flow. But it has to be noticed that fan objects are often not directly related to advocating the building of democratic institutions, but rather directly related to shaping feelings, eliciting affect, and staging co-performance. Therefore, if fandom publics are criticized for not being explicitly pro-democracy, the critique is fair but driven by a misplaced cause. The political implication of fandom publics does not lie in democratization but in other interesting ideas that are often found in the traditions of post-Marxism, post-colonialism, and post-modernism.

Post-Marxism critiques look at fans' active participation in fan objects as immaterial and free labor. Much of the fan activities covered in this book, such as vivid discussions on the fan objects, collaborative translation of foreign content, crowd-sourced reviews and ratings of cultural products, and emotional devotion to human fan objects (i.e., celebrities), could be seen as voluntary labor that helps the cultural industry to produce and sell their products. The aesthetic and social benefits fans derive from their participation should not be the legitimization of exploitation because fans do not really have the power to participate in the economic decision making that is based on capitalist ownership (see Fuchs, 2014). This critique is powerful because it is indeed true that fans do not have any meaningful ownership of either the content producers (such as Walt Disney) or the dissemination channels (such as Youtube). Therefore, whatever decisions made by these companies have little ethical accountability to the users. But what the Chinese realities have suggested is that capitalism is not a singular word at all. Chinese fans are not dealing with a homogeneous system called capitalism and, rather, they manage to find their way to advance their interests in a labyrinth of various capitalist forces. The foremost tension is the one between global versus local capitals. For many years, Chinese fans were allowed to enjoy content produced by foreign cultural industry without paying a cent through using local Internet services such as Youku or Baidu. Their fan activities such as collaborative translation are not so much exploited by the foreign cultural industry but pretty much by the local Internet industry. Only in recent years has the local Internet industry, strengthened through such exploitation of local users' free usage of foreign content, started to pay for some of the foreign content, with the money coming from advertisements inserted into the content.

I argue that the problematic side of this fan labor lies not in the fact that they are exploited but in the lack of consciousness about the exploitation enacted on the fans. In a way, it is similar to what Marx has termed as "false consciousness." Fans may neglect the capitalist exploitation simply because they gain enjoyment and pleasure out of their fan labor, wrongly considering the exchange a fair deal. So the problem does not lie in fans being labor, but in their comfort with being exploited in such a way. As long as they are content with the current exploitative relationship between the Internet companies and them, they would continue using the commercial platforms and do not turn to alternatives. However, I disagree that fans stand no chance in discovering their exploitative relationship with the digital capitals and becoming aware of possible resistance measures. A good illustration is how the online translation community encompasses an array of fully commercial, half commercial, and fully voluntary groups. Although not all of our interviewed translators resist the idea of selling their translations, a significant number of them have no plan to work for the Internet companies. Further, I argue that such consciousness of exploitation is more likely to be constructed when fans are actively engaged than when they are passively involved. Media and advertising companies have long played the game of attention economics, selling audiences' attention to advertisers through providing free or cheap content. When audiences passively pay attention to media content, they are less likely to communicate with other audiences, to understand the production process of the content, and to demand even just partial ownership of the content. When audiences become prod-users, as evidenced in Chapter 5, the awareness of structure, the sense of ownership, and the spirit of volunteerism are much higher than other fan communities. So are fandom publics free and immaterial labor? The answer is yes, but being labor does not automatically deny the potential of being politically progressive. Labor, since Marx popularized its usage, has always been a concept that contains the potential of liberation. The working class was hoped to be the agent of social revolution. The immaterial labor, according to Hardt and Negri (2000), possesses the heightened powers of subversion precisely because of its importance in late capitalist economy. However, it is simplistic and against the historical lesson we have learned (Sim, 2013) if we have to be forced to choose between the post-Marxist concept of labor and the cultural–political concept of participation as one true answer. My take on this debate is that fandom publics can be both immaterial labor and civic participant, which are not contradictory categories.

A post-colonial reading of fandom publics turns our focus to concepts such as globalization, neo-imperialism, or "the global networks of power" (Hardt and Negri, 2000, p. 184). After a globalized economy has invaded every corner on the earth, those nations and cultures that are late to the process bear the pain of suffering from the imbalanced power between the "First" and "Third World" or the "North" and the "South." The fandom publics that form around foreign cultural products are most susceptible to the post-colonial critique, which reminds us that the active participation in consuming such products could cultivate a dangerous mindset that the West is a superior culture whereas the Oriental is primitive and needs to be civilized. The empirical evidence shown in this book is mixed with regard to this critique (see Chapter 6): the fans of foreign entertainment content such as political sit-coms exercise discretion when evaluating the authenticity of views expressed in the content. When the content concerns their everyday experience (e.g., Chinese politics), they are able to resist, or even reject, the discursive power embedded in the shows. When the content is presenting experience far away from their direct access (e.g., foreign politics), they seem to be easy to be persuaded by the shows. Do fandom publics reinforce the dominance of the West? The answer is that it depends on whether the fandom public has other sources of experience to resist the Western discourse.

In addition, in my other writings (Zhang and Zhang, 2015), I did notice that the post-colonization is particularly strong when it comes to shaping views of new (or imported) forms of cultural practices. For instance, the popular reality shows on Chinese TV are mostly modeled on foreign counterparts. Fandom publics who have learned about reality shows from participating in the consumption and reproduction of foreign content were convinced that the foreign shows are original, sincere, and truthful. In other words, their judgment of quality is shaped by the values embodied in foreign reality shows. But we have to remember that there are multiple fandom publics co-existing at the same time. Those who fancy foreign reality shows have to involve in constant fights against those who prefer local reality shows. The discursive contest between the two heightens, rather than reduces, the potential to reflect on either party's enjoyment and pleasure. The political significance of fandom publics is manifested in such discursive contests that are only possible when fans make their claims visible and engage in debating or feeling each other's views. Another point I want to make is that foreign cultural products in the context of Chinese fandom are not just from the West. Instead, cultural products from Japan and South Korea seem to enjoy greater popularity because of their closer "cultural proximity" (Straubhaar, 1991). There are critics who accuse the Japanese and Koreans of being new colonizers, arguing that they are no different from the West when they use cultural products to brainwash Chinese audiences. Ironically, many Chinese audiences enjoy the East Asian foreign content for the reason that these cultures are similar to the Chinese culture and South Korean producers seem to be very much willing to China-nize their products in order to cater to the taste of Chinese market. As Bhabha (1994) argued, if there is a process called colonization, it is not a one-way process during which the colonizer imposes its power on the colonized but a two-way process of negotiation that changes both the colonizer and the colonized. Colonialism is a hybrid and colonization is a hybridizing phenomenon. The political significance of fandom publics is manifested in this two-way process of influence and the potential for the weaker side (i.e., the Chinese fans) to modify the stronger side (i.e., the foreign cultural industry and the discursive power it represents).

Finally, is the concept, fandom publics, a grand narrative? I believe that the preceding discussions have already revealed the answer: no, fandom publics are pluralistic smaller narratives. Although multiple fandom publics may share some features, not all fandom publics go through the same trajectory of formation and manifestation. The actual concern behind grand narratives is the totalitarian tendency such narratives seem to suggest. A post-modern critique might worry that by naming social members fandom publics, this book attempts to totalize our understanding of the formation of social categories. This would be a completely wrong reading of my effort. Fandom publics suggest one way of social formation among many other ways, which co-exist without necessarily excluding each other. Moreover, even the members of certain fandom publics can flow in and out other social categories, depending upon which identity the individuals choose to foreground at the moment. What matters the most is the political implications of fandom publics, which are so pluralistic and unpredictable that I am hesitant to make any conclusions about whether fandom publics empower the citizens or the existing powers. What I can say about their political potential is that firstly, individuals are able to join publics that are not conditioned on their geographical and social positions, which opens up new dimensions for many individuals to form publics; secondly, the mediation of new ICTs is so key that it becomes part of the politics of survival and recognition played by fandom publics; and, thirdly, the co-performance of fandom publics gain themselves visibility and such visibility is the very center of political contests.

Therefore, instead of being subject to the post-modernist critique, I have to admit that this book should be subject to the critique of post-modernism. The question now becomes, do fandom publics suggest that "anything goes" (Feyerabend, 1993)? Similar to the post-modernist artists' effort to collapse the hierarchy of high and low culture, this book suggests a collapse of the boundary among fields (Bourdieu, 1993), such as the political field, the cultural field, and so on. The argument is that fandom publics are both cultural and political. Whereas the cultural dimension is evident, fandom publics are no less political than other social formations such as social movement groups, civil society organizations, and radical dissidents. The concept of "double-coding" (Jencks, 1986), which means that post-modernist arts appeal to both insiders and outsiders of the artist field, is appropriate here to function as an analogy of the double-roles fandom publics play. Another analogy I can make here is how post-modernism envisions an alternative form of temporality, if the terms such as modernism and post-modernism inherently identify themselves with historicity (McHale, 2007). Modernism exists in an "ever-renewing newsness" kind of temporality so post-modernism can only differentiate itself by adopting one of the following four alternative forms of temporality: (1) a temporality of stasis; (2) a form of apocalypse and the end of history; (3) an even more frantic pace of innovation and obsolescence; (4) an option of multiple and uneven times. I agree with McHale that what have emerged in the empirical observation in this book suggest the fourth option. The multitude of fandom publics as well as the multitude of social categories among which fandom publics only occupy a portion shows that social formations in the network society can take many forms: some are personalized, ICT-mediated and visible, but others are hierarchical, ICT-deprived, and invisible; perhaps some social members are involved in both kinds of social formations at once. So if the question asks whether fandom publics suggest that anything goes, the answer is no, but fandom publics do suggest that many things go. When I say many things go, however, I don't mean that many things hold an equal amount of power. For instance, when post-colonialism says the colonizer could be influenced by the colonized, it does not mean that the colonizer and the colonized always have the same amount of power.

This book thus concludes by discussing power seen in the formation and manifestation of fandom publics. A Weberian understanding of power sees power as the capability of one party to coerce another party into doing something that is against the latter party's autonomous will. A Marxist understanding of power emphasizes the critical resources that enable their owners to exploit those who do not own such resources. A Gramscian understanding of power is more subtle than the above two views and hegemony developed by the ruling class takes the outlook of values and norms for all, sustaining its control through winning the consent of the ruled. A Foucaultian understanding of power is that power is everywhere and comes from everywhere: not only the ruling class but also the ruled class can be sources of power; in fact, what differentiates the powerful from the powerless is not the demarcation of classes or any social categories. As Foucault (2002) argued, whoever is able to define knowledge has the power and thus authorities, both social (e.g., schools) and political (e.g., the state), are more likely to have power than others. My understanding of power, however, is undeniably post-modernist and along the line of Baudrillard's (1998) concept, seduction. Instead of overt coercion or covert disguise, power as seduction emphasizes the complicity between the so-called powerful and the so-called powerless. To seduce is to perform, in the sense that there must exist a need to communicate. To seduce is also to make believe, to get the seduced to accept the meaning of the performance as natural and genuine. Therefore, power as seduction has to be materialized in performance (Alexander, 2011) and I further argue that it has to be materialized in co-performance. How to make the seduced believe the seducer is not just through successful performance by the seducer for the seduced, but through staging the seduced to be part of the performance, to become one performative element itself, to believe the meaning of their actions through acting. Alexander (2011, p. 5) talked about how "meaning must seem to come from the actor if it is to seem authentic, not from scripts, props, power or audience." But who else would feel more authentic than the acting actors themselves? No matter whether their performance is staged to follow a pre-written script and made possible through using props, the actors cannot disbelieve their own actions when they are acting out the script and have to treat the setting made of props as if it is real. Power as seduction thus manifests itself through keeping the seduced on stage, acting out scripts written by the seducer, co-performing with the seducer, and getting lost in the role-play to the extent that the seduced believe that the stage is their life world and the acting is their action.

The asymmetrical nature of power is maintained in this view of power as seduction but the asymmetry is achieved and maintained with much bigger difficulty and subtler mechanisms. Remember that the seducer cannot hide behind the curtain and must be part of performance in order to persuade the seduced that the propped setting is real. A successful seducer should be able to make the seduced believe that the script is the only story and it is everyone's story. However, there always exists the possibility that the seduced, for any reasons, divert from the script and improvise their performance; they may even sneak in props they think that should belong to the stage. What is even more interesting is the possibility that the seduced act out their own script and the seducer, as part of the show, has to continue the hijacked performance along with the seduced. In such kind of situation, we may claim that a power reconfiguration has been done. Actually I think that the co-performance of seduction is never fully dominated by one party, either overtly or covertly. Indeed, seduction is a co-performance full of snares and lures set up by both the seducer and the seduced. Instead of coercing the other party into the performance, both parties naively believe that their performances can over-power the other party's to make the show theirs. Most of the time, the show is neither fully acted out as the script suggests nor completely constrained by the propped setting. It is a constant competition between the seducer and the seduced to siege the stage and the competition might well become the source of pleasure of the co-performance. Power is seduction and when one party wins hearts and minds of the other party, show is over, seduction stops, power vanishes, history ends.

Bibliography

Alexander, J. C. (2011). *Performance and power*, Polity Press, Cambridge.

Baudrillard, J. (1990). *Seduction*, Palgrave Macmillan, Basingstoke.

Bennett, W. L. and Segerberg, A. (2012). The logic of connective action: Digital media and the personalization of contentious politics. *Information, Communication & Society*, 15(5), 739–768.

Bhabha, H. K. (1994). *The location of culture*, Routledge, London.

Bourdieu, P. (1993). *The field of cultural production: Essays on art and literature*, Columbia University Press, New York.

Boyd, D. (2010). Social network sites as networked publics: Affordances, dynamics, and implications, in *Networked self: Identity, community, and culture on social network sites*, ed. Z. Papacharissi, Routledge, New York, pp. 39–58.

Castells, M. (2006). Informationalism, networks, and the network society: A theoretical blueprint, in *The network society: A cross-cultural perspective*, ed. M. Castells, Edward Elgar, Cheltenham, pp. 3–48.

Chadwick, A. (2013). *The hybrid media system: Politics and power*, Oxford University Press, Oxford.

Corner, J. and Pels, D. (2003). Introduction: The re-styling of politics, in *Media and the restyling of politics: Consumerism, celebrity and cynicism*, eds J. Corner and D. Pels, Sage, London, pp. 1–18.

Feyerabend, P. (1993). *Against method*, Verso, London.

Foucault, M. (2002). *The order of things: An archaeology of the human sciences*, Routledge, London.

Fuchs, C. (2013). *Social media: A critical introduction*, Sage, London.

Hardt, M. and Negri, A. (2009). *Empire*, Harvard University Press, Boston, MA.

Ito, M. (2012). *Introduction*, in *Networked publics*, ed. K. Varnelis, The MIT Press, Cambridge, MA.

Jencks, C. (1986). *What Is Post-Modernism?* St. Martin's, New York.

Kadushin, C. (2012). *Understanding social networks: Theories, concepts, and findings*, Oxford University Press, Oxford.

Latour, B. (2005). *Reassembling the social: An introduction to actor-network-theory*, Oxford University Press, Oxford.

Livingstone, S. M. (2005). Introduction, in *Audiences and publics: When cultural engagement matters for the public sphere*, ed. S. M. Livingstone, Intellect Books, Bristol, pp. 9–16.

McHale, B. (2007). What was post-modernism. *Electronic Book Review*. Retrieved from www.electronicbookreview.com/thread/fictionspresent/tense.

Meng, B. (2010). Moving beyond democratization: A thought piece on the China Internet research agenda. *International Journal of Communication*, 4, 501–508.

Papacharissi, Z. (2014). *Affective publics: Sentiment, technology, and politics*, Oxford University Press, Oxford.

Price, V. (1992). *Public opinion* (Vol. 4), Sage, London.

Sim, S. (2013). *Post-Marxism: An intellectual history*, Routledge, New York.

Straubhaar, J. (1991). Beyond media imperialism: Asymmetrical interdependence and cultural proximity. *Critical Studies in Mass Communication*, 8, 39–59.

Taylor, C. (1994). *Multiculturalism: Examining the politics of recognition*, 25, 25.

Van Dijk, J. (1999). *The network society*, Sage, London.

Van Dijck, J. (2013). *The culture of connectivity: A critical history of social media*, Oxford University Press, Oxford.

Wellman, B. (2005). Little boxes, glocalization, and networked individualism, in *Digital cities*, eds M. Tanabe, P. van den Besselaar, T. Ishida, Springer, Heidelberg, pp. 10–25.

Zhang and Zhang (2015). Fandom of foreign reality TV shows in Chinese cyber sphere, in *Networked China: Global dynamics of digital media and civic engagement: New agendas in communication*, eds Chen, W. and Reeve, S., Routledge, London, pp. 197–213.

Index

activism 25–6; online activism 102
actor network theory 127; actors 9, 27, 56, 127, 139; actants 127–9; mediator vs. intermediary 127; translation 127
agency 4, 63, 69–70, 86, 127–8
authenticity 83, 132–3, 137
audiences 2, 5; vs. publics 8

Baidu Post Bar 15, 79–81
Beitaixi 51, 54, 56, 58
big Vs 56, 111–12, 119
blogs 49, 53–5, 73
Bonnie 51, 54, 56
Bourdieu, Pierre 31–2, 59, 138
Bulletin Board System (BBS) 15, 52–3, 55, 79

celebrity 107; activism 124, 133; culture 107–9, performance 113–15, 119, 133; relationship with fans 110, 119; users 110–12;
censorship 25, 32–4, 36–7, 70, 72, 79–80, 102, 111
Chicago School of Sociology 2
China Independent Film Festival 34, 58
China Internet Network Information Center (CNNIC) 16–21, 54, 91, 111
cinephilia 31; history of online cinephilia 34–5
civil society 25, 101–2, 138
citizens 22, 25, 102; vs. folk 47; vs. Gong 6–7
civic culture 69–72
collective action 89–91, 101–3; and network structure 96–9
community 1; online gaming community 91, 103; online movie fans community 44, 47; online translation community 60, 65–7, 70–2, 132, 136 vs. publics 2, 40–1

co-performance 130, 139–40; by fan publics 131–2; imagined audience in 131; style of 131; aesthetics of 132–3
cultural consumption: money spent on 17; time spent on 18; as economic activity 22; as political activity 23
cultural identity 23, 85
cultural production 31; statistics of 19–21
crowd 2, 4; vs. publics 4–5

democratization 25, 134–5
Douban 54–5, 91–2; and its network structure 95–9

fan(s): activism 61–64, 71–72; culture 18, 62; object(s) 5, 10–11, 50, 52, 62–3, 71–3, 75, 86, 89, 91, 103, 108, 110, 120, 127–9, 135
fandom 3, 10, 61–4; of celebrities 107; of movies 31–2; of transcultural TV 78
Fengruan 65
Fraser, Nancy 1–2, 5
Fiske, John 2, 62, 84

Gong vs. Si 6–8
Gu, Xiaobai 50, 56,
Guan vs. Min 7

Habermas, Jurgen 1–2, 5. 31–2, 40
House of cards 81–2
Huang, Xiaoxie 54, 58

Information and communication technologies (ICTs) 3, 8–9, 24–6, 55–6, 110, 125–6, 128
identity 5, 38, 53, 72–3 of being a Chinese 23, 84–6; as "here and now" 85
immaterial labor 61, 63–4, 71, 136
indigenous 84–6, 133

Jenkins, Henry 3, 61–4, 69, 72

Latour, Bruno 9, 27, 127–8
Li, Kaifu 112, 114, 118

mass 2–3, 4; vs. publics 4–5
mass media 5, 25, 34, 41, 44–6. 51, 56–8, 65, 110, 124, 129
mediation 2–3, 5, 7, 9, 41, 44, 49, 55–7, 110, 124–5, 127, 130, 138
Mizoguchi, Yuzo 6
movie industry 36–7, 43, 51, 57–8, 128; history of 32–4; pirate movie industry 41
My Love from the Star 75

network behavior 92–3, 120
network logic 3, 8, 49, 55, 57, 88, 103, 125–8
network of powers 44, 46, 57
network society 3, 8; as a theory 125–7
network structure 88, 92, 97–9, 103, 120, 132; objects vs. people as nodes 97, 108, 111, 115, 119; relationship formation 97, 103
networked individualism 8, 126; performance style of 50–2
networked public(s) 8, 88, 125

Pan, Shiyi 112–5
participatory culture 63; partcipatory media vs. civic culture 69–71
PM 2.5 112–3, 133
politics: of survival 134–5; of recognition 134–5
Post-Colonialism 136–7, 139
Post-Marxism 135–6
Post-Modernism 138
popular culture 15, 17, ; material formats of 21; scholarship of 21–4; critique on the scholarship of 25–6
power: as seduction 139–40; Baudrillardian 139; Foucauldian 139; Gramscian 139; Marxist 139; Weberian 139
private movie watching (PMW) 41–4
prod-users 71–2
public sphere: Habermasian 1, 31; subaltern 46; critique of 2, 5
public(s): affective 130; regular 43, 49–50; subaltern 32, 40–1, 43–4, 46–7, 55–7; fandom 128–9, 130–3; issue 108, 119, 130; mediated 124–5; relational

concept of 8–9; vs. publicness 6; vs. publicity 6; visibility of 8; Weibo publics 111, 119
public culture 61
public opinion 124, 129

Rear Window to Movies 35, 46, 53, 57, 128, 131, 133; counter-discourse of 35–8
real name verification 110–1
Renren 54, 91–2, 95–9

social capital 56, 88–9; bonding 94, 99–100; bridging 94, 99–100
social network
Social Network Sites: and collecitve action 89; diversity of 88; in China 91; interest-oriented 90, 101–3; relationship-oriented 56, 89–91, 103–4
Social Network Theory 125–6
social relationship 89, 103, 129; as Guanxi 108–10
super nodes 108, 120; vulnerability of 119

technological centralism 26–7; vs. technological essentialism 26; vs. technological determinism 26
television program: drama 23, 63, 65, 69, 76–8, 80, 82, 84–6; political drama 76, 81; reality show 64, 78, 137
Tengjin, Shu 51, 54, 56
ties: strong ties 89–90, 99, 101; weak ties 89, 97–9, 101, 125
TLF 66, 68
transcultural television (TV) 76
trending topics 111

unofficial culture 23–4

Wechat 55–6, 120
Weibo 54–5, 80, 110, 112, 119–20
Weixidi 55–8

Xici.net 35, 53
Xu, Xiaonian 112, 114–7

Yao, Chen 54, 110, 112, 113–6
YDY 65, 78–9
Yeeyan 65–8, 70, 72–3,
YYeTs 65–6, 70, 78

Zimuzu (subtitle groups) 65, 68